Hegel

Classic Thinkers Series

Daniel E. Flage, *Berkeley*

Bernard Gert, *Hobbes*

Dale E. Miller, *J. S. Mill*

A. J. Pyle, *Locke*

Andrew Ward, *Kant*

Hegel

J. M. Fritzman

polity

First published in 2014 by Polity Press

Polity Press
65 Bridge Street
Cambridge CB2 1UR, UK

Polity Press
350 Main Street
Malden, MA 02148, USA

ISBN-13: 978-0-7456-4724-1
ISBN-13: 978-0-7456-4725-8 (pb)

A catalogue record for this book is available from the British Library.

Typeset in 10.5 on 12 pt Palatino
by Toppan Best-set Premedia Limited
Printed and bound in Great Britain by T. J. International, Padstow, Cornwall

For further information on Polity, visit our website:
www.politybooks.com

For Gwendolyn Kelly Garrison, the avatar of India, "the one sole country under the sun that is endowed with an imperishable interest for alien prince and alien peasant, for lettered and ignorant, wise and fool, rich and poor, bond and free, the one land that *all* men desire to see, and having seen once, by even a glimpse, would not give that glimpse for the shows of all the rest of the globe combined."

Mark Twain, *Following the Equator:*
A Journey around the World, Vol. 2
(New York: Harper & Brothers, 1906), p. 26.

Contents

Acknowledgements   viii

1   Introduction   1
2   Hegel's Life and Influences   12
3   Hegel's *Phenomenology of Spirit*   31
4   Hegel's *Logic*   79
5   Hegel's *Philosophy of Nature* and *Philosophy of Spirit*   94
6   Hegel's *Philosophy of Right*   109
7   Hegel's *Philosophy of History*   118
8   Hegel's Lectures on Philosophy and Religion   127
9   After Hegel   136

Notes   154
Suggestions for Further Reading   161
Index   177

Acknowledgements

I owe unrepayable debts of gratitude to:

Emma Hutchinson, my editor at Polity Press, who has the patience of Sītā.
Caroline Richmond, my copy editor at Polity Press, who has the writing style of Gaṇeśa.
The anonymous reviewers for Polity Press, who have the wisdom of Sarasvatī. This book is a book because of them.
Alison Stone, who believed that I could write this book and recommended me to Polity Press.
My teachers: the late Clarence Bauman, Thomas N. Finger, the late Albert N. Keim, Manfred Kuehn, Kem Luther, William L. McBride, Calvin O. Schrag, Willard M. Swartley, et alia.
My students; they're my best teachers.
William A. Rottschaefer, who read the entire manuscript of this book, thereby preventing many errors and several stupidities.
My colleagues, for whom, if I couldn't reflect their light, I'd be filled with envious hatred: Randall E. Auxier, Sepideh Bajracharya, Aaron Bunch, David Campion, Rebecca Copenhaver, Edward Cushman, Andrew Cutrofello, Robert A. Kugler, Joel Martinez, John McCumber, Clayton Morgareidge, Jay Odenbaugh, William A. Rottschaefer, Nicholas D. Smith, Richard Dien Winfield, Emily Zakin, Rishona Zimring.
My co-authors, who allowed me to join them in the sun: Samantha Park Alibrando, Gina Altamura, Katherine Elise Barhydt, Nathan Baty, Wendy Lynn Clark, Isabelle C. DeMarte, Jeffrey A. Gauthier,

Molly Gibson, Sarah Marchand Lomas, Sarah Ann Lowenstein, Meredith Margaret Nelson, Kristin Parvizian, Brianne Riley, McKenzie Judith Southworth.

"I used to think gratitude a heavy burden for one to carry. Now I know that it is something that makes the heart lighter. The ungrateful man seems to me to be one who walks with feet and heart of lead. But when one has learnt, however inadequately, what a lovely thing gratitude is, one's feet go lightly over sand or sea, and one finds a strange joy revealed to one, the joy of counting up, not what one possesses, but what one owes. I hoard my debts now in the treasury of my heart, and, piece of gold by piece of gold, I range them in order at dawn and at evening."

Oscar Wilde, *Selected Letters of Oscar Wilde*, ed. Rupert Hart-Davis (Oxford: Oxford University Press, 1979), p. 276.

1

Introduction

Why study Hegel? So far, philosophy has had only two heroic moments – times where it cast aside everything that is external and became fully itself. The first is Neoplatonism, which begins with Plotinus in 3 BCE and lasts several hundred years. The second moment is German idealism. Hegel is the greatest of the German idealists. Not the most brilliant or creative: that would be Schelling. But it is Hegel who thinks things through to their conclusions and links them together. The world today would be almost unimaginably different without him. Hegel's philosophy decisively influenced both Marx and Lenin. Without them, communism would never have existed, there would have been no Soviet Union or communist China, and the First World War would have concluded quite differently than it did.

Martin Luther King Jr. was influenced directly through reading Hegel, especially the *Lectures on the Philosophy of History*, and indirectly through studying philosophical personalism while a doctoral student at Boston University. Personalism, by the way, is the view that ultimate reality – God, if you prefer – is a person. Whereas Aristotle claims that God is the Unmoved Mover, wholly unaffected and indifferent to the universe, a personalist such as King believes that God is in a loving relation with the universe and – like a person – God has thoughts and feelings. The history of the civil rights movement would have been substantially different without Hegel.

Hegel is also important for philosophy. The beginnings of Anglo-American philosophy – one thinks, in this context, especially of

G. E. Moore and Bertrand Russell – are marked by a rejection of Hegel's philosophy. Twentieth-century French philosophers such as Simone de Beauvoir and Jean-Paul Sartre, as well as German philosophers such as Martin Heidegger, Theodor Adorno, and Jürgen Habermas, develop much of their philosophies in conversation with Hegel. By contrast, more recent French philosophy is defined by a concerted rejection of his philosophy. Indeed, David Carroll writes that, for Jean-François Lyotard, "the central problem is still, as it has been since at least Nietzsche, how to escape from or exceed the recuperating powers of the dialectic."[1] Carroll further observes that

> there is really no critical philosopher in France in the last twenty years – this is especially true of Foucault, Deleuze, Derrida, as well as Lyotard – who has not made this one of, if not the most pressing of all critical tasks. The political implications of all of their work could even be argued to be directly rooted in their critiques of the Hegelian and Marxist dialectics.[2]

Carroll's point is reinforced when we recognize that Marx's own notion of dialectic is a further articulation of Hegel's. More recently, an Analytic Hegelianism has emerged as philosophers working in the Anglo-American tradition, such as Robert Brandom and John McDowell, have written extensively on Hegel, urging that his arguments are still pertinent.

Hegel is doing a lot of things, as we will see, but his central project is one of reconciliation – with a twist. Hegel wants to demonstrate that, in the modern era, nature and society are not finally alien to us. We can be at home. And, if we feel estranged, we must discover in the very conditions that seemed to cause our estrangement the basis for reconciliation. That is always his main theme. Now, this makes Hegel sound like a profoundly conservative thinker. If we do not feel at home in our society because of its many injustices and inequities, it might seem that he tells us to get over it, deal with it, stop whining, accept that things are for the best, and smile. That is not Hegel! It is not Hegel because he is not trying to reconcile us to actually existing circumstances – although this is what he sometimes seems to suggest – but rather to reconcile us to circumstances that he presents as rational. So, there is in Hegel a call that we be actively engaged in transforming our world and making it into a home.

Hegel frequently discusses spirit or mind (*Geist*). By this book's conclusion, readers will have a good grasp of this concept. As a first approximation, though, they will not go wrong to think of spirit as synonymous with human culture. Hegel claims that spirit emerges from nature but cannot be reduced to nature, and so spirit cannot be comprehended with the methods that are appropriate for the natural sciences.

If there is a single concept that is associated with Hegel, it is dialectics. People with only a limited exposure to Hegel's dialectics frequently believe that it consists in three steps. First, there is the thesis, a partial statement of the truth that is mistaken for the entire truth. Second, there is the antithesis, a corrective to the mistakes of the thesis which nevertheless misses the aspects of the thesis that are correct. Finally, there is the synthesis, which incorporates the correct aspects of the thesis with the correctives supplied by the antithesis. The synthesis then itself becomes another thesis, again giving rise to another antithesis, and then to another reconciling synthesis that becomes yet another thesis. This process continues until we reach the final synthesis that actually is the full truth and so does not require a correcting antithesis.

This account of Hegel's dialectics is itself only a partial comprehension that requires correction. Before criticizing, however, let us first note three features that it perceives correctly. First, it recognizes that truth emerges from error. Moreover, as we will see many times throughout this book, truth necessarily emerges from error. So, the history of philosophy is not, for Hegel, a catalog of howlers and blunders that might have been avoided. Rather, it is only by attempting to correct the perceived inadequacies of previous views that philosophy develops. Second, this account recognizes the importance of history. Truth cannot be seized in an instant but rather must develop through philosophers continually responding to and correcting each other. Earlier philosophers literally could not think what later philosophers can. Finally, this account implicitly suggests a holism in which partial truths are progressively corrected so that their one-sidedness is overcome.

However, this account must be supplemented. Although the thesis comes first in the order of narration, it actually emerges as a reaction to the antithesis. That is, what we are calling the thesis is recognized *as* a thesis only after it has been contested by the antithesis. Prior to that, the thesis is not explicitly articulated. Instead, it may be believed to be so obvious that individuals may not even recognize that they believe it. (This is an experience that many people have when they first visit another country.) Only after the antithesis appears is the thesis seen as a thesis and as a view that is, in principle, contestable. In this sense, the antithesis creates the thesis against which it protests.

This is why the antithesis is not, ultimately, alien from the thesis. The thesis is the product of the antithesis. Shifting perspective slightly, it is equally correct that the antithesis actually emerges from within (what will subsequently come to be recognized as) the thesis.

The thesis does not take kindly to the corrections offered by the antithesis. Even if the antithesis were content to correct only the perceived failings of the thesis, the thesis would resist. The thesis does not perceive its own failings. However, the antithesis challenges the very existence of the thesis. Just as the thesis believes that it expresses the whole truth, failing to perceive that its articulation is partial, so the antithesis also claims to possess the whole truth. Neither the thesis nor the antithesis recognizes any merit or legitimacy in the other. And so they struggle. As they fight, the thesis responds to the attacks of the antithesis by employing the very tropes and categories of the antithesis. By responding in this way, the thesis thereby becomes the antithesis. To be sure, the thesis may continue to disagree vehemently with the antithesis. However, in adopting the preferred descriptions and forms of argument of the antithesis, the thesis has already lost. It has irretrievably altered into the very form of the antithesis. This is the synthesis! The synthesis is best described not as the resolution of the thesis and antithesis, but rather as the thesis becoming a position within the antithesis.

An especially clear example is found in Hegel's first major publication, the *Phenomenology of Spirit*, when he chronicles Enlightenment's struggle with Religion. Enlightenment here plays the role of the antithesis, denouncing Religion as baseless superstition that is contrary to reason and experience. What Enlightenment fails to see is how Religion emerges through Enlightenment's very opposition to it. Before Enlightenment, Religion does not exist as an explicit set of beliefs. Instead, what will retrospectively be recognized as Religion initially exists as a thoroughly integrated aspect of the life of a people, as people's implicit worldview, expressed in their rituals and practices. It is only after Enlightenment appears, denouncing Religion as superstition, that Religion can then be experienced as a specific and contingent, and so as a contestable and optional, aspect. Enlightenment does not recognize this. What Religion, now explicitly articulated as Religion, does not perceive is how its own response to Enlightenment accepts Enlightenment's own categories. Religion *argues*. It maintains that it is not superstition but instead rational.

Indeed, Religion claims that it is more rational then Enlightenment. In responding in this way, Religion thereby takes on Enlightenment's own categories. Religion may still reject many of Enlightenment's specific assertions, but Religion articulates its rejection in the language of Enlightenment. At this point, Religion becomes not an alternative to Enlightenment, but merely another position within Enlightenment itself.

This example also allows us to comprehend the positing of the presuppositions. For Hegel, the presuppositions are posited retrospectively. It is not only that we can see, after the fact, that one thing was the beginning of something else. Crucially, it is also that what later emerges changes the very meaning of the thing from which it began. Religion exists *as* Religion – as a set of articulated beliefs that can be rationally defended, rather than as rituals that are inseparably integrated into the life of a people – only after, and as a result of, Enlightenment's depicting Religion as superstition. After Religion emerges as Religion, though, it can then be seen retrospectively as something quite ancient. As the life of a people, it is ancient. As a set of articulated beliefs, it is recent.

A final way in which the fashionable account of Hegel's dialectics is inadequate is that it supposes that there is a final synthesis – Hegel's own system – that does not itself become yet another thesis then to be opposed by an antithesis. This is one interpretation in the scholarly literature. In this book, however, I will argue that a better reading is that Hegel's system is not the culmination of dialectics but rather its comprehension.

Hegel lived almost two hundred years ago. His world is markedly different from our own. Nevertheless, many of the challenges that he faced are still with us. Comprehending how he articulated those problems and understanding his proposed solutions can provide guidance for us. I have already suggested that Hegel's project is best seen as one of reconciliation. I would like to discuss this further, urging that Hegel seeks to overcome various forms of dualism and skepticism. Skepticism would have us believe that there could be substantial constraints on our ability to know what the world is like, to know that other people also have minds, and to know about God. Now, there is a sense in which skepticism can be empowering, as Nietzsche later recognizes. If we doubt that some claim is true or that a theory is correct, we can be motivated to investigate further, do research, and see if we can learn more and comprehend matters more thoroughly. This type of skepticism is beneficial.

There is another type of skepticism, however, that is stultifying. This second type of skepticism asserts that, in principle, we can never know the world, whether other persons have minds, and about God. This skepticism further tells us that there is no point in investigating or doing research because we can never know what we would seek to know. It can take various forms, some more obvious, others less so. For example, this skepticism asserts that one gender can never comprehend others, that a culture can never understand others, that the universe is stranger than we can ever imagine, that we can never know what other persons are really like or what they believe, that – try as we might – the world is ultimately mysterious.

Hegel's response is that we should be skeptical of this very skepticism. Rather than heeding its counsels of despair, we should instead investigate, do research, observe and talk with others, and thereby discover what we actually can know. When it turns out that we do not know what we thought we did, then we should investigate further and try to correct the errors in our beliefs. We should not conclude, as insidious skepticism would advocate, that we cannot really know much or anything and then quit trying. Through overcoming previous mistakes and correcting errors, we learn more than we knew before. This is why, moreover, Hegel rejects a priori methods and conceptual analyses. We can discover what can be known only by attempting to know, partially succeeding, and then trying again.

All of this is to suggest that Hegel is not claiming to have achieved a final certainty – although there is a fashionable interpretation of him that asserts otherwise – but rather that he holds that we should strive for knowledge and correct errors when they are detected. In this way, moreover, mistakes and errors are not entirely negative. False theories can still have been useful – Ptolemaic astronomy could predict eclipses, despite believing that the earth is the center of the universe – and the discovery of a theory's limitations can motivate us to overcome them. When we learn that we have not adequately comprehended another person, culture, the universe, or even God, we do not despair in the face of an ultimate mystery. We renew our efforts.

Is it not the case that Hegel places an unconditional faith in reason, in our ability to know? True, he does. Paradoxically, however, so does the insidious skepticism that he opposes. This skepticism asserts that we cannot know – and how, we may sensibly ask, does it know this? Actually, the choice between Hegel and skepticism is quite simple: Should we try to know, making corrections as needed; or should we prefer an ignorance that does not even try?

Let me briefly discuss several other important themes in Hegel.

When Hegel criticizes worldviews and philosophies, he uses internal critique. He does not argue against those other positions because they contradict his own views. He recognizes that, were he to proceed in that way, the others could acknowledge that his system contradicts them – and then urge that this is why his system should be rejected. In order to avoid such gainsaying, Hegel instead shows that perceived alternatives to his system fail by their own standards of success. Such a position does not fail because it contradicts his system, it fails because it contradicts itself. Hegel then argues that a successor position emerges that addresses this contradiction. In this way, he seeks to show that what initially appear as alternatives to his own system are instead aspects, moments, within it.

This suggests that, for Hegel, philosophy must be a system that emerges historically. It is insufficient merely to chronicle the different articulations of philosophy, compiling a list of them, and noting their similarities and differences. Rather, philosophy must be a system that shows how previous articulations contributed to its own realization. Since later articulations become possible only as responses to earlier articulations, philosophy is necessarily historical.

As we will see in subsequent chapters, Hegel is also concerned to overcome a number of dualisms, and he opposes immediacy. The latter is the term he uses to refer to positions that advocate either that there are experiences that are unconceptualizable or that there is something – such as God or the universe itself – that is beyond human comprehension. In response, Hegel maintains that all experience is conceptual, mediated, and that there is nothing that cannot be comprehended. He argues, moreover, that the very attempt to assert that there is something that is ultimately mysterious involves conceptualizing it.

As noted above, Hegel also opposes dualisms, and, in this sense, his philosophy is a holism. Many of these dualisms find expression in the philosophy of Immanuel Kant, but they are deeply embedded in Western culture. In ethics, there are tensions between following our inclinations and doing what is moral, as well as tensions between achieving the best consequences and acting from the proper motives. In politics, there are tensions between the individual and the larger community, including the state. There are tensions between explaining the natural world, on the one hand, and comprehending humans and culture, on the other. There are tensions between faith and reason, as well as between humanity and God. With every dualism, Hegel attempts to demonstrate that both sides are one-sided, that each side is a partial truth that mistakes itself for the whole truth, that both sides are mutually co-determining, so that one side can be fully comprehended only by including what initially appears to be its adversary, that the estrangement experienced in one side is redoubled in the other, that one side emerges only when its opposite appears, that, even though both poles are mutually co-determining, we must nevertheless begin from one pole to see both aright.

Hegel published the *Phenomenology of Spirit* in 1807. Although the majority of its interpreters believe either that this book should be read as telling a single linear narrative or that it is actually two distinct stories slapped together, it is most usefully read as telling the story of Western civilization from three successive standpoints. Hegel first tells this story from the perspective of what he calls "shapes of consciousness," an era's worldview. He next tells it from the perspective of the social conditions that made possible those shapes of consciousness. Finally, he tells this story from the perspective of religion and philosophy. This book is notoriously difficult to comprehend. One of the reasons is that Hegel discusses things at a highly abstract level – and he often discusses several things at once, things that have some important features in common.

Another reason that the *Phenomenology of Spirit* is so hard is that Hegel's transitions can seem abrupt and arbitrary. Why did he go in that direction, readers wonder, rather than some other? It is helpful here to see Hegel approaching the story of Western civilization from a retrospective standpoint. But he tells it prospectively! What I mean is this. Writing in 1807, Hegel knows how history has turned out so far. So, when he tells the history of Western civilization, he knows which events were important and which can be ignored. He narrates that history from the beginning, however, and so it is not always obvious why things had to happen the way he says. Well, they did not have to happen that way. At the time, they were contingent and something else might have occurred. Given that they did happen, however, they become necessary. It is one of Hegel's deepest lessons that what was contingent can become necessary.

Here is a simple example. Suppose that the only way I can reach New Delhi by tomorrow is to catch a flight early this morning. It is possible, of course, that I might miss my flight. People do that every day. And if that happens, I will not reach New Delhi by tomorrow. Given that I do reach New Delhi tomorrow, however, then it was necessary that I caught my flight. So, although Hegel maintains that his transitions are necessary, this necessity is the result of their already having happened.

Many interpreters of Hegel believe that his concept of necessity is stronger than this and that each shape of consciousness must transition to a specific successor. I will later discuss the limitations of this.

Let me say a few more words about the *Phenomenology of Spirit*. Initially, it seems that Hegel is going to write a traditional book on epistemology, the theory of knowledge, explaining how an individual can know something. In a sense, that is not wrong. In another sense, it is.

To generalize to the extreme, modern philosophers from Descartes through Kant believe that, before we try to know anything else, we must first determine what sorts of things we can know. Hegel rejects this tradition. He claims that we only discover what we can know by actually trying to know things, failing, and then trying again. We can provisionally know what sorts of things we can know by retrospectively seeing what sorts of things we have actually been able to know. But we can do no more than that. So, rather than first attempting to determine, a priori, what can be known, Hegel instead investigates actual attempts to know.

Another way that the *Phenomenology of Spirit* is not a traditional book on epistemology is that Hegel believes that knowledge can be explicated only at the social level. To put this in a slogan, it is society that knows in the first instance, and individuals know only because society knows. What does that mean?

First, it means that individuals cannot determine what counts as knowledge or what the criteria for knowledge are. Whether some individuals can be correctly said to know something is a matter of whether others in their society regard them as knowing it. In science, for example, a scientist knows that a theory is true only when it has been recognized as true by other scientists. Before passing this process of peer review, an individual scientist does not know that a theory is true. This explains why Hegel begins with individuals trying to obtain knowledge but then switches to discussions about society. His approach to knowledge is quite distinct from the individualist perspective to which we are accustomed, and that also makes it difficult to comprehend the *Phenomenology of Spirit*.

There is something else that is even more radical. Hegel believes that humanity ultimately constitutes an extended mind, a shared consciousness. We believe, unreflectively, that each individual has a mind. Two heads are better than one, we say, but they are still two heads. Hegel thinks, however, that, if the two heads are thinking together, or even thinking against each other, they then should be regarded as a single mind. I will discuss this in greater detail in the chapter on the *Phenomenology of Spirit*, but it is helpful to anticipate Hegel's views.

Following the *Phenomenology of Spirit*, Hegel wrote the *Science of Logic* as well as the *Encyclopedia of the Philosophical Sciences* (which is divided into three books: *Logic, Nature, Spirit*). The *Logic* of the *Encyclopedia* is an abridgement of the *Science of Logic*. For the purposes of this book, we do not need to discuss them separately. The *Logic* is divided into three components: Being, Essence, and Concept. It is incredibly easy to get lost among the *Logic*'s trees and so to miss the forest.

There is a continuing debate about whether the *Phenomenology of Spirit* merely introduces readers to Hegel's system while remaining outside of it, as Moses remained outside of the Promised Land, or whether it is itself a component of the system. I suggest that the *Phenomenology of Spirit* both introduces the system and is a part of it. The *Phenomenology of Spirit* tells the history of Western civilization, as I have suggested above, from three successive perspectives: the shapes of consciousness, their social contexts, and religion and philosophy. The *Logic* narrates that same history from the perspective of concepts. Being is the moment where things are described as they appear. However, Being can explain neither why similar things are similar nor why things appear as they do. These failures lead to Essence, which tries to explain appearances by postulating hidden forces. However, Essence cannot explain why things would be caused to appear as they do, and it does not recognize that, in addition to being changed by other things, things can change themselves. Finally, the Concept explains things by pointing to their purposes. It is crucial to recognize that these three levels of explanation are not mutually exclusive but rather are nested together. Essence contains Being and the Concept contains both. Again, Hegel's perspective in the *Logic* is retrospective, although his narrative is presented prospectively. Further, the *Logic* is not only a history of the ways in which people have thought (a category theory) but also a discussion of what there actually is (a metaphysics).

In the *Philosophy of Nature*, Hegel argues that the results of contemporary science can be arranged in a hierarchical order, from those aspects that are most distant from human culture to those which are nearest. He is concerned to show that we need not feel estranged or alienated from nature. Rather, nature is the condition of the possibility of human culture. In the *Philosophy of Spirit*, Hegel chronicles the development of spirit, beginning with the individual (subjective spirit), moving to society (objective spirit), and concluding with art, religion, and society (absolute spirit).

The chapters on Hegel's *Elements of the Philosophy of Right* and on the *Philosophy of History* discuss objective spirit in greater detail, and the chapter on his lectures on Aesthetics and on Religion further discusses absolute spirit.

I have tried to write this book so that it does not presuppose any previous knowledge of philosophy and still provides a useful orientation to Hegel – an impossible task, perhaps, but many things are impossible until someone does them. If you need help, try Wikipedia, at http://en.wikipedia.org/, *The Internet Encyclopedia of Philosophy*, at www.iep.utm.edu/, or *The Stanford Encyclopedia of Philosophy*, at http://plato.stanford.edu/.

Finally, Bertolt Brecht "never met a person without a sense of humor who understood Hegel's dialectic."[3] Neither have I.

2

Hegel's Life and Influences

What I will do in this chapter is to discuss Hegel's life so that readers will have an understanding of the context in which his philosophy is situated. I also want to indicate some of the influences on him. Before proceeding further, however, a brief discussion of context.

A thing is the thing that it is, Hegel believes, as a consequence of the set of relations in which that thing is positioned. Change those relations, change the context, and the thing itself changes and becomes something other than it was. Since the relations are continually changing and, moreover, a relation doesn't form a self-consistent set, things are always on the move. Hegel's context isn't ours. Perhaps, later, readers may decide that it wasn't his either. Nevertheless, that context isn't wholly alien from ours. I intend to insert Hegel in our context, as much as is feasible, so that we comprehend him from our perspective. This will involve situating him in contemporary debates as well as interpretive controversies about the meaning of his texts. Reading Hegel this way risks distorting him, to be sure, but it has two considerable advantages. First, the Hegel we encounter will be more accessible, less strange, than he might otherwise seem. As we progress, we will discover that he becomes less familiar and more interesting. The second advantage is that Hegel will be found to have something to say about contemporary debates. He won't be talking about historical curiosities. Not that he ever did, but explaining why apparent curiosities are actually of decisive importance would require digressions and detours that, while scenic, might try the patience of readers who prefer traveling to touring. There is yet a third advantage to this way of reading Hegel: we may eventually find our own context strange.

Hegel's life is, apart from his philosophizing, uneventful and so can be quickly narrated. He was born in Stuttgart on August 27, 1770. Stuttgart is in Swabia, which was regarded as backward by persons from other parts of Germany. Hegel always spoke with a Swabian accent. He had a sister, Christiane Luise (1773–1832), and a brother, Georg Ludwig (1776–1812).

Hegel went to seminary with Hölderlin and Schelling in Tübingen (1788–93). All three were enthusiastic supporters of the French Revolution. This is an enthusiasm that Hegel never lost. He worked as a tutor in the homes of wealthy families in Bern (1793–6) and Frankfurt (1797–1801). During this time, he wrote "The Life of Jesus," "The Positivity of the Christian Religion," "Fragments on Religion and Love," and "The Spirit of Christianity and its Fate." Hegel portrayed Jesus as a moral teacher and he attempted to articulate a philosophy based on love.

From 1801 to 1807 Hegel was in Jena, initially in order to work with Schelling, who was a professor at the university there. The two men collaborated on a journal, for which they wrote most of the articles, and Hegel published his first book, *The Difference between Fichte's and Schelling's Systems of Philosophy* (1801). His *Phenomenology of Spirit* was published in 1807, and it is with this book that he becomes the philosopher whom we recognize as Hegel. It seems that the friendship between Hegel and Schelling was based primarily on a shared philosophy. This ended with the *Phenomenology of Spirit*, which contained several sharp criticisms of Schelling. Hegel wrote the concluding sections while Napoleon was invading Jena. He saw Napoleon from a distance and later wrote to his friend Friedrich Immanuel Niethammer (1766–1848) that he had seen the emperor, this world soul, sitting on horseback.

While Hegel was in Jena, he impregnated Christiana Burkhardt, his landlady, which resulted in a son, Georg Ludwig Friedrich Fischer (1807–1831). When Hegel worked as a newspaper editor in Bamberg (1807–8) and then as the headmaster of a high school (*Gymnasium*) in Nuremberg (1808–16), they remained in Jena. In 1811 Hegel married Marie Helena Susanna von Tucher (1791–1855), with whom he had two sons, Karl Friedrich Wilhelm Hegel (1813–1901) and Immanuel Thomas Christian Hegel (1814–1891). While in Bamberg and Nuremberg, Hegel published sections of his *Science of Logic*, in 1812, 1813, and 1816.

Hegel finally received an academic appointment, at the University of Heidelberg (1816–18). His son Georg Fischer lived in an orphanage after Christiana Burkhardt's death, but he came to Heidelberg to live with Hegel's family in 1817, the same year that Hegel published *Encyclopedia of the Philosophical Sciences*.

Hegel then received an appointment at the University of Berlin (1818–31). He published the *Elements of the Philosophy of Right* in 1820. His *Philosophy of History* is based on lectures he gave in 1821, 1824, 1827, and 1831. While in Berlin, he also gave lectures on Aesthetics, Religion, and the History of Philosophy. He died, possibly of cholera, on November 14, 1831.

So they say.

Joe Hill (1879–1915) didn't die. Neither did Hegel.

After 1831, his followers divide into two groups, the so-called Right and Left (or Young) Hegelians. The Right Hegelians are more socially and religiously conservative, interpreting Hegel as supporting the Prussian state and as an orthodox Lutheran. The Left Hegelians, by contrast, read Hegel's philosophy as advocating freedom – and hence, his philosophy, even if not the man himself, as implicitly critical of the state. They also read him as an atheist who jettisons the traditional God of theism and replaces God with Humanity. Ludwig Feuerbach (1804–1872) is the culmination of this trajectory. Karl Marx (1818–1883) begins as a Left Hegelian but takes his leave. To simplify, Marx comes to believe that the Left Hegelians' emphasis on religious and theological concerns is insufficiently radical and that what is crucial is a rejection of such speculations accompanied by a turn to real existing material conditions. We don't need to discuss these issues any further now, but readers with a sense of dialectics will already suspect that the truth lies in seeing how these opposing views are one-sided, and so false, expressions. Briefly: what is required is to see how Hegel's advocating freedom and criticism of the state is, for him, internal to the state itself; how his supposed atheism is his belief in God and that he is, if not an *orthodox* Lutheran, a fully *consistent* Lutheran – indeed, a Lutheran who is more Lutheran than Luther himself; and how not only are religion and theology the expressions of real existing material conditions but also that those conditions can be comprehended solely through religion and theology.

I want to write a few words about the metaphysical and non-metaphysical Hegel. I will discuss this in more detail later. Here, what is important is that, until the twentieth century, Hegel is read as a metaphysician. There are debates about whether his metaphysics goes beyond the critical philosophy of Immanuel Kant (1724–1804) – more later – or if Hegel is a throwback to some sort of pre-critical metaphysics that Kant had already shown to be untenable. Nevertheless, regardless of whether Hegel's metaphysics was celebrated or condemned, he was read as doing metaphysics. Beginning in the last quarter of the twentieth century, a non-metaphysical interpretation has become increasing fashionable.

Now, here's a tip about reading academic writing. Whenever scholars say that something is "fashionable," it's certain that they will immediately criticize it.

The non-metaphysical interpretation of Hegel sees him as completing Kant's critical philosophy and doing so in a way that doesn't fall back into pre-critical philosophy. Unlike most previous philosophers, who claim that it is possible to have actual knowledge of God, freedom, and the soul, Kant maintains that humans can have knowledge about only those things which are possible objects of experience. He further restricts experience to that which can be detected by the five senses. Kant sneers at the claim that individuals can have any experience that transcends the senses – for example, in his book against the mystic Emmanuel Swedenborg (1688–1772), *Dreams of a Spirit-Seer* – but Kant simply assumes that there cannot be any such experience. The non-metaphysical interpretation of Hegel believes that he is continuing this trajectory. Its advocates are willing to concede that Hegel himself doesn't always follow this trajectory, that he backslides into metaphysics. They are also willing to concede that this non-metaphysical interpretation of Hegel's philosophy is, to some extent, a rational reconstruction, one that emphasizes those aspects of Hegel's thought that are intelligible without his metaphysical commitments.

There are two primary objections advanced against the metaphysical reading of Hegel. First, it is said to be pre-critical, representing a return to errors that Kant had overcome rather than a move beyond the position reached by Kant. Second, it is asserted that the metaphysical reading isn't credible. Regarding the first objection, I will indicate in this book why Hegel's metaphysics represents a move beyond Kant's critical philosophy rather than a throwback to a position which hasn't yet reached Kant's level. The non-metaphysical interpretation is correct in believing that Hegel carries forward Kant's critical philosophy and thereby completes it. However, that interpretation fails to recognize that Hegel can move beyond Kant precisely because of his metaphysics. I will discuss these further points throughout this book.

In regards to the second objection – even if a metaphysical reading of Hegel's philosophy is required in order to progress beyond Kant, it is nevertheless too incredible for us to believe – one is tempted to respond by invoking Oscar Wilde, who wrote: "I can believe anything, provided it is quite incredible." There are several decisive reasons to reject this dismissal of Hegel's metaphysics as too incredible. First, if appeals to incredulity were conclusive, then we should reject quantum mechanics without further ado. Second, such appeals, if allowed to proceed unchallenged, would make impossible any serious criticisms of ideology, as critiques of ideology frequently suggest that the social relations in which we are situated, with their accompanying practices and our experiences of our motivations, aren't transparent. Finally, however, those who advert that Hegel's metaphysics is too incredible to be credible aren't cognizant of developments in (what passes for) mainstream Philosophy of Mind, Epistemology, and Metaphysics. In those areas, theories have been advanced that relevantly converge on Hegel's metaphysics. This doesn't itself provide evidence of the correctness of either those mainstream theories or Hegel's metaphysics, of course, but it does show that the latter can't be dismissed as too incredible when similar views are seen as meriting serious consideration.

Let me now discuss the main influences on Hegel's philosophy. There is a real sense in which Hegel is influenced by the entire history of Western philosophy. Indeed, it would be difficult, perhaps impossible, to find any significant Western philosopher who didn't influence him. This is especially true if we note that influences can be not only positive – where a philosopher regards predecessors as proceeding on the proper path and so seeks to further or complete their projects – but also negative – where a philosopher considers predecessors as fundamentally misguided or one-sided and so aims to reject or overthrow their projects. Nevertheless, I can't discuss the whole history of Western philosophy here. What I will do instead is highlight the main influences on Hegel – influences that we can discern, not always those that Hegel himself acknowledges – saying a few words about each.

So that readers don't get lost, let me add that the most important of these influences are **Aristotle**, **Spinoza**, **Kant**, **Herder**, and **Schelling**. I'll also write their names in boldface when we encounter them below.

We begin with what Hegel himself identifies as the beginning of Western philosophy: ancient Greece. (Although he had maintained that there is no philosophy in India, near the end of his life he concludes that there is genuine philosophy in India. Nonetheless, he still claims that, for the West, philosophy begins in ancient Greece.)

Parmenides (fifth century BCE) claimed that there is only one thing and that the evidence we have from our senses, that there are many things, is wholly illusory. He arrived at this startling conclusion by initially arguing that only Being is and that Nothing cannot be. If there isn't Nothing, then there is no way in which one part or aspect of Being could be separated or distinguished from another; without Nothing, Being can't have parts. Even if we could conceive of two different aspects of Being – and Parmenides maintained that we can't conceive this – the two aspects would immediately merge into one because Nothing wouldn't keep them apart. Parmenides' successor, Zeno of Elea (*c.* 490–430 BCE), introduced a number of paradoxes intended to show that motion and change are impossible, concluding that – although it seems that there are many things, some of which move – there is actually only one immovable thing, Being. Being itself can't move because it encompasses all Being and so there is no place it could move to.

Hegel rejects this line of argument. In his *Logic*, he argues that, although we mean for there to be a distinction between Being and Nothing, insofar as Being is conceived as the most general description or category, we can't articulate any difference between Being and Nothing. So, although Parmenides and Zeno intended there to be a distinction between Being and Nothing, they themselves couldn't say what that distinction is. (Parmenides and Zeno were in a bind here, because they claimed that Nothing can't even be *thought*, and so they can't even think the difference between Being and Nothing.)

The sophist Gorgias (*c.* 485–380 BCE) wrote *On Non-Being* (or *On the Non-Existent*), a work that is now lost, as a parody of Parmenides' argument. Gorgias asserted that nothing exists; that even if something did exist, it would be impossible to know it; that even if it could be known, it would be impossible to communicate this knowledge; and, finally, that even if this knowledge could be communicated, it wouldn't be understood. This move from Being to Nothing is eminently Hegelian.

Hegel believes that no philosophy is wholly incorrect, that there is a partial truth in each philosophy that is mistaken for the whole truth. What needs to be done, in examining a philosophy, is to recognize its correct but partial insight while also seeing that, because it is partial, it is not the final truth. Parmenides was correct to believe that, ultimately, everything is finally one. He was incorrect to believe that this one is a pure identity that excludes difference. One way to put this point, although it will sound paradoxical now, is that Hegel doesn't believe that Being is opposed to Nothing, not ultimately, but that Being contains Nothing.

Heraclitus of Ephesus (*c.* 535–475 BCE) rejected Parmenides' monism. Monism is the claim that there is only one basic substance – in Parmenides' case, that there is only one thing, Being. Heraclitus believed that all things emerge from fire, that fire is what is most fundamental, and so, in that sense, he could be considered a monist. Nevertheless, whereas Parmenides maintained that there is only one thing, Heraclitus insisted that there is a plurality of things. And, while Zeno claimed that movement is impossible, Heraclitus made change fundamental to his philosophy. He believed that everything is in continual motion, that change is constant. He claimed that it is impossible to step into the same river twice, for example, because the water that is flowing now isn't the same water as earlier or later.

Hegel agrees that change is a central property. He argues that change occurs because things become contradictory with themselves and so must alter to overcome those contradictions. This process of overcoming contradictions means that change is rational and progressive.

Plato (*c.* 424–348 BCE) was influenced by Pythagoras (*c.* 570–495 BCE), who maintained that everything is number. It's not clear what Pythagoras meant by this. He may have intended to convey that everything has an underlying mathematical structure. He would have likely arrived at such an insight by studying the harmonics of musical instruments. In any event, Plato was dissatisfied with Heraclitus' belief that everything is in a constant flux because he thought that this didn't account for stability and persistence throughout change. If everything is always changing, why are we still able to identify a horse as a horse, and the same horse, during different periods of its life? Moreover, how can we identify different horses as horses? There must be some underlying feature, Plato believed, that persists throughout the changes that makes horses the horses that they are. Plato called this underlying feature the *form* of a thing. The form of a thing is what makes that thing the thing that it is.

As an initial approximation, Plato's form can be thought of as a definition of a thing, a definition that states what a thing is and also, at least implicitly, how that thing differs from all other things. An example of this is *prime number*. Suppose, to follow the pattern of many of Plato's dialogues, an individual, asked to define "prime number," responds by giving a list of prime numbers: 2, 3, 5, 7, 11, 13, 17, 19, etc. We would respond by saying that we don't want examples of prime numbers, instead what we want to know is what makes those numbers prime – which is: a prime number is any natural number greater than 1 that is evenly divisible – divisible without a remainder – only by itself and 1. Now, we know what factors make a number a prime number. We can now tell for any number, moreover, if it is a prime number: see if any other number other than itself and by 1 evenly divides into it. The process is laborious for large numbers, but there is a process. So, in principle, we can't be fooled into believing that a number is prime when it isn't.

According to Plato, Socrates (c. 469–399 BCE) believed that everything, or almost everything, can be defined this way, giving the necessary and sufficient conditions that make a thing the thing that it is. Such an analysis would not only tell us what, say, virtue is, but it would also provide, in principle, a means to determine whether any specific thing or action is an instance of virtue. Another consequence of this would be a rejection of cultural relativism. There would really be a form for (almost) everything, and so what a thing is wouldn't depend on any group's opinions.

Socrates also believed that these definitions, which he called "forms," are what is actually real and that individual things exist as the things they are because they participate in their *forms*, which makes those things be what they are. Not only this, Socrates thought as well that the forms are perfect, eternal, and unchanging, and that they exist in a separate and higher plane of existence than this world.

Hegel rejects the view that there are hidden essences existing beneath or behind things, essences which make these things the things that they are. In his discussion of the topsy-turvy, or upside-down, world in the *Phenomenology of Spirit*, Hegel suggests that such notions do no conceptual work. If objects had hidden essences which were the cause of those objects appearing as they do, but were nevertheless distinct from the objects' appearances, then the essence might be the opposite of its appearance. So, what appears to be vice might have the essence of virtue, punishment could be reward, and so forth. We realize what objects are from the objects themselves rather than from essences.

Aristotle (384–322 BCE) agreed with Socrates that things have definitions – which Aristotle called *universals* rather than *forms* – but he insisted that these universals don't exist in a separate and higher plane of existence and that things don't participate in them, as

Plato's Socrates maintained was true of the forms, but instead universals are instantiated in the things. Aristotle argued that the notion of forms existing separately doesn't explain anything. Not participation but instantiation. This enabled a limited relativism, for Aristotle, as virtues are indexed to cultures. It is only a limited relativism, however, because he argued that there is an overarching purpose for humans – being as much like the gods as it is possible for human beings – and so he claimed that this sets the final standard for determining whether persons are living to their fullest extent.

Hegel agrees with Aristotle that the universals of particulars are instantiated in those particulars, and so he joins Aristotle in rejecting Plato's Socrates' suggestion that universals, or forms, could exist separately and apart from particulars. Hegel is even more radical than Aristotle on this point, though, as he maintains that the universals aren't behind, beneath, or in (pick your metaphor) the particulars but, rather, are the ways in which particulars appear. A bit of precision is called for here. Hegel isn't a nominalist, urging that universals are no more than names we give to particulars grouped in various ways, ways that might be useful but are nonetheless arbitrary. Hegel insists that universals really do exist, but they are the ways in which particulars appear to us. Talk here of "appearances" might be potentially misleading. In saying that universals appear, a distinction isn't being made between how things appear and how they really are, such that they might ultimately be different than how they appear. A rope can initially appear to be a snake, true, but it is a rope and not a snake because, when examined further, it appears as a rope.

Hegel also moves beyond Aristotle by emphasizing the role of history. One way to express this point, quickly, is that Aristotle believed, as did Plato's Socrates, that universals are unchanging, and so he would reject the claim that they could develop over time. For Hegel, by contrast, they do develop. The clearest example of this is Hegel's view that freedom develops historically. The Oriental World recognized that only one individual, the pharaoh, was free. The Greeks and Romans saw that some persons, citizens, were free. In the Germanic World, the modern world, we realize that all persons are entitled to freedom. What is crucial is that Hegel isn't making only an epistemological claim, he is also making an ontological claim. It isn't that people comprehend freedom while freedom itself exists unaltered. Rather, freedom itself develops. It is not merely what counts as freedom that changes, but also what freedom really is. And, given Hegel's views about universals, we could have anticipated that this would be his position. Recall that a universal is, for him, the way that a thing appears. If freedom appears substantially different at various times, then it is freedom itself that develops, not merely the perception of it.

Hegel also differs from Aristotle in two other ways that are worth mentioning here: regarding the constitution of society and the prime mover.

When Aristotle compared humans to other creatures, he selected bees. This is because he considered the community of bees, the hive, to be the actual creature and individual bees to be parts of the hive (as, we might say, the organs of the body – heart, liver, lungs – are parts of the body). So, Aristotle regarded the city-state, the *polis*, as the actual creature and individuals as parts of it. Another way to put this point is to say that, for Aristotle, the city-state is the fundamental unit of analysis. Hegel instead claims that society and the individual are mutually co-determining; the fundamental unit is a dyad consisting of both society and the individual.

The moon, sun, planets, and stars are, Aristotle theorized, in a vortex motion around the world, arranged based on the heaviness of the materials composing them. The prime mover exists at every point along the periphery of the universe, as the prime mover is pure form with no matter composing it. The planets and stars are alive, since they move. They desire to be as much like the prime mover as possible. They can't simultaneously be at every place, as the prime mover is every place along the perimeter, and so they move in circular orbits around the earth so that, over time, they will have been everywhere they could be. The prime mover is the teleological, but not the efficient, cause of the universe. That is to say, the prime mover doesn't directly exert any force on anything in the universe. Since the prime mover is perfect, it doesn't think about, and isn't aware of, anything less perfect than itself, and so it thinks only about itself. Indeed, as pure form and no matter, the prime mover is solely thought, a thought that thinks itself. It causes movement in the universe because other things want to emulate the prime mover as much as possible.

Hegel's absolute plays a similar role in the structure of his philosophy, although the differences between the absolute and the prime mover are as important as the similarities. Whereas Aristotle's prime mover is unchanging, Hegel's absolute develops historically. And whereas the prime mover is entirely unaffected by the universe, the absolute is the collective result of the universe

– principally, indeed, the result of human actions. The prime mover is eternal and so always already everything that it ever will be, whereas, as just mentioned, the absolute is a result. Hegel's result is an extended mind, a collective consciousness, that potentially encompasses all of humanity. The prime mover always functions as the teleological cause of everything, as all things want to be as similar to it as they can. Since the absolute develops historically, its function as a teleological cause is retrospective. That is, looking back on the past, Hegel discerns how things have been aiming to construct the absolute. And how is Hegel's absolute absolute?

Hegel's absolute is absolute because there is nothing external to it that would limit it. It may be viewed, initially, as having two components: nature and spirit. As nature, it encompasses the universe, inorganic and organic. As spirit, it is human culture in all of its manifestations. Hegel denies that any progress occurs in nature. The changes there are cyclical: day follows night, the seasons follow each other, generations are born, reproduce, and die. Only at the level of spirit, according to Hegel, is there progress. What progresses is human freedom. Someone might think that human culture is insignificant when compared to the vastness and grandeur of the universe. However, Hegel regards nature as the condition and backdrop for spirit. It is not only that there is progress only at the level of spirit; spirit, not nature, is self-determining. Things happen in nature as they must, but humans decide what sort of culture and lives they will have – what they will be. No individual decides these things, of course, but they are the results of our collective decisions and actions.

Neoplatonism, a philosophy that flourished during the third and fourth centuries CE, attempted to combine the teachings of Plato and Aristotle. Following the suggestion of Socrates, in Plato's *Republic*, that the forms themselves exist as forms because they participate in the Good, Neoplatonists believed that the One is logically prior to all other things. The Neoplatonic One is similar to Parmenides' Being. While Parmenides maintained that Being is one and so the apparent plurality of things is false, the Neoplatonists believed that this plurality is real because it emanates from the One. They also claimed, however, that all of the emanations are less real, pure, perfect, and divine than the One and that each successive emanation is less than its predecessor. While the Neoplatonists regarded the One as always already fully existent, Hegel believes that the Absolute is a result that is constructed through history. It is, primarily, a human achievement. In retrospect, persons can imaginatively project who they have become into the past and then see history as the development of something that was already there. This is consistent with possible alternative futures (which would now be the present).

Christianity and Martin Luther (1483–1546) can be discussed together, as Hegel's views of Christianity are largely a radicalization of Luther's. Hegel regards Christianity as the revealed or consummate religion, where religion develops as far as it can and still remains religion and not a transition to philosophy. Hegel sees Christianity as pivotal in the progressive realization of human freedom. Christianity introduces a notion of the worth of the individual and of human dignity that had been largely absent in earlier times. With the death of Christ, moreover, the transcendent God of theism dies too. What rises is not Christ but rather the believing community that worships together.

Philosophy begins in the modern era with René Descartes (1596–1650), Hegel believes, because Descartes implicitly broke with a mythological worldview. Whereas Michel Eyquem de Montaigne (1533–1592) was skeptical of the quest for knowledge and so suggested that persons who are raised as Catholics or Protestants should continue to worship in their tradition, Descartes feared that this skepticism threatened the progress of science and knowledge. In a move to out-flank skepticism, Descartes attempted to doubt everything that can be doubted. It is not that Descartes actually believed that these things are all false. Rather, because they can be doubted, they shouldn't be accepted as true until they have been proven. His goal was to find something that can't be doubted, so that this might serve as the foundation of knowledge. He claimed that the one thing that can't be doubted is that one is doubting. Even if the skeptics doubt everything else, Descartes maintained that they can't deny that they are doubting. Since doubting is a form of thinking, Descartes urged, the skeptics can't doubt that they are thinking. Thinking requires a thinker, moreover, and so the skeptics can't deny that they exist. So, Descartes arrived at "I think, therefore I exist" (*cogito ergo sum*). Although I have described this as though it were an argument, and "therefore" (*ergo*) suggests this, Descartes denied that *cogito ergo sum* is an argument and instead insisted that it is an immediate insight. Descartes was a dualist, believing that there are two basic ontological substances, matter and mind (this isn't quite accurate, since he believed that both matter and mind are created by God). Matter is extended substance, extended in space. Mind could exist without matter. Hegel sees Descartes' *cogito* as a great advance, as it implicitly recognizes that persons are accountable only to each other and that philosophy must be founded on subject, not substance.

The distinction between subject and substance will become clearer after we discuss **Benedict de Spinoza** (1632–1677). Whereas Descartes was a dualist, believing that there are two basic substances, mind and matter, Spinoza was a monist. That is to say, he believed that there is only one substance, which he identified with both nature and God. God doesn't create nature, according to Spinoza, God is nature. Substance expresses itself in an infinite number of attributes. We know two – mind and matter. Attributes have modes – ideas for mind and material objects for matter. Spinoza believed that there is a parallelism between the attributes: for every mental mode there is a corresponding material mode and vice versa. Like an algorithm, substance expresses itself necessarily and deterministically. Spinoza denied that there is free will. All determination is negation (*omnis determinatio est negatio*), every specification of a thing says how that thing differs from other things, and so things can be defined only negatively, stating how they differ from other things. Substance would have a positive determination were it not infinitely greater than all determinations. In his *Ethics*, which is really a metaphysics, Spinoza presented his ideas as a series of deductions from what he takes to be intuitively obvious axioms.

In the Preface to his *Phenomenology of Spirit*, Hegel says that the key to comprehending his philosophy is to realize that it consists in subject as well as substance. I will explain subject in a moment. Hegel would agree that Spinoza's substance aptly describes inorganic nature. Hegel would add, though, that it doesn't describe human culture. Human culture develops historically, not according to a pre-existing algorithm, and so Hegel has no need to deny free will. Humans can project possibilities into the future and then work to realize them. This is largely what Hegel means by subject. He agrees that all determination is negation, arguing that this demonstrates that the only thing that is fully real is the Absolute, which is subject and substance. Hegel's absolute is a result, however. It is the totality of all finite determinations. Whereas the attributes and modes are the expression of Spinoza's substance, Hegel effectively reverses this. His absolute is the expression of finite determinations.

The Enlightenment (eighteenth century) rejects appeals to tradition, religion, and authority. It believes that all claims must be evaluated by reason. Its motto – Kant claimed in his essay "What is Enlightenment?" – is "dare to know." In social relations, it advocates equality. Hegel is in many ways an advocate of the Enlightenment, but he is critical of some of its aspects. In rejecting appeals to tradition, the Enlightenment views reason as ahistorical, so that propositions that legitimately function for one group of persons as reasons should also be accepted by all others as reasons. If others don't accept them, this is evidence of superstition or stupidity. Hegel, by contrast, sees reason as historically developing and culturally conditioned. The Enlightenment also had difficulty recognizing that a claim can be examined only in light of other claims. Wholly to reject tradition would be to imagine that it is possible to examine a claim without appealing to any others or to examine all claims at once. The points just made hold, mutatis mutandis, to Enlightenment's views on morality.

Hegel is an advocate of the French Revolution (1789–99), which overthrew the monarchy – trying and executing Louis XVI (1754–1793) and his wife, Marie Antoinette (1755–1793) – and established a form of democracy. However, he sees its Reign of Terror (1793–4) as an inevitable consequence, not as a contingent misfortune. The French Revolution advocated for human freedom and equality but was unable to articulate a notion of equality that would allow some individuals to have, at least for a set time, more responsibility and power than others. In order for society to function, there must be individuals who serve as legislators, judges, and executives. When they do serve in these ways, though, they are no longer formally equal to others and so they become targets for prosecution and execution. Other persons then fill those roles, and they too become targets. The rise of an emperor, Napoleon Bonaparte (1769–1821), becomes almost inevitable. Hegel thinks that the chief shortcoming of the French Revolution is that it was not able to conceive of a notion of equality that would be consistent with individuals having various powers and duties. What is crucial to add, though, is that this latter concept of equality becomes thinkable only as a consequence of the Reign of Terror. Hegel addresses these issues in his *Elements of the Philosophy of Right*.

The philosophy of **Immanuel Kant** (1724–1804) can't be quickly and easily explained without approaching a caricature. Kant's philosophy can be seen – retrospectively, that is; this isn't how Kant would have understood it – as a synthesis of two traditions, Rationalism and Empiricism.

Such empiricists as John Locke (1632–1704) and David Hume (1711–1776) claimed that all knowledge arises from sense experience. As Hume recognized, however, if all knowledge arises from

the senses, then it is difficult rationally to justify our belief in induction and causality. We observe previous regularities, but why believe
that those regularities will continue in the future? We observe that
a certain event preceded another event, but – since we never seem
to observe causation as such – what justifies the belief that the first
event caused the second?

Such rationalists as Descartes and Spinoza agreed that much of
human knowledge comes from sense experience, but they claimed
that there is some knowledge that doesn't. This knowledge is sometimes called innate. This shouldn't be taken to mean that people are
born with this knowledge in a fully articulated state but, rather, that
this knowledge doesn't arise from sense experience. Rationalists
frequently claimed that we can innately know that there is a God
and that we have an immortal soul. One difficulty they confronted
was that many people say that they don't have this knowledge and
further deny that there is a God, etc. The rationalist reply, that these
persons really do have this innate knowledge but that they aren't
thinking clearly, isn't persuasive.

In his *Critique of Pure Reason*, Kant synthesized the empiricist and
rationalist traditions by distinguishing between matter and form,
or content and structure – a distinction that is at least as old as
Aristotle. Kant claimed that experience has two components. What
he called the matter of experience is given to us, although the matter
of experience is itself never experienced, and the mind provides its
form. Only when the mind has structured the matter of experience
do we have experience. I will say a few more words about this. I
will describe it as though it is a process that occurs in time, one part
of the process occurring after another. This isn't accurate, though,
because the process itself isn't temporal.

The matter of experience is given to us in what Kant calls the
forms of intuition or the forms of sensibility: space and time. The
matter of experience isn't itself in space and time. Rather, space and
time are forms that our minds provide. The mind then takes the
matter of experience, now in space and time, and imposes twelve
categories of the understanding; the most relevant are existence,
causality, number, and relation. Only after the understanding has
imposed its categories can we have experience – although the distinction between sensibility and understanding suggests that there
could be representations that are spatial and temporal but non-
conceptual. (This is enormously more complex than I'm indicating;
I'm completely ignoring, for example, the imagination's role in
generating schemata so that everything is synchronized.) This

allowed Kant to claim that we can know, a priori, that everything we experience will be in space and time. He could also claim, in response to Hume, that we can know, a priori, that every event has a cause. We need to investigate to discover an event's cause, but we can know a priori that there is one. In sense experience, determinism holds. Every event is caused by another event (or other events) that wholly determines it. Kant believed that experience conforms to Euclidian geometry and Newtonian mechanics, so that all movement is the result of the application of external forces. All of our knowledge comes from sense experience, but experience itself is the result of the matter of experience being structured by the forms of sensibility and the categories of the understanding. This is universal: all persons, everywhere, at all times, have experience through this process.

What about God, the soul, and human freedom? Because all knowledge comes from sense experience, we can't know anything about these because they aren't things that we could experience. We can believe in anything that goes beyond sense experience, Kant holds, as long as it isn't contradictory. We can believe that there is a God, that we have an immortal soul, and that there is freedom, where our actions aren't caused by any previous event, although Kant adds that, in principle, we can't comprehend how freedom would be possible. (I remind readers that I'm simplifying.)

In his *Groundwork of the Metaphysics of Morals*, Kant claimed that we should always do our duty. We can determine what our duty is by universalizing our maxims for actions and then seeing if those universalized maxims can be consistently willed. A maxim is a rule that describes the purpose of an action. If I add some red pepper to the dal, for example, I do so in order to make it tasty. My maxim would be something like "I may add pepper to dal, or to food in general, whenever that would make it tasty." Suppose if I wonder if this maxim is ethically permissible. I universalize it so that it applies not only to me, but to everyone. The maxim becomes "All persons may add pepper to food to make it tasty." This is ethically acceptable. Even if everyone acted on this maxim, and if everyone knew that everyone acts on it, there would be no problem. I can consistently will it; that is, I can want the maxim to hold and that everything required for the maxim to be possible should hold too. The maxim doesn't contradict or undermine itself.

Perhaps, though, I don't have any pepper and I also don't have any money to buy some. I really want tasty dal, though, and so I'm tempted to steal some pepper. Is that ethically permissible? In this case, my maxim would be "I may steal pepper whenever I want tasty dal and can't buy pepper" or, more generally, "I may steal whenever it's in my interest to do so." Universalizing this: "All persons may steal whenever it's in their interest." This maxim does undermine itself and so can't be consistently willed. How? If everyone acted on it, and if everyone knew that everyone follows this maxim, then the institution of private property would collapse. This wouldn't trouble someone who intends to abolish private property, of course. However, our example instead involves someone who wants there to be private property – indeed, is committed to the institution of private property – but also wants to steal something. Kant's point was that this individual really wants everyone else not to steal but also to make an unjustifiable exception for herself or himself. He believed that persons are frequently tempted to prefer their self-interest – or, less frequently, the interests of others – over their duty, and so the moral life is one of struggle to overcome inclinations and to be moral.

Because Kant held that the world that we experience through the senses is governed by Newtonian mechanics, in his *Philosophy of Material Nature* he maintained that matter is inherently lifeless. Organic organisms seem to be alive, with the ability to move themselves and to have purposes and goals. Kant believed that the human mind is incapable, in principle, of ever comprehending how organisms are actually the result of external forces, and so we must proceed as if organisms were alive, can move themselves, and have purposes. This assumption isn't actually true, nor is it constitutive, but it is regulatively useful.

Hegel objects to what he regards as the dualisms in Kant's philosophy – between matter and form, sensibility and understanding, duty and inclinations, constitutive and regulative. Kant assumed that things as they are in themselves, apart from the ways in which we know them, could be radically different than how we experience them. Hegel believes that we experience things as they really are and that the only way that they could be different is that they might be experienced differently in the future. What initially appears to be only intricate marks on paper becomes philosophy after I learn the Devanāgarī script and then learn to read Sanskrit. Whereas Kant believed that the mind imposes concepts on the matter of experience, Hegel thinks that we experience things as they really are; things really are conceptualized.

Kant approached morality from the perspective of the individual and so believed that duty and inclinations will be frequently opposed. Hegel attempts to describe a set of social institutions – the family, civil society, and the state – organized in such a way that inclinations support duty. He also maintains that the best metaphor for the universe is an organism, not a mechanism, and so he claims that the claims that Kant thought were only regulative – that organisms are alive, can move themselves, and have purposes – are constitutive.

Johann Gottfried von Herder (1744–1803) argued that Kant was mistaken to believe that the process by which the mind constitutes experience is the same for all persons. How persons experience the world, Herder maintained, depends upon the categories of their language. We think in language, thought is wholly linguistic, and so persons who speak different languages experience the world in significantly different ways. Herder also maintained that ethics isn't universal but that it is grounded in a culture's social mores and customs. He denied that one culture is superior to another. Different cultures are all on the same level.

Hegel agrees that thought is linguistic and that persons who speak different languages experience the world in significantly different ways. He also believes that morality is rooted in mores and customs. However, he disagrees that no culture is superior to another. Instead, some cultures are superior to others, and this superiority is based on the extent to which human freedom has been realized. He believes that cultures develop historically and geographically. As I explained above when discussing Aristotle, Hegel thinks that the Oriental World knew only that one is free, the Greco-Roman World knew that some are free, but only the Modern World, what Hegel refers to as the Germanic World, knows that all persons are entitled to freedom. This development isn't merely historical but also geographical, moving from East to West. Hegel claims that some cultures are stuck in the Oriental World and that they can't be historically developed beyond that. This is a point at which we must think beyond Hegel.

Johann Gottlieb Fichte (1762–1814) is the source of many ideas that Hegel subsequently appropriates. Fichte rejected Kant's distinction between things as we experience them and things as they are apart from our experience of them. Kant believed that things as they are in themselves could be radically different from the way we experience them. Fichte held that we experience things as they actually are. It is possible that future experiences will correct or enlarge previous ones, of course, but not that things could be radically different than any way we could experience them. Fichte also held a theory of social recognition, where human beings become individuals with rights and responsibilities by being recognized by others as such. What Hegel adds to these is a notion of historical development.

Johann Christian Friedrich Hölderlin (1770–1843) and **Friedrich Wilhelm Joseph Schelling** (1775–1854) were Hegel's roommates when he was in seminary. From them, he takes the ideas that philosophy must be a system where all of its aspects are interrelated, and that there is an absolute, a single principle, of which philosophy – indeed, the world – is the expression. Again, Hegel adds the notion of historical development. More, he comes to think of the absolute not as an unknowable ground out of which the world emerges but, rather, as something that is entirely conceptualizable, the totality of the ways things are connected with each other, as well as the knowledge of those connections.

In the next chapter, on the *Phenomenology of Spirit*, we will see in detail how Hegel builds on, and departs from, his former roommates.

3

Hegel's *Phenomenology of Spirit*

This chapter will provide an overview of Hegel's most famous work and consider various interpretations. It will also discuss why Hegel believes that philosophy must be a system and how that system is to be constructed.

There has been a continuing debate about whether the *Phenomenology of Spirit* is one book or two. That is to say, some philosophers claim that it contains a single and sustained argument. Others maintain, however, that Hegel began intending to write a book on epistemology, mainly responding to Kant. Approximately halfway into the book, these latter set of interpreters maintain, he decided instead to write about social and political philosophy, art, and religion.

I will adopt the reading advocated by Michael N. Forster in his book *Hegel's Idea of a Phenomenology of Spirit*.[1] Forster argues that Hegel's *Phenomenology of Spirit* tells the story of Western civilization from three perspectives. The first occurs in the chapters on "Consciousness," "Self-Consciousness," and "Reason." These narrate that story from the perspective of individual shapes of consciousness. A shape of consciousness could be thought of as a worldview. The second perspective is found in the chapter on "Spirit," which focuses on the social contexts in which those shapes of consciousness are situated. Finally, the "Reason" and "Absolute Knowing" chapters examine the attempts to articulate God's nature, or that of the Absolute, through art, religion, and philosophy, culminating in Hegel's own philosophy.

I want to discuss briefly the context of Hegel's *Phenomenology of Spirit*. In many ways, this text is a continuation of Kant's philosophy, especially his *Critique of Pure Reason*, but it is a Kant that has been informed by Herder. That is to say, Kant believes that reason is the same for all persons at all times, in all places, in every culture. Indeed, Kant so wholly believes this that it never occurs to him that it is a thesis that requires an argument for its defense. Herder, by contrast, recognizes that different cultures have different languages and that a language allows its users to comprehend aspects of the world that are not apparent to those who speak another language. Herder further maintains that patterns of reasoning and thinking differ from one linguistic group to the next. Whereas Herder thinks that there are different cultures with divergent ways of conceptualizing their world, Hegel adds that the history of the West, and especially of Western philosophy, can be seen as constituting a progression. It is Hegel's insight that reason itself has a history, that what counts as reason is the result of a development. This is something that Kant never imagines and that Herder only glimpses.

This means that, while Kant could be content to focus on the individual knower – since reason is universal, it couldn't matter who that knower might be – Hegel thinks that attention must be paid to what counts as knowledge in a specific society. As a consequence, he cannot remain at the level of the individual knower but must move to the social level.

The preface: some basic hegelian concepts

The Preface to the *Phenomenology of Spirit* was written after Hegel had completed the rest of the work. No doubt, a full understanding of the Preface would require that it be read both before and after reading the *Phenomenology of Spirit*. Here, I will draw attention to a few of its most salient points.

Commentaries have often interpreted the Preface as Hegel's defensive anticipation of criticism. It is true that he grouses about uninformed criticism. However, it would be wrong – that is, not subtle – to see this as his attempt to delegitimate any critical engagement with his text. Rather, Hegel tells his readers what such engagement must consist in.

First, Hegel claims that philosophy doesn't consist in a set of doctrines or propositions. Rather, it is a process of thinking. What might seem like philosophical propositions are meaningless apart from the thinking process that produced them. What is this process? Hegel calls it *dialectic*. It consists in taking some claim to truth and asking what must be the case in order for this claim to be not merely true, but even possible. In his *Phenomenology of Spirit*, as we shall see, Hegel frequently shows that a claim must be inadequate because the conditions which would make it possible are ones that the claim itself explicitly denies or repudiates.

Second, Hegel maintains that the only legitimate form of criticism is an internal criticism, whereby it is shown that a philosophy fails by its own standard for success. External criticism, by contrast, rejects one philosophy because it is incompatible with another. The mere fact of incompatibility, however, cannot itself motivate the acceptance or rejection of either philosophy. To put this point in other words, proponents of a philosophy that has been rejected on the basis of an external criticism have no motivation to agree with that rejection. Rather, they may respond by rejecting the philosophy that provides the external criticism. They do have a compelling motivation to agree with the rejection of their philosophy, though, when it has been shown to be inadequate by an internal criticism. In that case, the philosophy has been shown to be inadequate based on that philosophy's own standards for adequacy.

Third, Hegel believes that no philosophy is ever wholly mistaken. Rather, it is inadequate – a partial truth that misunderstands itself as the whole truth.

I will now discuss some of Hegel's most important points in the Preface. The goal is not a thorough explication. That would be impossible in this introductory book, and perhaps in any book. Rather, I hope to say enough so that readers may then make their own way across this challenging terrain.

Hegel claims that science is a system. That's nice to hear, but what does he mean by science and what is a system? Hegel's goal is to make philosophy into a science. As a first approximation, we could say that a science is a body of knowledge that can claim universal agreement. This isn't quite correct, though, since Hegel believes that philosophy itself develops over time; it has a history. So, to say that philosophy is now a science would be to claim that it can claim the agreement of the educated Westerner. We will see later that Hegel believes that this claim can be extended to all persons, but for now we can say that science is potentially universal. Its method is that of internal criticism, showing how positions fail by their own standards of success. Someone who follows this process will see why previous positions are inadequate and why Hegel's own position is finally adequate. That's the promise.

Hegel says that philosophy shouldn't be edifying. Why not? As Hegel understands edification, it really is a matter of telling us that those things that we have already unquestioningly accepted should continue to be accepted, whereas philosophy frequently shows that those things are incorrect. Philosophy isn't edifying because it shows how things that passed for common sense weren't accurate. Hegel will later talk about philosophy as a path of despair. Nevertheless, it is clear that he anticipates a new era and that his *Phenomenology of Spirit* will play a principal role in its inauguration.

Hegel believes that every philosophy is a further development, articulation, of a previous one – or ones – that is perceived as inadequate. This is what he is referring to when he speaks of a wealth of shapes that are self-originating and self-developing. However, he is referring not only to philosophy when he discusses shapes – although philosophy is generally what is most central to his focus – but also to cultural forms in general, such as politics, art, and religion.

At this point, it will be useful to say a few words about Hegel's sometime friend Schelling. They were roommates in seminary, along with the poet Hölderlin. Although he was five years younger than Hegel, Schelling was precocious and had published several philosophical systems while still in his early twenties. Many people believed that Hegel was merely Schelling's follower, a hanger-on with no real talent.

Schelling and Hegel both put the Absolute at the center of their philosophies. What's the Absolute? It might be thought of as God, but, if so, then it must be Spinoza's God that is identical with nature. (As we will see in a moment, "God that" rather than "God who" is appropriate when discussing Spinoza's God.) Spinoza's God is not a God that transcends the universe – existing outside and independently of it – but rather a God that *is* the universe. God is *Absolute* because it is not dependent upon anything else, whereas all things depend upon other things for their existence and continuation, and because there is nothing external to it. Could there be two or more Absolutes? No, because those two things – "things" for want of a better word – would exist in some relation to each other and so they would actually be only aspects of the Absolute. In the religious vernacular, they would be false gods.

Back to Schelling. It is useful to discuss his views because Hegel articulates his own position in repudiating Schelling's. So, what does Schelling think? He thinks that the Absolute is above or beneath (pick your metaphor) thought, knowledge, and language. It is prior to any distinction between subject and object, regardless of whether that distinction is thought of as the subject of knowledge (the knower) and the object of knowledge (the known) or as the subject and object of a grammatical sentence, such as "DJ Gulab Jammin" (subject) plays bhangra (object). There's literally nothing that can be *said* about the Absolute, according to Schelling, and it can't be an object of knowledge. The Absolute can, however, be *felt*, and it is art that most completely occasions an experience of the Absolute. This is a unique experience, of course, because people can't describe or say – even to themselves – what they felt.

Schelling's views about the Absolute are the target of Hegel's gibes about A=A, philosophy that's shot from a pistol, and that all cows are black at night. Schelling's Absolute may be experienced immediately, if it can be experienced at all, without any preparation or work. And, in his Absolute, there is no distinction between one thing or another – indeed, there isn't one thing and another, there is just the Absolute. By contrast, Hegel believes that the Absolute can be fully known and that it can be expressed in language. This isn't fully accurate, but as a first approximation we could say that Hegel's Absolute consists in the articulated relations of all things with each other.

Not as substance but as subject. To understand this, it is useful to say a few more words about Spinoza. Schelling developed his notion of the Absolute from Spinoza's substance. According to Spinoza, there is really only one thing: substance, which is God, which is nature. Substance expresses itself in an infinite number of attributes – contemporary Spinoza scholars debate whether "infinite" as used by Spinoza means "denumerable" or rather "as many as there are." In any case, Spinoza claims that humans experience only two attributes: mind and matter, or thought and extension. He also claims that there is no such thing as free choice or free will; they are illusions, and everything that happens is causally determined by previous things. Substance is itself free, according to Spinoza, because there is nothing external to it that could determine, cause, or limit it. Whatever happens is an expression of substance's own nature. However, substance does not think or decide what to do. To put the point uncharitably, but accurately, Spinoza's substance does what it does. Moreover, substance does what it does without having any goal or purpose.

Hegel might allow that such a notion is adequate to explain mudslides, but he maintains that it is wholly inadequate to explain human actions, much less those of animals or the movements of plants. Whereas Spinoza's metaphor for the universe would be a machine that has no maker and no purpose – certainly an odd machine – Hegel's metaphor would be an organism. An organism does have purposes. As we will see when we discuss his philosophy of nature, Hegel thinks that the Absolute comes to know itself through humans, who are its vehicles, in Charles Taylor's phrase.[2] So, when Hegel says "not as substance but as subject," he means that the best model for the Absolute is finally humanity itself.

Truth is the whole. The briefest way to begin to express Hegel's view would be that the truth involves comprehending how things fit together. An example might begin to make this clear. If we know a person only as a professor, we don't know the full truth about her. We don't know her as a friend, chef, woman, rabbi, mother, daughter, niece, or mayor. The truth of this person is the totality of these aspects, as well as comprehending how these aspects complement or work against each other. Hegel's point is that a specific philosophy – of, say, Spinoza or Kant – isn't the full truth. The full truth would be not only the entire history of philosophy but also a recognition of how each successive philosophy is engendered as an attempt to overcome perceived inadequacies in its predecessors. And that comprehensive recognition is what Hegel's philosophy claims for itself. It is not one more philosophy in a series of philosophies but instead the comprehension of the series *as* a series.

Reason as purposeful activity. Reason itself is, according to Hegel, something that changes and develops historically, articulating itself to overcome its own previous inadequacies. Hegel is not merely maintaining that the ancient Greeks' understanding of reason is different from that of the medievals, for example, which in turn is different from that of the Enlightenment. His point is more radical: reason *itself* is something different in the ancient world than it is in the medieval, and both differ from what reason is in the modern world. The butterfly is the development of the caterpillar – the butterfly is the truth of the caterpillar, Hegel would say – but the butterfly isn't a caterpillar. What allows us to say that these different things – reasons (plural) – are still, at a higher level of analysis, instances of the same thing – reason (singular) – is that we can tell a story of how reason develops from the time of the ancient world to the modern.

Spirit – what's that? In 1910 J. B. Baillie translated the title of Hegel's *Phänomenologie des Geistes* as *Phenomenology of Mind*, while in 1977 Arnold V. Miller translated it as *Phenomenology of Spirit*.[3] Okay, so what does Hegel mean by *Geist*? The briefest answer would be that this means "human culture." This isn't accurate – I will explain why in a moment – but readers won't go too far wrong if they substitute "culture" for "spirit." To talk more about this, I will briefly discuss Aristotle's view about what a society is – and anticipate a lot of what I will later discuss more fully.

Aristotle believes that humans are, by nature, social animals. Further, he believes that human nature is something fixed, static, and unchanging. All persons in all places at all times are social animals. When Aristotle compares humans to other animals, he always picks *bees*. Why bees? Because, in the case of bees, the organism is not the individual bee but the hive. Just as one can understand an individual human cell fully only once one understands how it functions within the structure of the living body, although this analogy wasn't available to Aristotle, so one understands an individual bee fully only once one has understood the hive of which the bee is a member. Aristotle believes that an individual person is fully human only within the context of a city-state. Thus, he believes that the *polis* – the collective community – has a metaphysical priority over the individual.

Hegel disagrees with Aristotle on two points. First, while he agrees that humans are social animals *by nature*, he denies that human nature is fixed, static, and unchanging. Instead, Hegel believes that human nature is dynamic – that is, he believes that human nature itself changes and develops over time. Second, he denies that the collective community is prior metaphysically to the individual. Rather, the collective community and the individual mutually co-determine each other. Hence, Hegel would agree with Aristotle that there is no individual outside of a (linguistic) community. However, he would equally stress that there can be no community without individuals. Let us grant that Hegel is correct that human nature changes over time. Is this change merely random? No, for Hegel believes that human nature is developing towards a goal, and that this goal is the maximization of freedom. How is that possible?

Back to Aristotle. Recall his doctrine of the Unmoved Mover, which is pure form with no matter. Aristotle believes that the Unmoved Mover is the best and greatest thing. The Unmoved Mover is perfect. It is functionally equivalent to what we call God.

The Unmoved Mover is fixed, static, and unchanging. Aristotle believes that the Unmoved Mover is unchanging because it is perfect and so it could only change into something less perfect. Thus, the Unmoved Mover does not act. It only thinks. Further, it thinks about the most perfect thing – that is, itself. Since it does not change, its thought does not change. The Unmoved Mover is a thought that thinks itself. Aristotle believes that everything tries to become as much like the Unmoved Mover as possible. Perhaps it comes as no surprise that he believes that human nature, like the Unmoved Mover, is unchanging.

Hegel has a concept in his system which serves much the same function as Aristotle's Unmoved Mover. Hegel calls it Absolute *Geist*, Spirit, or sometimes just the Absolute. But, for Hegel, *Geist* is developing dynamically towards greater freedom. So too, according to Hegel, is human nature. This is not all. Hegel believes that *Geist* does not exist transcendently, but only immanently within the material world. *Geist* can exist only as embodied *Geist*, and matter can exist only insofar as it embodies *Geist*. While Hegel considers himself an orthodox Lutheran, he seems much closer to certain forms of mysticism. In any case, we can say – perhaps with some inexactitude – that Hegel really believes in only one person of the Christian trinity, the Holy Spirit, and that he thinks that the Holy Spirit exists solely within the world. The consequences of this are quite radical. God can see things only by looking at them though someone's eyes. More shocking, perhaps, God can think only through human thoughts. Indeed, God is not unchanging; God develops towards greater freedom insofar as humans develop towards greater freedom.

Hegel believes that world history can be divided into three stages. In the first, the Oriental stage, persons know only that one person, the ruler, is free. In the second, the Greco-Roman stage, persons know that some persons, the citizens – but not non-citizens, which include women, children, slaves, and foreigners – are free. Finally, in the third, European stage, persons realize that all persons are free. Hegel is *not* claiming that in the modern world all persons actually are free. He is quite aware that there still is plenty of oppression. Instead, he is claiming that all persons have a right to freedom, and that everyone knows this, regardless of how they act.

A moment ago, I said that, for Hegel, *Geist* is wholly immanent within the world. That is not quite precise. Hegel also believes that *Geist* can act behind the backs, as it were, of persons so that their actions result in freedom being increased, even if this is not what they intend. Hegel calls this "acting behind the back" the *Cunning of Reason*. He thinks that, most often, *Geist* acts behind the back of what he calls World-Historical Individuals, persons such as Caesar and Napoleon. Although these persons may be concerned primarily to increase their own power, or perhaps the power of their country, they don't anticipate the full meaning of their actions. *Geist* is able to manipulate them in such a way that freedom is increased for everyone. More precisely, their actions have unintended and unanticipated consequences which eventually result in promoting freedom.

Hegel believes that humans discover – as well as create or constitute – their human nature in two related ways. One way is through having other persons recognize that nature. (Recall here that Aristotle believes that one of the main benefits of friends is that they enable me to discover the sort of fellow I am: if my friends are all kind and gentle people, then chances are that I am as well; while if my friends are all obnoxious louts, it is hardly likely that I am any different.) The second way is through activity, principally labor. By seeing the products of their labor, persons come to create and discover their nature.

This brings us to Hegel's famous master/slave – or lord/bondsman – dialectic. The story goes like this. Two humans both insist that the other recognize him as a free person while being unwilling to grant the other person that same recognition. A fight occurs in which each person tries to destroy the other, since the other's refusal to grant recognition is a threat to his personhood. The loser of the fight begs to be allowed to live as a slave – or bondsman – of the lord and promises to recognize the lord as a person. Thus, the lord now is able to be recognized as a person and so is able to create and discover his human nature. The bondsman, unfortunately, has no such luck but must obey the orders of the lord. So the bondsman gets to work: washing clothes, cleaning, cooking meals, digging wells, planting gardens, weeding, etc. A dialectical reversal may now occur, however, at least according to one fashionable interpretation.[4] For the bondsman can create and discover his human nature through the products of his labor. Hence, while the lord is dependent upon the bondsman's recognition to know his nature, the bondsman is independent of the lord, since the bondsman can discover his nature in the products of his labor. So, the bondsman now is implicitly free. (We will see later why the bondsman's view that he can be free as long as his thoughts are free results in Stoicism, which proves to be freedom not in its fullest sense but merely an early station on the way.)

We can also compare Hegel's views about society with those of John Locke, who thinks that society is simply an aggregate of individuals. Individuals are to society, for Locke, as stones are to a heap. Just as being in a heap of stones does not affect what the stones are, so being in a society doesn't affect who individuals are. Aristotle, as we just saw, disagrees, claiming that the society is the organism itself and that individuals are individuals only because they are a part of society. Aristotle would deny that an individual who was raised by and still lives with wolves is a human being, for example, whereas Locke would claim that this individual was a human. They differ because Aristotle thinks that being part of a human society is necessary for an individual to be human. Hegel's view – predictably – is a synthesis of those of Aristotle and Locke. Individuals have agency, Hegel maintains, but their agency is itself a result of the society in which they live. Consider that someone living in the eighth century couldn't have aspired to be a radio talk-show host.

However, society is itself an agent. We have a glimpse of this when we speak of collective entities as though they were themselves individuals: Halliburton wonders if it will be fined, the USA seeks better relations with Mexico, Nigeria worries about an AIDS epidemic. This can be explained further by briefly discussing the hypothesis of the extended mind. Andy Clark and David J. Chalmers claim that the mind can extend beyond the physical brain, beyond an individual's body or skin.[5] They claim that any processes which would be regarded as mental if they were to occur in the brain should be considered mental when they occur outside the brain.[6] As a thought experiment, they consider Otto, a man in the early stages of Alzheimer's disease who supplements his failing memory with a notebook that lists addresses. Since those addresses would be considered part of his mind if he had memorized them, they should be so considered even though they are written in his notebook. The notebook is an aspect of Otto's extended mind.[7]

Hegel wouldn't disagree with Clark and Chalmers's extended mind hypothesis, but he would be critical of their lack of speculative daring. He would be more impressed by Edwin Hutchins's *Cognition in the Wild*, Karin Knorr Cetina's *Epistemic Cultures*, and Lynn Hankinson Nelson's *Who Knows*.[8]

Hutchins intends "to show that human cognition is not just influenced by culture and society, but that it is in a very fundamental sense a cultural and social process. To do this I will move the boundaries of the cognitive unit of analysis out beyond the skin of the individual persons and treat the navigation team as a cognitive and computational system."[9] No individual sailor knows the location of or can project the trajectory of the USS *Palau*, a helicopter transport ship, as it sails through San Diego's harbor. Rather, its charts, instruments, maps, and sailors together are the extended mind that guides the *Palau* through the harbor. Hutchins also suggests that it isn't individuals who have expertise but rather the extended mind of which the individuals are parts. Knorr Cetina and Nelson argue that it is the scientific community itself that knows, in the first instance, not individual scientists. "Communities know," Nelson maintains, "individuals only derivatively so."[10] Hegel would respond by saying that even this does not go far enough. It is humanity itself that knows – that is to say, Spirit.

Hegel believes that Spirit irreducibly emerges from Nature. Although Spirit depends upon Nature for its existence, there is a break or rupture between them. This is why the methods of natural science are not adequate to study Spirit. Is this story of Spirit emerging from Nature true? Hegel will maintain that such a story is necessary in order for us to find the world meaningful. He will then argue that, since such a story is necessary, there is no reason to doubt that it is true.

Philosophy must provide a ladder so that people can realize the Absolute – more about what that means later – and Hegel intends for the *Phenomenology of Spirit* to be that ladder. It will begin with what might be the most elementary philosophical position and subsequently show the inadequacies of each such position until its readers arrive at the concluding section, Absolute Knowing. What they will know then isn't yet another position but rather the pattern that has run through all of the sequence of positions, making them part of a sequence.

The Understanding is the mightiest power. Hegel distinguishes the Understanding from Reason. Reason comprehends a thing within its set of relations. It recognizes that a thing is only the thing that it is as a result of its relations. One might consider an individual, for example, who is the person she is only because of her relations to others: children, friends, parents, teachers, neighbors, ancestors, decedents, et al. The Understanding, by contrast, attempts to comprehend a thing by disregarding its relations. As such, the Understanding necessarily fails. The Understanding believes that it has succeeded in comprehending a thing without having to consider its relations – relations which actually constitute it and make it the thing that it is – when it is actually only ignoring those relations. Why then does Hegel claim that it is nevertheless the mightiest power? Because, although it fails to comprehend a thing that has been ripped from its relations, the Understanding frequently provides (without recognizing that this is what it is doing) a new set of relations in which that thing is now situated, thereby making that thing something other than it was. It can only be considered the same thing because a story can be told about how it alters when it is removed from one set of relations and inserted into another. Again, though, the Understanding doesn't recognize that this is what it is doing.

An example: A woman who tries to define herself independently of her family may do so by emphasizing her connections to her friends, to her co-workers, or to a political struggle in some other country. In doing this, the woman will herself change, thereby acquiring – peradventure – a partially new set of relations. But she is still the same person, perhaps you say, so doesn't this suggest that things have some essence that allows them to remain the same despite being in other relations? So, isn't Saul Kripke correct when he claims that a proper name picks out one unique thing or person, an essence? And, if there aren't essences, how is it that this woman in the example continues to be identified as the same person, even as she enters into new relations and de-emphasizes or perhaps even loses others? Hegel's answer will be to deny that there are essences involved here and instead will say that this woman is considered to be the same person because a narrative can be told that tracks her throughout the changing relations into which she enters and departs. The Understanding is the mightiest power because it can sever a thing from its constituting relations, thereby dissolving that thing and creating something new – or killing it.

Here, death enters. This process can be applied not only to ideas and persons but to entire societies. The temptation is to turn away in horror, or sadness, and refuse to comprehend what has happened. However, Hegel emphasizes the importance of tarrying with the negative, not looking away but rather tracking this process, not despairing at death but being hopeful of the possibility of new life. Since Spirit is not an entity or thing but this very process, it thereby becomes other to itself. Indeed, it will be only in Absolute Knowing, the concluding section of the *Phenomenology of Spirit*, that Spirit will be able to look back over the terrain it has traversed and recognize that those various shapes are its own previous shapes.

The negative is the self. The self is, for Hegel, not some positive thing but rather the failure to be identified with any thing. That failure, however, is actually a success. That is, the self has the ability to reflect on, and to abstract from, any of its positive characteristics. The self's negativity consists in its ability to take a distanced view of itself. As such, the self is not a being but instead a becoming or a potentiality. Philosophy too is a process. As noted before, it is not a set of statements, claims, or arguments, but rather the continued self-undermining of positions which assert that they are the full truth when they are only partial aspects of the truth. Truth is a bacchanalian revel, says Hegel in one of his most memorable phrases, where everyone dances but also, whenever anyone drops out of the dances, another takes that place – and so the dance can also be viewed as complete stillness. What does this mean? Think of a waltz. On the one hand, there is constant movement. But, since the pattern of movement – the dance – is fixed, on the other hand, the movement can also be seen as following a prescribed pattern and so as also stationary.

So, what is the point? The point is that the history of Western philosophy can be described in the same way as the dance. As one position fails and so is rejected, another takes its place. But Hegel speaks of a bacchanalian revel, a dance where everyone is drunk. Why must they be drunk? They are drunk in the sense that they lack awareness of being part of the dance. Once they achieve that awareness, though, philosophy as the love of wisdom or knowing becomes actual knowing. It isn't that Actual Knowing discovers some additional fact that previous shapes failed to recognize. Rather, it discovers that those previous shapes are part of a series. Truth, then, is its own self-movement. It is the engendering of shapes and their eventual rejection as inadequate, so generating still new shapes that attempt to overcome the inadequacies of the previous ones.

We learn by experience that we meant something other than we meant to mean. If there is a single sentence that encapsulates Hegel's central teaching in the *Phenomenology of Spirit*, this is it! Each shape of consciousness will discover that what it said isn't what it meant and that what it meant isn't what it meant to mean. The easiest example of such an event would be a legal contract. A person might intend to mean one thing when she writes and signs a contract, but a court may nevertheless decide that what this contract actually means isn't what she intended it to mean. What she meant isn't what she meant to mean.

Hegel frequently claims that these shapes succeed each other with necessity, and sometimes he adds that this necessity is logical necessity. Clearly, this notion of necessity has little to do with necessity as contemporary logicians understand it. So, what is he talking about? Many commentators have claimed that, given some specific shape, there is some minimal way of altering it such that, uniquely, some specific other shape will result. This *prospective interpretation* – which I introduce in order to contrast it to the correct *retrospective reading* – claims that there is something – generally, a self-contradiction – within each specific shape which necessitates a transition to another particular shape. For example, Forster writes:

> The "necessity" of a transition from a shape of consciousness A to a shape of consciousness B just consists in the complex fact that while shape A proves to be implicitly self-contradictory, shape B preserves shape A's constitutive conceptions/concepts but in a way which modifies them so as to eliminate the self-contradiction, and moreover does so while departing less from the meanings of A's constitutive conceptions/concepts than any other known shape which performs that function.[11]

Here, the transition from shape A to shape B isn't *necessary* if all that B does is eliminate A's self-contradictions and preserve its constitutive conceptions/concepts. Other shapes, C or D, might do that too, in which case the transition from A to B would be only contingent, not necessary. For the transition to be *necessary*, B also must be closer to A's constitutive conceptions/concepts than any other shape. This means, however, that a transition that initially seems to be necessary won't be if there is some other shape that does what B does but that departs even less from A's constitutive conceptions/concepts than B did.

There is another problem for the prospective interpretation. Suppose that both B and C would eliminate A's self-contradictions and preserve A's constitutive conceptions/concepts. How can we tell whether B or C departs least from A's constitutive conceptions/concepts? Recall that A's implicit self-contradiction can be overcome only by eliminating some of its constitutive conceptions/concepts while preserving the others. Assuming that B and C are not identical, then the constitutive conceptions/concepts of A which each eliminates and preserves must be different. Here is a simple example: Let A's constitutive conceptions/concepts be p, ~p, and q; B eliminates p but preserves ~p and q; C eliminates ~p but preserves p and q. In this case, B and C are equally distant from A.

Suppose that D eliminates ~p, preserves p and q, but introduces r. From the perspective of A, before any transition, it might seem that B and C depart less from A's constitutive conceptions/concepts than D. But that isn't correct. A's constitutive conceptions/concepts include p and ~p. Since these are contradictories, and since anything can be deduced from a contradiction, s can be deduced from them. So, D's introducing s could just as well be described either as making explicit one of A's implicit constitutive conceptions/concepts or as D's drawing attention to one of A's implicit constitutive conceptions/concepts that no one previously had bothered to notice.

The prospective interpretation is hopeless because there is no way to show that a shape that is the successor to another is somehow uniquely necessary. It simply assumes that there really is one unique successor shape that would be the least change from a previous shape than all possible changes. This isn't credible. As seen above, pick any proposed minimal change and others that are equally minimal could be proposed. Without discussing mereology, the metaphysics of parts and wholes, the prospective interpretation also assumes that a change could be designated as minimal – or, indeed, as a change at all – apart from some context. Such an assumption would be most unHegelian. Most importantly, there is no reason to believe that a sequence of shapes would be generated in any such manner – certainly not if what is referred to is the sequence of philosophies that emerged in the West. The prospective interpretation thinks of necessity as a push forward. That is to say, it focuses on some specific shape and believes that the emergence of a unique successor is required.

However, Hegelian necessity is not *pro*spective but, rather, *retro*spective. That is, Hegel focuses on a specific shape and recognizes that, since this shape actually exists, all of the previous shapes were necessary in order for this shape to exist. Had any of those shapes been different, then this specific shape would have been different too. Hegel's sense of necessity is a deflationary one, one that is wholly compatible with contingency. What happens next is wholly contingent, at any moment, but what has happened was completely necessary. An example: It is contingent that a soldier survives a war. Given that this soldier subsequently has children, though, it becomes necessary that she did survive. Had she died during the war, her children wouldn't have been born. The retrospective succeeds where the prospective fails. (Perceptive readers will have recognized that the argument in the previous paragraphs is itself an example of how a shape is found inadequate and so replaced by a successor shape.)

Agreement with others. As noted earlier, Hegel rejects appeals to feeling, intuition, conscience, or common sense. The limitation of each of these is that it can be gainsaid. Someone who asserts that the truth of something is intuitively obvious, for example, has no reply – except stupidly to repeat the same assertion – to the counter-assertion that the falsity of that same thing is intuitively obvious. Hegel believes that this is no way for philosophers to behave. Rather, the proper way is to appeal to reasons that are recognized as such by others. This again is his internal criticism, where a position is shown to be inadequate according to its own standards of adequacy.

Hegel talks at some length about the speculative sentence or proposition. What's that? Let's depart from Hegel's own examples and select one that is more prosaic. Here are some sentences: "Angelica is feline," "Angelica is cute," "Angelica is skittish," and "Angelica is playful." Each of these sentences has a subject ("Angelica") and then predicates some quality of that subject ("feline," "cute," "skittish," and "playful"). The grammar misleadingly suggests that the subject has an existence, or an essence, that exists apart from and independently of these predications. The speculative sentence recognizes, however, that the subject goes into its predications, such that it is nothing but the sum total of predications into which it can enter. If we subtract from her all of the qualities that can be predicated of her, we lose her too. So, the speculative sentence describes in different words the point that we have already seen about relations.

Introduction

Much of the Introduction can be seen as Hegel's rejection of the turn in philosophy to epistemology, the theory of knowledge, that is initiated by Descartes, culminates in Kant, but still continues to the present. Ancient and medieval philosophers generally agree that metaphysics is first philosophy. That is to say, they believed that before doing anything else in philosophy, it is first crucial to investigate the basic nature and constituents of reality. They asked such questions as: "Is there one or more substances?" "What is the nature of space and time?" "Does God exist and, if so, can God's existence be proven?" Descartes rejects this approach and instead claims that epistemology must be first philosophy. Before we begin to know anything, he maintains, we have to inquire about our ability to know. This endeavor culminates in Kant, who claims that what is most crucial is to determine what can be known by reason alone, a priori, without any information from the five senses.

Hegel rejects this entire approach. The fear of error, he urges, is the error itself. Such philosophers as Descartes and Kant fear that they will mistakenly believe that they know things that are actually false and so – before they know anything else – they first attempt to see what can actually be known. Hegel believes that such projects are doomed to failure because the only way actually to find out what can be known is by making claims to knowledge and seeing if those claims are subsequently undermined. This is the point of his writing a *Phenomenology of Spirit* – the only way to know what can be known is to examine how knowledge presents itself. Attempting to discover what can be known, before actually knowing anything, is like deciding you won't get into the water until you know how to swim. The proper approach, Hegel says, is first to get into the water, because only then can you learn to swim. Insofar as knowing is thought of as an instrument or medium – a mistake, Hegel thinks – then the question arises as to the nature of the object of knowledge, the thing that is known, independent of that instrument or medium. We have, in other words, Kant's thing-in-itself, the object as it actually is apart from human cognition: something outside of space and time, something to which such human categories as cause and effect, number, and relation can't be meaningfully applied. Although Kant himself intends to bypass skepticism, his way of articulating matters actually gives rise to skepticism. Is the object as it is in-itself, apart from any knowing of it, anything like the object as known? And if the answer is that the object as known isn't similar to the object as it is in-itself, or if the answer is that we can never know whether they are similar, then this is a failure of knowing. Matters aren't helped if we are told that we need be concerned only with the object insofar as it is an object of knowledge. Kant distinguishes the object as it appears to us from the object as it is in-itself, apart from the ways it appears to us. Rather than knowing the object, we know only its appearances. Kant believes that this is sufficient, whereas Hegel recognizes that this replays the very skepticism that Kant had intended to leave behind.

It is the object itself that must be known, according to Hegel, rather than appearances of the object. He notes that this will be a path of despair. Many times, as we journey on this path, we will believe that we have finally achieved knowledge, only subsequently to discover that this knowing was false knowing – that is to say, incomplete and partial. We must persevere on this path, though, as there is no other way to knowledge. As noted already, Hegel rejects appeals to personal conviction and authority because he recognizes that such appeals can immediately be gainsaid by the counter-appeals that make opposite claims.

Although Hegel writes of a necessary progression of shapes, I suggest that we read this in a deflationary way, so that the progression is necessary in the sense that, given where we are now, the previous shapes have become necessary. Had any of them been different – which they might well have been – then our present shape would be different too.

Hegel also writes of "determinate negation." This is an important concept in his philosophy. The basic idea is that, when a philosophical position is refuted, negated, it isn't wholly rejected. Rather, the false claims that it makes are rejected but the ones that are true – or, at least, still appear to be true – are retained. Hegel uses the German word *Aufhebung*, translated as "sublation," to express this. Determinate negation cancels a position that has been rejected. However, determinate negation also preserves, changes, and transcends that position.

As we have seen so far, Hegel emphasizes the importance of internal rather than external criticism. He also uses this notion to bypass skepticism. Skepticism arises when we wonder whether what we believe to be knowledge of an object really is *knowledge* of the *object*. Perhaps the object is actually quite different from the way it seems, the worry goes, and maybe there is no way ever really to know what the object is like. To take this concern to another level, we could also ask whether there really is an external world at all. Perhaps everything that seems external to the mind is somehow produced by the mind itself. This would be solipsism, of course, the view that all that exists is an individual's consciousness and everything else is an illusion. It seems impossible to overcome this form of skepticism, since all of our evidence for objects external to our mind is a result of how they appear to us. How can we know that how they appear is how they really are? Indeed, how can we know that they have any reality beyond their appearances?

It might seem that any way out of these difficulties will involve either being dogmatic or an infinite regress. Individuals might dogmatically *assert* that they know that the object as it appears is how the object really is. This approach fails because other persons may experience the object differently or make a counter-assertion. There is no way to adjudicate between these competing claims.

Alternatively, individuals might appeal to authority, feelings, conscience, or tradition to support their claim that they know that the object as it appears is how the object really is. In this case, though, their appeal to authority (or whatever) will likely be challenged. Then, they must appeal to something else to justify their earlier appeal to authority.[12] This appeal to something else will also be challenged . . . and so we fall into an infinite regress. We thus seem to confront a dilemma between dogmatism and infinite regress. Neither will help us. Dogmatism gives us a standard but no reason to accept it. Infinite regress promises a standard, but we never reach it.

Fortunately, Hegel has a third alternative. Before discussing it, however, I must first explain an oddity about how he uses the term "knowledge." Contemporary epistemologists disagree about whether a belief must be justified to count as knowledge, but almost all agree that the belief must be true. A justified false belief, then, would not count as knowledge. When Hegel uses "knowledge," however, he means only that the belief is justified, not that the belief is also true. (For our purposes here, a belief is *justified* if the person who has that belief can give some reason – a reason which would be accepted as a reason by the person's peers – to support the belief; of course, in order for a belief, even a false one, to be justified, it is necessary that the belief be thought true by those who believe it.) "Knowledge," for Hegel, is not only justified *true* beliefs; it also includes justified false beliefs. Hegel uses "knowledge" and "knowing" where contemporary epistemologists would instead use "conviction" and "being convinced." With this in mind, we can now understand Hegel's alternative.

Hegel's way out of the dilemma between dogmatism and infinite regress is to bracket questions about whether the knowledge is true – that is, whether the justified belief is actually true – and instead consider knowledge only as it appears to consciousness. Hegel recognizes that all knowledge as it appears to consciousness already distinguishes between claims about some object and the object about which those claims are made. In discussing a green chili, for example, we can distinguish between (1) the claim that the chili is green and (2) the chili that we experience as green (but which we might experience as white if we are now seeing it under a green light). So, both claims about an object *and* that object present themselves to consciousness. Hegel will drop questions of the object as it exists independently of consciousness. Insofar as such questions are retained, they are transfigured into inquiries about claims to knowledge of an object, and that object itself, as these appear to consciousness. This distinction provides a standard of truth because the *knowledge* of the object can be compared with the *object* of knowledge, as both appear to consciousness, with the object of knowledge functioning as the standard. The claim that the chili is green can be compared with the chili that we perceive, for example, and we might notice that we are seeing the chili under a green light, and so we would realize that the chili would be white under normal light. If the knowledge of the object (the claim that the chili is green) does not correspond to the object of knowledge (because the chili is white under normal light), then the knowledge of the object must be reformulated to match the object of knowledge (we might conclude that the chili is white). As a result, the standard is the object as experienced (the chili). Things are a bit more complicated, though, as Hegel also maintains that, because the standard is the object of knowledge as it appears to consciousness, this reformulation (recognizing that the claim that the chili is green must be rejected because the chili is white) leads to a change in the standard too. Why?

There is always the danger of misunderstanding Hegel if his views are explained using terms other than those he uses. There is an even greater danger, however. This is that we use the terms that Hegel uses and use them as he would – so that we can speak "Hegelese" – but not understand what we are saying. Indeed, if we are really good at speaking Hegelese, we might not even realize that we don't know what we are talking about. Since we can speak Hegelese well, moreover, others also won't realize that we don't understand what we are saying, either because they don't speak Hegelese and so have no idea what we are saying or because they do speak it and what we are saying sounds good to them.[13] If we use terms that everyone already understands, even though they aren't Hegel's terms, we are less likely to fool ourselves and others into believing that we have understood things when we haven't.

Let's try explaining Hegel's arguments in the Introduction by using the terms "theory" and "experience" used in contemporary philosophy of science. If we do this, then we can say that Hegel's argument is that a theory always makes a distinction between its claims and its object (or object domain, the thing that the theory is about). Scientists don't compare a theory's claims with something which hasn't been experienced; rather, they compare those claims with the object *as* experienced. Insofar as the theory doesn't accurately describe the experienced object, the theory must be revised. If the theory makes some predictions about how the object will behave under certain conditions, and the object doesn't behave that way, then the theory must be modified. Most contemporary philosophers of science agree that experience itself is theory-laden. That is to say, what we experience is partially a result of the theories we accept. We see a hammer fall because of gravity, for example. Lacking a theory of gravity, Aristotle couldn't have seen this. Since experience is theory-laden, changing our theory about an object also changes our experience of the object. As a consequence, the experienced object is the standard that tests the truth of the theory, but changing the theory changes the standard too.

How does this happen? Kenley R. Dove exemplifies one interpretation, according to which Hegel himself doesn't do anything other than recording what he observes.[14] Dove accepts the prospective interpretation of necessity. He argues that the shapes of consciousness present themselves in a logically necessary sequence, and so Hegel needs only to record the ways in which each shape proves to be inherently contradictory, collapses, and so engenders the subsequent shape. Hegel's dialectical method is wholly phenomenological, Dove maintains, and consists in his merely watching and reporting the unfolding of the shapes. On this view, the new object, and so the new standard, arises on its own.

In section 87 of the *Phenomenology of Spirit*, however, Hegel writes that the new object appears as a result of a reversal of consciousness and that this reversal is something which we contribute. I discussed above the difficulties with the prospective interpretation of necessity – insurmountable, in my view – and advocated a retrospective reading. On this reading, we see with hindsight which earlier shapes were necessary. Those shapes were necessary because they made our current shape possible. But there is a bit more than that going on here. From their own perspective, they don't recognize that any given shape represents an attempt to overcome the difficulties with a previous shape. At most, they recognize that shapes change over time, like fashions in men's ties: earlier this, now that, later the other thing. What we contribute, according to Hegel, is a recognition that the shapes of consciousness form a *progressive series* of shapes. And this recognition is made possible because this is how Hegel tells the story. This suggests that there are alternative ways of telling the story. Someone – Martin Heidegger would be an example – might propose that the shapes are a regressive series, where each shape incorporates only the failures of its predecessor. Someone else might say that there isn't really any *series* at all, just one thing happening after another. Hegel seemingly denies that there can be alternative versions of his *Phenomenology of Spirit*, but his real claim is that, when we have finally considered matters, we won't find those other versions adequate. So, there is an element of rhetoric in Hegel's presentation. This would only be a criticism if there were an alternative to Hegel's strategy – if, that is to say, some version of the prospective interpretation could be made plausible. I see no hope for that and so don't consider the mere presence of rhetoric in Hegel's argument a point of criticism.

Consciousness: Sense-Certainty

Hegel structures the *Phenomenology of Spirit* so that it proceeds from the most immediate to the most mediated. By "immediate," Hegel means an experience that wouldn't have conceptual content and by "mediated" he refers to something that would have conceptual content. An example will make this clearer. Consider any object, say, a pencil. The experience of this pencil has conceptual content. The pencil can be described as an object, cylindrical, seven inches long, one-quarter inch in diameter, yellow. To have an experience without conceptual content would be to be unable to describe it using any terms that could be applied to any other things. The section on Sense-Certainty describes the attempt to refer to something immediately, without using concepts. In the Preface, we noted Hegel's claim that we learn by experience that we meant something other than we meant to mean. This will happen here. Sense-Certainty will assert that it can immediately refer to something, without using concepts, but we will see that it is unable to do this. Hegel will express this point by saying that Sense-Certainty will discover that it must use universals. That is to say, it must use concepts which don't uniquely apply to any particular object but which instead apply to a wide range of objects. The pencil is yellow, but so are pears.

Let's take a step away from Hegel's text for a moment and ask who believes in sense-certainty. Is Hegel describing a position that exists only theoretically, as a point in conceptual space? No. Let's consider five instances of sense-certainty. First, the distinction in Kant's *Critique of Pure Reason* between the forms of sensibility (alternatively, the forms of intuition) and the categories of understanding could suggest that humans can have representations which, although temporal and spatial, are non-conceptual. Such a non-conceptual representation is an example of "sense-certainty" because it would be the merest felt presence of a thing, a bare this-here-now, without being able to describe or conceptualize it further in any way.

Second, in his essay "Knowledge by Acquaintance and Knowledge by Description," Bertrand Russell argues that we have two kinds of knowledge: that based on acquaintance and that based on description.[15] Russell seems to mean by knowledge by acquaintance what Hegel calls sense-certainty – the view that there can be an immediate experience of something, an experience that has no conceptual content, that can't be described using any universals. Often, theories of foundationalism in epistemology take knowledge by acquaintance to be properly basic. Epistemological foundationalists claim that there are some beliefs which either don't require any justification or are self-justifying. If someone says that Bengali is the fourth most widely spoken language, we can ask what evidence supports this claim. Foundationalists maintain that there are some claims for which demands for justification aren't appropriate, such as knowledge by acquaintance.

Third, it is sometimes asserted that no one but a woman can know what a woman feels. This may mean that it is only with great difficulty that a man can have the depth of feeling, sympathy, and imagination to comprehend how a woman would experience things. That is correct, of course. It might also mean, however, that a woman's experience is literally indescribable, that it can't be articulated, that it wholly lacks conceptual content.

Fourth, sometimes similar claims are made for religious experience, especially mystical experience, where persons will claim that they have had some experience that in principle can't be communicated to others because it goes beyond, or lies beneath, any concepts. Again, it is sometimes asserted that mystics have a knowledge that can't be expressed in language: "Those who know don't say and those who say don't know." (There's a snarky reply: "Yes, so they say.")

Finally, rejecting Russell's view that names are disguised descriptions of the person (or thing) named, Saul Kripke proposes instead that names are "rigid designators" that pick out the same person (or thing) in every possible world which contains that person.[16] Kripke proposes that a name is linked to a person through an initial act of "baptism" – Kripke's word – whereby a person is named. Since Kripke denies that description plays any role here, he is committed to maintaining that this person can be referred to immediately, without using any concepts or universals.

Hegel will show that Sense-Certainty can't say what it means or mean what it says. Let's pause a moment and ask whether Sense-Certainty has to *say* anything. Why couldn't it assert that it has an immediate experience or knowledge of something, that this experience or knowledge doesn't have conceptual content, that it can't be articulated with universals, that it can't be expressed in language, that it can't be communicated, and that Sense-Certainty fully accepts this? Hegel's response would likely be that even to describe this experience or knowledge *as* "experience" or "knowledge" is already to have said something. Why not call it "ignorance" instead? He would then observe that, while it asserts that it has some experience or knowledge that is its alone, Sense-Certainty also demands that others recognize that it has this experience or knowledge. To see this, let's return to the example above. When epistemological foundationalists claim to have knowledge by acquaintance that is properly basic, they aren't noting some curiosity about themselves – like someone who says he gets hiccups whenever he watches football – but rather are claiming that they know something that can't be doubted and that this then justifies at least some of their other beliefs. A woman who asserts that only another woman can understand what a woman feels says this in order to claim that there are some things that men aren't qualified to discuss. Those who assert that they have mystical experiences often use this to support pronouncements about what others should or shouldn't be doing. Kripke believes that he can refer directly to a specific individual and name her "Madhuri," to give an example, and that this name will rigidly designate her in all possible worlds in which she exists. Since he claims that this naming doesn't involve any descriptions – and so, presumably, any concepts or universals – he hence believes that he can immediately designate this specific person throughout her entire life in all possible worlds where she exists rather than only, for example, on 15 May 1967 in Bombay. Hence, it is not that Hegel demands that Sense-Certainty speak when it would be happy to be quiet or that he puts words in its mouth. Instead, Sense-Certainty speaks on its own and then Hegel asks what it means to say.

Sense-Certainty claims that it can immediately refer to something – say, *this here now*. But those words are all universal terms. They can refer to a specific thing but they can refer to other things too. Moreover, to refer to any specific thing and not to some other thing requires contrasts: this not that, here not there, now not earlier or later. Sense-Certainty would surely concede that a sentence that is true can't become false by being written. But if we write "now it's night," that sentence becomes false when we read it the next morning. Hegel's point is that what "now" means depends upon its context of use – which is to say that the attempt to refer immediately to something, without using concepts or universals, fails.

Sense-Certainty makes another attempt. It first tried to refer to something immediately by focusing attention on the object that is being referred to: "this here now." That failed, as we have just seen, because those terms have a meaning only when contrasted with other terms. In its second attempt, Sense-Certainty emphasizes the subject that is doing the referring. When *I* say "this here now," a specific object is referred to because *I* mean to refer to it. Sense-Certainty now claims that it is *my* immediately intending to refer to something that is important. But who is this *I*? Each individual uses "I" when referring to the self. An example: Salman says "I'm going to visit my father" and Abhishek says "I'm going to visit my father." Although both of them say "I," each refers to himself, and so it is no surprise that Salman goes to see Salim and Abhishek goes to see Amitabh. Another example: I go to a colleague's office. On the door, I see a posted note, "I'm in Room 223." I don't think "No, *I'm* not in Room 223," but rather understand that my colleague is in Room 223. The point is that "I" can refer to a specific individual only in a particular context, which requires that this "I" be distinguished from any other "I."

Yes, this is all obvious – so what? So, Sense-Certainty's attempt to refer to something immediately, because that's what "I" mean, fails because "I" itself proves to be a concept, a universal.

In section 109, Hegel explicitly notes that there has been a reversal. Sense-Certainty meant to refer immediately to some specific thing, without invoking any universals, but instead it finds itself referring, against its own intentions, to universals. What Sense-Certainty meant it couldn't say and what it said it didn't mean. That Sense-Certainty couldn't say what it meant must be understood simultaneously in both senses of that expression: Sense-Certainty is unable to *express* what it meant, and Sense-Certainty itself doesn't *know* what it meant.

In that same section, Hegel also mentions the ancient mystery religions of Ceres and Bacchus, eating bread and drinking wine (perhaps also a reference to the Eucharist), and that animals aren't excluded from this wisdom. What is he talking about? Sense-Certainty first asserts that it can refer immediately to things but then discovers that all of its attempts to do so involve concepts and universals. It might then conclude that there is some unbridgeable gap between those universals and the specific thing to which it wished to refer. By eating their food – in the case of carnivores, their prey – animals show that there is no such gap. In eating bread and drinking wine, moreover, believers commune with and participate in the divine.

We have seen that Hegel repeatedly emphasizes the importance of internal criticism, and we have a nice instance of that at work in the section on Sense-Certainty. Sense-Certainty asserts that it can refer to things immediately, but Hegel shows that it nevertheless surreptitiously employs universals. Hence, Sense-Certainty fails by its own standard for success. This section also provides a fine example of determinate negation. Although Sense-Certainty is mistaken in asserting that it is possible to refer *immediately* to particulars, it correctly believes that particulars can be referred to.

Consciousness: Perception

Perception can be seen as an inversion of Sense-Certainty. The latter claimed to be able to refer immediately to particulars but nevertheless found itself using universals. Perception recognizes that reference requires universals but won't be able to articulate how those universals relate to each other or how they connect to the particular.

Perception claims that a thing has many different properties. Salt, for example, has a certain texture, taste, and color. Nice. Questions arise, however, that Perception isn't able to answer successfully. How are an object's properties able to link with each other and with the object? Suppose we say that an object is merely a concatenation of its properties, such that the object is identical to, and nothing over and above, its properties. This doesn't seem correct, as we recognize that an object can remain the same object even though some of its properties change. Salt remains salt, for example, even if red food color is added so that the normally white salt is now red. Suppose we then maintain that the object is distinct from its properties, such that an object has properties but isn't identical to them. In that case, though, how can objects be distinguished from each other? It seems that objects are identified on the basis of their properties. If the object is something other than its properties, it seems that there will be no way to distinguish one object from another.

Following John Locke's suggestion, we might distinguish between primary and secondary properties, such that the object is identical to the concatenation of its primary properties while its secondary properties could come or go without making that object other than it is. Even supposing that there is some non-question-begging way to distinguish primary from secondary properties – a way that doesn't involve merely stipulating some properties as primary and others as secondary – we still won't know how it is that primary properties could concatenate together to form an object or how secondary properties could link to them. Nor do we really know whether there is some essence that underlies the primary properties.

We saw that Sense-Certainty attempted to resolve its difficulties by focusing first on the object and then on the subject. This is true of Perception too. Recognizing its inability to resolve the above problems at the level of the object, it then tries to resolve them at the level of the subject. It proposes that what counts as an object or as a property is a matter of how the subject – that is to say here, consciousness – views things. A heap of stones is a single object, a heap, insofar as the subject considers it as one. Alternatively, it can be viewed as many individual stones, insofar as that is how the subject regards it. Leaving aside the difficulty of how or why the subject would have any basis to make such perspectival discriminations, all of the above problems are replicated at the level of the subject. Is the self something that *has* thoughts, desires, and memories while remaining distinct from them, as Descartes believes? Or is the self merely the concatenation of its thoughts, desires, and memories, as David Hume suggests with his so-called bundle theory of the self?

How are a self's thoughts, desires, and memories able to link with each other and with the self? Suppose we say that a self is merely a concatenation of its thoughts, desires, and memories, such that the self is identical to, and is nothing over and above, its thoughts, desires, and memories. However, a self can remain the same self even though some of its thoughts, desires, and memories change. Aamir remains Aamir, for example, regardless of whether he is thinking about Karisma or Kareena. It might be asserted that the self is distinct from its thoughts, desires, and memories, such that a self has thoughts, desires, and memories but isn't identical to them. In that case, though, how can selves be distinguished from each other? It seems that selves are identified on the basis of their thoughts, desires, and memories. (A science fiction excursus from

Hegel's text: We distinguish Karisma from Kareena, in the first instance, because they look different. True enough, but what happens if each loses all of her thoughts, desires, and memories while acquiring all of the others?) If the self is something other than its thoughts, desires, and memories, it seems that there will be no way to distinguish one self from another.

Perception is unable to overcome these problems of the one and the many. It can't provide an account that links the properties either with each other or to an object, it can't explain how an object remains the same object when its properties change, and it can't explain how objects can be distinguished if an object isn't identical to its properties. Perception then attempts to overcome these difficulties at the level of the subject, only to see them replicated. Perception correctly suspects that the object is the result of consciousness' own activity, as we will see, but it does not yet have the resources adequately to articulate that.

Consciousness: Force and Understanding

The object results from consciousness' own conceptual activity, but this hasn't yet been recognized. The section on Force and Understanding represents one last attempt to resist this conclusion. Consciousness doesn't yet perceive its own activity and product.

But how can the object be the result of consciousness' activity – readers may interrupt – isn't this backsliding into solipsism? To see why that is not the case, recall the analogy with theory introduced above. There, we noted that theory makes predictions about the object. If those predictions are inadequate, the theory is modified. Since our comprehension of the object is based on our theory of it, however, to modify the theory is also to modify what we take the object to be. It is, in other words, to modify the object. At any moment, what the object is taken to be is itself a result of the theory of the object. In turn, the theory is something that consciousness produces. Hence, it isn't solipsistic to say that that the object is a result of consciousness' activity.

Earlier, we noted that Hegel distinguishes between the Understanding and Reason, where the former attempts to comprehend a thing without attending to the set of relations in which that thing is embedded, while the latter recognizes that the thing is constituted through its relations and is unintelligible – indeed, doesn't exist – apart from them. In this section, we observe the Understanding attempting to overcome the difficulties that emerged in Perception. The Understanding makes a distinction between an inner force and its outer expression. It then claims that the object as it appears to us is an expression of a force that is the object. The object will then have two aspects: its appearance to us and the force that produces this appearance. The next suggestion is that the inner force behaves in a lawlike way, or is governed by some law, such that the object as it appears to us, its expression, is predictable and not chaotic. An example: Observing that the planets orbit the sun, the Understanding might suggest that there is some force – gravity – that produces planets' orbits as its expression.

Hegel believes that this appeal to force and its expression doesn't explain anything. In the case of gravity, for example, saying that there is some force that produces the orbits tells us no more than describing how the planets orbit the sun in a certain way. Talk of an inner force and its outer expression is superfluous.

We now come to one of Hegel's more difficult discussions, about what is called the inverted, topsy-turvy, or upside-down world (in German, it is the *verkehrte Welt*). There, the North Pole is south, vice is virtue, and so forth. Let's begin by asking which shape of consciousness Hegel criticizes with his discussion of this bizarre world. One of the difficulties in reading the *Phenomenology of Spirit* is that Hegel frequently criticizes several distinct philosophical positions simultaneously with the same argument. Here, he is criticizing the theory of the forms advanced by Plato's Socrates, various forms of Christianity, Kant's theory of morality, and scientific accounts of hidden forces. What all of these views have in common is that they posit another and truer level of reality. Let's take Plato's Socrates as an example.

In many of Plato's dialogues, Socrates begins by asking someone for an account of some moral quality, such as piety, courage, justice, or virtue itself. Frequently, Socrates' interlocutor responds by giving examples. Socrates then responds that he doesn't want examples of, say, courage but rather wants to know what form (feature or definition) makes these examples of courage. Socrates recognizes that prime number has a form – a positive integer greater than 1 that can be divided without remainder by only two positive integers: itself and 1 – and he assumes that this must be true of, if not all things, at least all moral qualities. The appropriate response – although none of Socrates' interlocutors makes it – would be that, unlike prime number, there may be no form that makes all of the examples of courage actual examples of courage. Analogously,

Ludwig Wittgenstein (1889–1951) suggests that there is no common feature that makes all games games.[17] While some games are competitive, played with balls, played with cards, involve chance, or require more than one player, other games don't have those features. Socrates maintains that, until we discover the form which makes courage courage, we won't know whether putative examples of courage really are examples of courage. He doesn't begin with examples of courage and then ask whether there is some feature possessed by all of them, and by no other things, that makes them examples of courage. Rather, he believes that it is possible that we are radically mistaken about what courage is and that each of our supposed examples of courage actually isn't really an example at all. He hopes to discover the form of courage and then use that as the standard by which to discern whether supposed examples of courage actually are instances of courage.[18]

Socrates' attempt necessarily fails because, except for self-contradiction, he has no standard by which to rule out any proposed form. It is only if we begin by identifying examples of courage that we can then consider whether a specific action is courageous. If we believe, however, that it is possible that all of the supposed examples of courage aren't really examples of it, then we have no standard.

This is where Hegel's discussion of the topsy-turvy world becomes relevant. If we begin by assuming that we could be radically mistaken about what courage really is, then we must allow that it is possible that what we take to be instances of courage are really examples of cowardice. This inversion whereby courage becomes cowardice can be generalized, of course, so that wisdom really is what we regard as stupidity, virtue what we consider vice, and so forth. Someone might suggest that God could tell us what courage really is, but what God recognizes as courage could be what we consider to be cowardice.

Someone else might suggest that Reason can provide a standard by which to discern correct from mistaken supposed instances of courage. If Reason is supposed to begin its work *de novo*, without starting with paradigm instances of courage, then at most it will exclude contradictory examples.

Stepping away from Hegel's *Phenomenology of Spirit* for a moment, it is unlikely that Reason, on its own, could even do that much. Paraconsistent logics developed from research in relevant logics.[19] A *paraconsistent logic* allows contradictions but puts constraints on what can be deduced from them.[20] There is no non-question-begging argument to show that Reason, on its own, uses traditional logic instead of a paraconsistent logic. If Reason employs the latter, then it couldn't exclude contradictory examples as illegitimate.

If we allow that there are inner forces that produce outer expressions, moreover, then what we consider the South Pole may actually be the North Pole, attraction could be repulsion, virtue vice, and so on.

The point of the topsy-turvy world is to underscore that the appeals to inner forces are explanatorily useless. The world of inner forces at best superfluously replicates the world that appears to us. At worst, it turns everything upside down to no purpose.

Self-consciousness: Lordship and Bondage

We are about to transition from the level of the individual (consciousness) to the social (self-consciousness). Some scholars have thought that Hegel changes his mind, at this point, about the sort of book he is writing. Beginning with a text that shares affiliations with much of the preceding epistemological trend in modern philosophy, especially Kant, these scholars believe that he then decides to explore issues in social and political philosophy. From Hegel's discussion of the topsy-turvy world, however, we can see why a move from the individual to the social is necessary.

Let's return for a moment to Plato's Socrates. Rather than beginning with examples of courage and seeing if he could discern some features that these examples have in common which would then allow him to say that any actions having these features would also be instances of courage, he starts by assuming that we could be radically mistaken about what courage is, and so he seeks a form of courage that will determine whether supposed examples of courage really are such. This approach makes possible the absurd result that what we regard as courage is really cowardice and vice versa. The point is that there is no way forward if we begin with the supposition that we could be radically mistaken, since the only constraint on theorizing is avoiding contradiction (and, as discussed above, it is not clear that there is even this constraint).

The upshot of this is that we must begin by treating specific examples of courage as paradigm instances, asking which features they share, if any. This then necessitates a move to the social, because what counts as examples of courage will be determined by public standards (usually implicit and often conflicted). Hegel will now discuss the emergence of these standards, exploring how society becomes progressively more conscious of what these standards are as well as increasingly aware that these standards are actually society's own creation rather than things naturally given and encountered.

To do this, Hegel initially backs away from societies and discusses life. Life is characterized by desire. In the first instance, naturally, this is desire for those things that are necessary for a specific living being to stay alive and to produce offspring. This level of existence isn't free, because it is wholly bound up with survival and reproduction. There can only be a level of freedom when there is a relative independence from nature. This occurs when desire is not only for survival and reproduction but also a desire to be desired. This moment represents the transition from nature to culture, spirit.

This desire to be desired begins in conflict. Each individual demands to be recognized as an individual but is unable or unwilling to extend that recognition to the other. Rather than having mutual recognition, then, we have a demand for recognition that isn't reciprocal.

In describing the struggle for recognition, Hegel writes as though it concerns two individuals. Insofar as this has a historical reference to ancient Greece, it is more likely a struggle between two groups. I have discussed Hegel's tale of lord and bondsman above and so there is no need to repeat it. What must be emphasized, however, is that this struggle is for *recognition* and so marks the transition from nature to culture.

Alexandre Kojève claims that Hegel's "Lordship and Bondage" section is the key to the entire *Phenomenology of Spirit*[21] and considers that all of Hegel's other discussions are variants of that section. Simplifying to the extreme, Kojève believes that history is on the side of the bondsman and that Hegel's text narrates his progressive liberation. This interpretation has been criticized.[22] One of the more telling objections to Kojève's interpretation is that the next shape of consciousness is Stoicism, which focuses on the Stoics' attempts to control their thoughts and reactions to external events, believing that it is irrelevant whether a person is an emperor or a slave. As a consequence, Stoicism can be seen as a continuation as much of the lord as of the bondsman. This suggests that we should attempt to interpret subsequent sections of Hegel's text not as the progressive liberation of the bondsman but rather as the progressive overcoming of the split between the lord and bondsman.

Self-consciousness: Stoicism, Skepticism, Unhappy Consciousness

Stoicism no longer attempts to control external events but instead focuses its efforts on maintaining an equanimity in the face of whatever happens. It has a negative attitude to both the lord and the bondsman. Whereas both the lord and the bondsman believe that they have some influence over their circumstances, Stoicism denies this and so claims that it doesn't matter whether a person is an emperor or a slave. To hold that it does matter would be to think that an emperor would have more ability than a slave to have things happen as that individual wishes them to happen. Stoicism maintains, however, that both emperor and slave lack any ability whatsoever to control the course of events. Stoicism believes that nothing in the external world can be controlled, or even influenced, by its actions. It views its own actions as occurring regardless of its intentions or desires. The most that it can control are its own thoughts and attitudes to what happens. Stoicism attempts to cultivate an attitude of indifference so that it is not affected by anything that happens. In making this attempt, Stoicism does achieve a level of freedom of thought, in that what it thinks isn't merely a response to whatever occurs in its environment. Since it isn't linked to a freedom to act, however, this freedom is merely formal and abstract. Stoicism extols truth, goodness, virtue, and wisdom. Since Stoicism has renounced any attempt actually to do anything, however, these don't have any content and so lack any determinate meaning. The self – the "I" – which emerges in Stoicism is one that seeks to transcend any distinguishing characteristics which would mark it as a specific individual and instead attempts to obtain a universal perspective. Insofar as thought is independent of any occurrences in the external world, the thoughts of one person would be no different than those of anyone else.

Whereas Stoicism claims that what is crucial is that thought should not be concerned with anything that happens in the world, Skepticism maintains that thought itself isn't essential. Skepticism recognizes that thought without content is empty thought, it isn't really thought at all, and so it loses all connection to reality. Whereas Stoicism hopes to obtain a universal standpoint, Skepticism maintains that any supposed universal standpoint is only that of some individual. Assertions made for the truth of any perspective – irrespective of whether this perspective claims to be universal and so denies that it is one possible perspective among many – can be gainsaid by counter-assertions. It is for this reason that Hegel compares Skepticism to squabbling children. When one child asserts something, the other child instantly asserts the opposite. If the first child were then to say that opposite thing, the second child would contradict it. Although the arguments of Skepticism initially seem significant, they are mere gainsaying. Skepticism recognizes that any claim can be contradicted by a counter-claim, and it realizes that this is equally true of its own claims. This leads to a duplication within thought. For every thought, there is a counter-thought.

Skepticism is the truth of Stoicism. The Unhappy Consciousness – it is generally agreed that Hegel here refers to medieval Christianity – attempts to go beyond Skepticism by reasserting the distinction between particular perspectives and a universal standpoint, as well as by further distinguishing inessential from essential thoughts. There is a sense in which the Unhappy Consciousness could be viewed as sequel of the struggle between the lord and the bondsman. Kojève's interpretation isn't adequate, but nor is it wholly misguided. With the Unhappy Consciousness, though, all persons take the position of the bondsman and the lord becomes God. People have no ability to accomplish anything; only God can do this. Positive qualities are attributed to God. People are then viewed, and view themselves, as deficient and lacking. True individuality is attributed to God alone, who occupies a universal standpoint. People experience themselves as separate from God and seek to overcome this distance. Their attempts, however, merely underscore their experience of the immensity of the distance between God and themselves. Experiencing itself as worthless without God, whom it can never reach, the Unhappy Consciousness isn't a happy camper. What the Unhappy Consciousness doesn't recognize is that both sides of this division are itself.

Reason: Observing Reason

Observing Reason understands external reality to be its own creation. How can this make any sense? Are rocks reason's creation? Yes, because we create the theory that allows rocks to appear *as*, and so to be, rocks. There is no thing-in-itself beyond, or behind, appearances. How a thing appears and how it can appear is what it is in-itself. Nevertheless, Observing Reason doesn't yet recognize its own activities in what it observes. It believes that the reason it finds in things is there independently of itself, not yet recognizing its own activity.

Observing Reason does not recognize that observation itself is a directed process that involves a focus upon specific things to the exclusion of others. What is observed is based on our interests; things as such don't present themselves for observation, we actively select them to be observed. Observation, then, doesn't equal perception.

Observing Reason attempts to distinguish between the essential and the accidental. It tries to distinguish sensibility, irritability, and so forth, and then relate them through laws. This produces only tautologies, urges Hegel, because all of these are only different aspects of the same thing. Statistical frequency by itself reveals nothing.

Observing Reason also seeks to reduce the organic to the inorganic. The relation of inner and outer in the inorganic is purely numerical, and so there isn't a necessary connection here. In the case of the organic, however, there is such a connection. Its parts affect and are affected by its other parts. It maintains homeostasis. We observe a rational progression in humans, moreover, but there isn't such a progression in nature, and hence there can't be laws that govern it.

Observing Reason introduces logical and psychological laws. Logical laws are merely formal. Observing Reason treats these laws as mere givens – it doesn't yet recognize them as its own product. Modus ponens, to depart from Hegel's text, is a valid form of inference only in systems that allow it. However, to insist that it is always and everywhere valid is to treat it as a given. Psychological laws are merely empty empirical generalizations. They take themselves to be laws which are descriptive of the way in which any individual will respond to a thing. They forget that how an individual will respond is conditioned by that person's circumstances. Moreover, they fail to recognize that individuals, having learned what these supposed laws are, may act in ways that violate the laws, precisely because of the laws' predictions.

Physiognomy and phrenology. These two sciences of Hegel's day claim that a person's inner dispositions and moral character can be read from that person's face or the shape of the skull. Hegel's point is that there isn't any way to read the face; actions alone can be read, and so he would disagree with George Orwell's assertion that "at 50, everyone has the face he deserves."[23] The idea of phrenology is that certain parts of the brain govern specific dispositions and moral characteristics, such that greater, or lesser, development will have a corresponding effect on the shape of the skull. Hegel entirely disagrees with physiognomy and phrenology, as both fail to recognize that human consciousness has an interiority that can be read only through an individual's actions. Hegel says that a punch to the head is the proper response to someone who claims that, although we appear to be good persons, our skulls actually reveal us to be rascals. He further says that these sciences are like someone who considers the penis only as a way to piss and doesn't recognize its role in copulation and reproduction. Indeed, these sciences, says Hegel, would reduce knowledge to pissing. His point, to step back from the potty mouth for a moment, is that these sciences attempt to reduce knowledge to a purely natural phenomenon, rather than recognizing that knowledge involves standards – ones which we have created. Readers might believe, and hope, that such sciences must be long dead. However, MacIntyre convincingly shows that they are still healthy and active.[24]

Let's step back again, for a moment, from Hegel's text and ask a seemingly naïve question: Why the attitude? Hegel's official position – which he flagrantly violates in this section – is one of internal criticism, whereby he shows that a view fails by its own standards. Okay, maybe he can be defended here. He could say that the people who propagate physiognomy and phrenology recognize the distinction between inner thought and outer expression that these sciences would deny. They would object to being classified and treated as rascals because of their faces or head bumps, despite their intentions and the quality of their actions.

But, still, Hegel says that where and who we are now is a result of our history, such that – given where and who we are now – our history is necessary. Had it been different, which it certainly could have been, we would now be different too – if *we* would even be here now. Okay, but, in that case, why is Hegel so viciously sarcastic in discussing these two shapes of consciousness?

Slavoj Žižek correctly observes, in one of his many books, that the venom in Hegel's criticisms is a defensive desire to distance his own views from physiognomy and phrenology. Of all the shapes of consciousness examined in the *Phenomenology of Spirit*, these are the closest to his own. Hegel thinks that Spirit is, finally, its expression, that there is no hidden reality behind or beneath it. Spirit is what it does. From a certain perspective, this is infinitely far from physiognomy and phrenology. From another, however, they are so close as to be almost indistinguishable. To prompt his readers to adopt the first perspective, Hegel explodes with invective. To anticipate, Hegel will show that a person's moral character is judged by looking at this individual's actions. Persons who consistently behave badly are bad persons, regardless of what they assert their inner intentions to be. Indeed, what they intend is best determined by what they actually do, and so they may not be the best judges of their own intentions. Persons may have to confess that what they thought were expressions of tough love, for example, were actually instances of gratuitous cruelty.[25]

Reason: rational self-consciousness makes itself actual

The standards that individuals act upon are, in the first instance, standards which they unthinkingly take from their society and internalize. Individuals may, however, articulate standards for themselves that are at variance with those of their society. They may choose either still to conform to their society's standards or to violate them. If the latter, then we get three possibilities: Pleasure and Necessity, the Law of Heart and the Frenzy of Self-Conceit, or Virtue and the Way of the World.

Pleasure and Necessity. Seeking pleasure in another person always leads to seeking it in still another. This is experienced as an alien necessity that is externally imposed. In Neel Mukherjee's debut novel, *Past Continuous*, for example, Ritwik Ghosh is unable to understand or control his self-destructive sexuality.[26] He is driven to seek out increasingly more dangerous venues for sexual encounters with strangers. Ritwik experiences this not as a rational expression or as connected with any of his other goals but instead as a force that is imposed upon him and that he cannot resist.

In the Law of Heart and the Frenzy of Self-Conceit, individuals claim that they follow their consciences. The problem, however, is that conscience can say almost anything. When, in Mark Twain's *Huckleberry Finn*, Huck decides to keep secret the location of Jim, an escaped slave and his friend, he does not follow his conscience but violates it. Conscience seeks to make itself master of the universe and thereby becomes a source of evil.

Virtue and the Way of the World. The Way of the World is Adam Smith's invisible hand. By seeking only their own self-interest, individuals nevertheless create, as an unintended by-product, a society that works for the benefit of most – if not all – people. What is crucial here is that individuals may develop and express their individualities, within the constraints that the world allows, of course. Virtue, by contrast, demands that individuals exchange their individualities for a disinterested and universal perspective. Whereas the Way of the World achieves a kind of virtue as an unintended by-product, Virtue aims at this directly. Virtue struggles with the Way of the World, but its struggle isn't serious; it is only a sham fight, because Virtue doesn't really want to overthrow the Way of the World. What it wants is for the Way of the World to remain safely in place and for Virtue to be seen as challenging and denouncing it. Virtue loves to kvetch.

Reason: individuality

Individuality that takes itself to be real: this is Kantianism. It demands that the expression be an outward manifestation of an inward intention. Here, individuals express the universal standpoint by means of their individuality.

The Spiritual Animal Kingdom and Deceit, or the Matter at Hand. Academics are often pointed to as the perfect examples of the Spiritual Animal Kingdom. The residents of this realm claim to be interested in something for its own sake – say, German idealism – but they are really interested in their own work. Although they claim to be interested in their own work because it is intrinsically interesting and because they hope to make a substantial contribution to their field, they are interested in it at least as much because it will further their own careers, leading to increased prestige, tenure, promotion, etc. In claiming to be interested in the matter at hand, they engage in deception, and possibly self-deception. This is a spiritual animal kingdom because these persons are interested in spirit (culture), but they resemble animals in that they appropriate it only to nourish themselves.

In his useful book on *Hegel's Absolute*, Donald Phillip Verene claims that the meetings of the American Philosophical Association are instances of the Spiritual Animal Kingdom.[27] No doubt, but ironically Verene's claim is itself another example. And, obviously, noting that Verene is a member of the Spiritual Animal Kingdom is still another instance. Rather than attempting to escape inclusion by identifying other members, we must instead vigorously affirm our membership. I am writing this book, for example, in the forlorn hope that it will bring me wealth, fame, and promotion.[28] There is this to be said, though, for the Spiritual Animal Kingdom. It doesn't matter what the personal motivations of these people are: the matter at hand gets promoted anyway. Since these people are shameless self-promoters who select a specific field because they believe that it will advance their careers, however, the matters at hand that get promoted may not merit that attention. Well, yes, that's what a rival would say . . .

Reason as Law Giver. By claiming to be interested only in the matter at hand, and only for its own sake, Reason has implicitly taken a universal perspective that prescinds from the motivations of any specific individuals. From here, Reason now emerges as that which gives the law – Hegel has Kant's moral law in mind – but this law is wholly formal, a priori, lacking any content. Because it is to be universal – applying to all peoples, in all places, at all times – it can't incorporate the customs, codes, or mores of any specific group. (More accurately, in order not to be entirely empty it must incorporate these, but it does so surreptitiously, denying, even to itself, that this is what it is doing.) As a consequence, this universal moral law must allow anything that isn't self-contradictory. Since any behavior can be described in alternative ways, some of which aren't self-contradictory and none of which is self-announcing as correct, this law actually permits anything.

Reason as Testing Laws. Reason can test laws only for self-consistency. Again, anything can be made self-consistent if it is described appropriately. The content of moral laws, however, is grounded in the customs, codes, and mores of a specific community. These are often implicit. Everyone knows what they are, even if no one can say what they are. An example: Everyone knows that, when riding on a public bus, one sits next to a stranger only if none of the nearby seats are empty. Everyone knows that, unless a person has limited mobility, one doesn't ask others to give up their seats. Everyone also knows that, even if a person has limited mobility, one doesn't ask to sit where someone else is sitting if there are empty seats nearby.

Since we are following Forster's tripartite text of the *Phenomenology of Spirit*, we now have reached the conclusion of its first telling, from the perspective of shapes of consciousness. Before journeying to the next telling, Spirit, it will be useful to spend a few moments taking stock of our trek. Let's ask what has been established. We began by asking what knowledge is. We discovered that knowledge couldn't be defined at the level of individuals but necessitated a move to the social level. This is so because knowledge must conform to standards, and these standards cannot be those of any individual but only those of a society in which an individual is situated. We then saw the failure of attempts to transcend those standards in favor of ones that would claim to be universal. Universal standards apply to all societies, true enough, but such standards are merely formal and so empty. They allow anything, prohibit nothing, and so fail as standards. As a result, we are thrown back on the standards of our society. These standards change, of course, and in retrospect we will regard those changes as cumulatively progressive. Specific standards can be criticized, and we can advocate that they be modified or replaced by others. Any radical change, however, will initially be experienced as evil and will succeed only if enough people are converted to its ways of thinking and seeing the world. Hence, while a Gandhi or a Martin Luther King Jr may claim to appeal to their oppressors' own better insights, they are as much instilling or indoctrinating the insights to which they would appeal.

Spirit: ethical order

According to Forster, Hegel's story is now retold, this time from the perspective of Spirit. Put otherwise, we could say that it is retold from the perspective of the cultural and social institutions that made possible the shapes of consciousness.

Hegel tells his readers that Reason becomes Spirit when it realizes that it is all of reality. I would like to take a moment to defend Hegel, as many readers may recoil on hearing this. What can it mean, they may ask, to say that everything in the world, and the world too, is Reason. Let's step back from Hegel's text and approach things from a different perspective. The logical positivists believed that there were observations, which could be described in observations sentences, that were independent of any theory. Theories are attempts to explain observations and to predict new observations, but the observations are the same regardless of the theory. According to the logical positivists, when Ptolemy disagrees with Newton, or Newton with Einstein, they disagree about theories but agree about observations.

Several later philosophers of science – most prominently Thomas Kuhn and Paul Feyerabend – disagreed with the logical positivists. Kuhn and Feyerabend argued that observations themselves are dependent upon theory. Change the theory and you change not only what you will see but also what you can see. Pick any observation you want, that observation is embedded within a theory. On this view, when Ptolemy, Newton, and Einstein disagree, they disagree not only about which theory best explains the observations but also about what the observations are. Although contemporary philosophers of science squabble about the details, they have largely accepted the claim that observations become observations only within the context of a theory and that there is no observation that is theory neutral or independent. Now, scientific theories are created by scientists. These theories are, to write like Hegel for a moment, the products of consciousness. So, it isn't fanciful for Hegel to claim that everything is Reason.

There is another way in which Reason is all of reality. Hegel thinks that all things are capable of being comprehended, that there is nothing that is ultimately mysterious or in principle unknowable, although many things may be unknown (such as exactly how many peas were in the matar paneer I had for dinner last night). He thinks this not only because he has an optimistic faith in Reason but also because he believes that observations are only observations within the context of some theory. In order for something even to be recognized as puzzling or as an anomaly is for it already to be embedded in a theory where it is implicitly intelligible. As a consequence, when Hegel writes that Reason is all of reality, he isn't maintaining anything that should startle a contemporary philosopher of science.

Reason had discerned that the world is rational – that it has a rational structure – and that knowledge must conform to a society's standards. What Reason doesn't yet know, what Spirit will discover, is that these standards are Reason's own creation. Persons encounter tradition and authority as things given to them, in the first instance, as one might encounter a boulder in a stream, without comprehending that tradition and authority are human creations. Spirit will learn this. The customs and laws of a people are that people's own creation. Spirit will learn this as we see how religious faith is initially opposed to and struggles with rational insight, only to be reconciled in morality.

Hegel begins his tale of Spirit's development by discussing the tragic conflict between the demands of divine and family laws, on the one hand, and the laws of the state as exemplified in Sophocles' *Antigone*, on the other. Ancient Greek society has neither the resources to mediate this conflict nor the mechanisms to determine when one set of laws will be subordinated to the other. It lacks the notion of individual rights over against the claims of the state as well as any check or limitation on the king's prerogatives. As a consequence, this conflict is experienced as a tragedy. Each side has right on its side but each is also one-sided and partial, unable to perceive the right that the other side possesses. This conflict re-emerges with Socrates, who demands a rational justification of customs and laws which they are unable to provide. When individuals recognize that no justification is forthcoming, they see no reason not to advance their own interests at the expense of the (no longer believed credible) public good. The Athenians correctly recognize that Socrates is a direct threat to their society. That they have no more adequate response than to execute him proves that their society is already bankrupt.

In the Roman Empire, we have universal law – universal, that is, as far as the empire extends – but this law sees rights primarily as rights to property. It hasn't articulated a notion of the rights of individuals. These property rights are formal and empty. They are a product of a society in which persons experience the empire as something external and over against them. They experience it as despotic. They don't recognize it as their own creation and they don't feel at home in it. Stoicism and skepticism flourish in this time. People do not believe that they can control or substantially influence their circumstances. They expend their energies, then, in controlling their own responses to things, believing the things outside their influence.

Spirit: self-alienated and culture

We next transition to the world of the courts of the French kings, especially that of Louis XIV, the so-called Sun King, before the French Revolution. The desire is now for wealth, and state power is perceived as a means to enhance one's wealth. The power of the state has only the legitimacy that force of arms can confer upon it. Power is successively taken from the nobility and centralized in the figure of the king, who grants titles and privileges as a way to consolidate his own power. The nobles are no longer relatively autonomous and independent but rather obtain or maintain their royal prerogatives solely by the grace of the king. These are distributed by the king so as to increase his hold on power. In order to be near the king, the nobles no longer live on their estates but rather at the king's palace.

Their desire to curry favor with the king results in a universe of flattery and deceit, where individuals say only those things that they believe will flatter the king, undercut their rivals, and promote their own interests. It might be thought that such a situation would create only a nest of lying vipers. It is that, of course, but it is something more. As in the Roman Empire, a certain interiority is promoted. In creating masks and managing impressions, the nobles can no longer act naturally or spontaneously but instead must cultivate the appearances they wish to project. They must develop tact: the ability to anticipate how their words and actions will be experienced by others. This demand that they must see themselves as they are seen by others, to assume an appearance so that they will be viewed as they wish to be viewed, promotes a certain ironic stance, where one adapts to the perceived requirements of various situations without fully identifying oneself with any of them.

So, we have *Rameau's Nephew* by Diderot. The Nephew takes great pride in his ability to play whatever part he believes is required in order to promote his material ends. Irony here is universal. The Nephew can play any role but maintains an inner distance from each of them. What it is crucial to recognize, though, is not that the Nephew has some inner self that retains its independence from all roles but rather that there is no self apart from the roles played. Maintaining an inner independence is merely another ruse and, moreover, one that is self-deceptive. The stance of the Nephew results in alienation from others and one's culture as well as self-alienation. What is positive here, though, is the notion that all institutions are our own creation, and so is the self. Also positive is the realization of everyone's dependence on others. This section is an internal duplication, a *mise en abyme*, within the *Phenomenology of Spirit*.[29] Spirit is also finally its own creation. Here, however, that dependence is experienced as negative, as a needing to conform and adapt, to conceal one's true opinions and feelings, to survive.

Spirit: Enlightenment

We now come to the opposition of religious Faith and Enlightenment. The first point to note is that the Faith opposed by Enlightenment is the Enlightenment's own creation. That is to say, in previous times, Faith permeates all aspects of life, and it is in Faith that all things have their meaning. Faith is not a separate sphere of life that could be opposed. Enlightenment so treats Faith. However, Faith, in response, accepts Enlightenment's understanding of it. Enlightenment regards Faith as no more than a concatenation of stupidly false beliefs and bad science, while Faith responds by urging that it is as rational, even more, than Enlightenment. In doing so, Faith ceases to be a way of life and becomes a set of beliefs that is in principle detachable from other aspects of life. Religion is a product of thought and a way of making sense of things – it is philosophy presented through myths and images – but Enlightenment fails to recognize this integrative aspect of Religion. Where Religion sees a stone as participating in the divine, Enlightenment sees no more than the worship of a *stone*.

Enlightenment values only usefulness and judges everything based on a criterion of usefulness. People too are valued only as useful. The French Revolution proclaims the equality of every man, but this is an equality that doesn't recognize that there can be legitimate differences in responsibilities.

Spirit: absolute freedom and terror

The state is too complex to be run directly by millions of equal individuals. Whenever someone steps into a leadership role, that individual is viewed as tyrannical, as declaring himself above and better than others, and so must be executed. The French Revolution gives way to the Terror and the Terror consumes the Revolution. Individuals have not yet understood that equality must be the equality of equality and inequality. Put otherwise, merely formal equality must be overcome in favor of a system that allows for inequalities in responsibilities and duties.

Spirit: morality

This is resolved in Morality. Here, Hegel has in mind Kant's theory of morals. At this level, the split between what individuals ought to do and their inclinations is internal to and constitutive of them. Nature prompts individuals to be happy, but duty demands obedience to the moral law. The reconciliation of happiness and duty, when it occurs, is a fortuitous accident, not something that can be achieved through care and planning.

But what is duty? We have seen already that Hegel regards Kant's ethics as formal and empty. At most, it prohibits self-contradictory actions, and so individuals need only describe their actions in non-contradictory ways to be permitted to do anything. This gives rise to duplicity and self-deception. Seeking happiness, agents describe their actions as motivated and conforming to duty. This permits any enormity.

Conscience. So we get appeals to conscience. Most people are inclined to have a deep respect for others who do things that are unpopular when they claim to be following their conscience. These conscientious persons, we tend to think, are following principles rather than doing what is easy or convenient. Indeed, some have gone so far as to assert that the voice of conscience is the voice of God. Hegel is deeply suspicious of appeals to conscience. This involves a return to a theme that we saw raised in the Preface: Hegel's rejection of appeals to intuition or feeling. The problem with appeals to conscience is that there is no external check on them. Professors who are scathing in criticizing students can claim to be doing their duty, for example, and so seek to mask their sadism and contempt – to mask these from others, of course, but also from themselves.

Conscience eventually evolves to become the Beautiful Soul. This character refuses to engage in any attempt to intervene in the world, believing that the world is so evil that any attempt to improve things would result only in soul-destroying moral compromises. To avoid such compromises, the Beautiful Soul holds back from any engagement with the wicked world. The Beautiful Soul is contrasted with the Practical Person, who regards a certain amount of moral compromise as an acceptable price to pay for getting things done. The Beautiful Soul and the Practical Person regard each other with disdain. The Beautiful Soul sees the Practical Person as morally compromised, if not corrupt. The Practical Person perceives the Beautiful Soul as a lazy lout who is happy to complain about things but isn't willing to do anything to help make them better.

Both the Beautiful Soul and the Practical Person need to forgive each other, but the former is more at fault. It is true that the Practical Person is prepared to cut corners and wink at misdemeanors to get things done. As Žižek recognizes, however, there is a sense in which the Beautiful Soul is itself the source of the evil it sees.[30] It is the Beautiful Soul, after all, who decides to regard the world as so thoroughly corrupt that any attempt to improve things will only sully itself. Alternatively, the world might be considered basically good but needing improvement and so perfectible and ameliorable. In addition, because it regards itself as having a pure conscience that is misunderstood by a wicked world, the Beautiful Soul isn't sufficiently self-critical about the ways in which its insistence on duty serves to mask its own self-serving motives.

Reconciliation is achieved, then, when the Beautiful Soul and the Practical Person forgive each other. Both accept that involvement in the world will result in mistakes and moral compromises. The appropriate response is not to do nothing, however, but instead for individuals to forgive each other, and themselves, and to try to do better in the future.

Religion

We now come to the third retelling of the story, this time from the perspective of Religion. To express briefly what will be learned in the section on Religion, Spirit discovers that it is itself the Absolute. Formerly, God was believed to be something distant from humanity, transcending the universe. In the section on Religion, however, it is seen that there is no gap between God and the world. Hegel chronicles the various attempts that have been made, historically, to conceptualize God. These range from thinking about God as light, as a plant or an animal, as an artist, or as a work of art, to God's having a human form. It is only in Revealed Religion, Protestant Christianity, that God is finally adequately comprehended. That isn't quite accurate, of course, because God can't be *adequately* comprehended from the perspective of Religion. The thinking of Religion is imagistic, mythical, not yet the fully conceptualized thinking that occurs at the level of philosophy. So, the accurate way to express the point would be to say that the concept of God advanced in Revealed Religion is the most adequate concept possible within Religion.

What is the view of Revealed Religion? What gets revealed there? At first, it seems the typical Christian view – and Hegel has been scolded for his parochialism in favoring Christianity over other world religions. And Hegel's *Phenomenology of Spirit* does read like a recounting of the Protestant view. But his text can be read in a more radical and startling way.

On the more traditional view, God is composed of three persons: Father, Son, and Holy Spirit. The Son is incarnated as Christ who then is crucified and resurrected. Hegel's story is a version of this but one with marked differences. Here, God becomes fully incarnated in Jesus, so that, when Jesus is crucified and dies, God dies. The distance between humanity and God is wholly overcome because God is no more. However, Hegel is a fan of dialectics, after all, and so the story doesn't end there. (Indeed, the story never ends, but I will discuss that in the chapter on Hegel's *Philosophy of History*.) On the traditional telling, God the Father raises Christ (God the Son) from the dead after Christ has been dead for three days. Forty days later, Christ ascends into heaven and the Holy Spirit is sent to guide the Church. (Given the history of the Church, one might wonder if it could have done any worse without divine guidance, but this is a book on Hegel.) For Hegel, by contrast, God dies with the death of Jesus. The resurrection, then, is that of the solidarity and love of the Christian community. The Christian community is itself the God that it worships. So, the charge that Hegel privileges Christianity over other religions is correct. Christianity is quite distinct from others. Some other religions have a notion of a god who becomes human and dies: Ram and Kṛṣṇa, for example, in Hinduism. No other religion, however, has a god who becomes fully human and dies – full stop. God continues, in a sense, but God continues through, in, and as the believing community that worships Him. The implications of this are considerable. Other religions claim that it is important to believe in God. Christianity, understood from Hegel's perspective, thinks it important that we believe in ourselves – and in the communities and social institutions we construct. Other religions think it important that we discern and follow God's will. Christianity believes that there is nothing beyond ourselves to which we are accountable. The death of God in Jesus frees us from all authority, according to Hegel, finally even from the authority of God.

In recent years, analytic philosophers have begun to reappraise and rehabilitate Hegel. This is all to the good, of course, but Hegel still remains a distant shore for them. So, Paul Redding reports that John McDowell accepts what he regards as a Hegelian "incarnation of reason." Such reason "doesn't need constraining from any *outside* . . . but neither does this *anthropologize* reason – after all, the idea of a god that became human would hardly be a compelling thought if that god were just *another* human being trying to live up to the norms of a god."[31] McDowell is correct that Hegelian reason is constrained internally, not externally. This certainly does anthropologize reason, however, and that is its central point. It is not that Christ is merely a human trying to live up to God's norms, but rather that Christ – God incarnate – is wholly indistinguishable from any other human. And Christ's final teaching is that God leaves it entirely up to us to construct, and try to live up to, *our* norms.

Absolute Knowing

The final section of Hegel's *Phenomenology of Spirit* is Absolute Knowing. It is rather short, some might think, if it is supposed to tell us everything. What is crucial to realize is that Absolute Knowing doesn't give us any new information. It is not another, let alone the final, shape of consciousness. Rather, Absolute knowing recollects where we have been. Hegel compares it to a gallery of images, where each image represents a shape of consciousness that has been lived through and subsumed. An even better metaphor, although one not available to Hegel, would be a motion picture. Here, each frame would represent a shape of consciousness or an aspect of a shape. Running the film would allow us to pass imaginatively through the terrain that we have already traversed. Now, however, we can comprehend how the shapes of consciousness stand in relation to each other. Hegel's *Phenomenology of Spirit*, then, may be considered to be a memory theater, "an imaginary building thought of as comprising various rooms and areas, each containing mnemonic objects and features that symbolize particular ideas, which can be visualized mentally as a systematic method of remembering those ideas."[32]

And what have we learned? That there is no independent or external standard for knowing, that knowledge is, finally, what we take it to be. There are genuine constraints on what can count as knowledge, of course. However, they are internal to our epistemic activities. As a consequence, those constraints can be evaluated and revised internally to those activities.

Hegel describes the *Phenomenology of Spirit* as the introduction to his philosophical system. In the next chapter, we will begin to investigate it.

4

Hegel's *Logic*

Hegel wrote two Logics. One is the first part of his *Encyclopedia of the Philosophical Sciences* – the *Philosophy of Nature* and the *Philosophy of Spirit* are the second and third parts, respectively – and the other is the *Science of Logic*. For our purposes here, in this book, we can treat the two Logics together, regarding the *Science of Logic* as a more detailed version of the so-called *Encyclopedia Logic*.

Before proceeding further, we need to discuss what sort of book the *Logic* is. To do that, we need to consider what sort of book the *Phenomenology of Spirit* is, as Hegel describes it as the introduction to his philosophical system. There are two main views regarding the relation of the *Phenomenology of Spirit* to Hegel's system. One maintains that it is an introduction to the system but is itself outside of the system. The alternative view claims that the *Phenomenology of Spirit* not only introduces the system but is also a part of it. I will urge that we adopt the latter reading, but let's now consider the former interpretation.

One prominent version of the first view, that the *Phenomenology of Spirit* is distinct from the system, interprets that text in ways that are significantly different from the reading proposed in the previous chapter. There, readers will recall that the *Phenomenology of Spirit* was read, following Forster, as telling the same story three times. It tells the story from the perspectives of the shapes of consciousness, the sociological and institutional contexts of those shapes, and religion. On that reading, moreover, we learn that knowledge consists in what is recognized by a society as conforming to its standards for knowing.

According to the first view, however, the *Phenomenology of Spirit* is a linear text that presents a single sustained argument. (Another alternative would be that Hegel begins by writing about epistemology, changes his mind about what his book is actually about, and then proceeds throughout the rest of the book to write primarily about social and political philosophy.) The first view also claims that the *Phenomenology of Spirit* is a text that *fails*. That is to say, it succeeds in showing the failure of all attempts to ground or base thought on something external to or other than thought. The *Logic*, then, represents a new beginning, one where thought is based on nothing less than itself.

There are a number of difficulties with this view. It commits Hegel to a foundationalist epistemology. That is, it has Hegel believing that justification must be in terms of something that is properly basic – something that either doesn't require justification or is somehow self-justifying. It also commits Hegel to internalism rather than externalism or reliabilism regarding justification. That is to say, internalism in epistemology holds that persons can correctly be said to know something only if the justificatory grounds, or reasons, are cognitively accessible to them. Many contemporary epistemologists argue for externalism. Externalism claims that persons can have knowledge as long as their beliefs are the result of reliable processes, even if the justificatory grounds aren't cognitively accessible to them. Although Keith Lehrer's scenario regarding a fictional Mr Truetemp is intended as a criticism of externalism, it nicely illustrates the view.[1] Lehrer imagines that Mr Truetemp has, unbeknownst to him, a thermometer (Lehrer calls it a "tempucomp") implanted in his brain such that, whenever he forms a belief about the ambient temperature, his belief is correct. Externalists would claim the Mr Truetemp *knows* what the temperature is. He *knows* what the temperature is, they would say, because his true belief is the result of a reliable cognitive process, even though he has no idea why, or even that, he is always able to state the temperature correctly. Although not all epistemologists are wholly persuaded that externalism is correct, most believe that internalism's insistence that knowledge requires that the justificatory grounds should always be cognitively assessable to the person who knows sets the standard for knowledge too high.

There's no compelling reason to attribute such a view to Hegel. If knowledge is a matter of conforming to a society's standards, moreover, then externalism is a closer fit than internalism, as externalism would adopt a third-person perspective on individuals, asking whether their claims are to be taken as knowledge rather than whether those individuals take themselves to be justified. (There is, nevertheless, a moment of truth in internalism. Hegel places great value on what he calls the right of subjectivity, which requires that individuals regard those social standards as legitimate and so as authoritative for them. This standard is not too high. Hegel doesn't require that individuals be able to give complete justifications of what they believe. That is, individuals aren't required to give a justification that presupposes a philosophical grasp of the systematic whole in which their beliefs are embedded. However, he does require that they be able to say something in defense of their belief and to have some sense of the standards to which they are asked to conform.)

Also, even if thought could construct a system based only on thought, that alone would not be a decisive reason to prefer it.

Hegel claims that philosophy must not have presuppositions. What does this mean? To continue the previous discussion, some philosophers have argued that Hegel's philosophy is generated wholly a priori, without any inputs from the world or reliance on information provided by the senses. These philosophers urge further that Hegel's system is then generated by thought thinking itself. Hegel begins the *Logic* by discussing Being, saying that it is the most general and indefinite concept. Although we *mean* for there to be a distinction between Being and Nothing, he urges that we can't *say* what that distinction consists in. Since Being is the most general concept, we can't specify how it differs from Nothing (and so it is clear here, by the way, that Hegel isn't talking about whether a thing *exists* when he discusses Being). We oscillate from Being to Nothing and then back to Being, meaning for there to be a distinction between the two but finding no distinguishing characteristic. From this continued oscillation, however, arises the concept of Becoming. When we focus our attention on Becoming as the to-and-fro movement between Being and Nothing, we realize that, in order for there to be Becoming, for Becoming to be, there must be something that becomes. As a consequence, we arrive at the concept of Determinate Being. Determinate Being has sufficient determinate content that it can be said to become.

In a nutshell, these are the first several steps of Hegel's *Logic*. He starts with Being because it is the most general concept. Doesn't this show that his system lacks presuppositions?

No.

Philosophers distinguish between foundationalism, discussed above, and coherentism. Coherentism denies that beliefs, or concepts, are ultimately grounded on some specific beliefs that don't have foundations or somehow could ground themselves. Coherentism denies, then, that beliefs or concepts are properly basic. Rather, it claims that beliefs mutually support each other as, analogously, the parts of a spider's web, a fishing net, or an arch mutually support each other. Coherentism claims that beliefs mutually support each other, and so a specific belief might help support another belief, but, in turn, this latter belief also helps support the former. A belief may then appear as a premise in one context but as a conclusion in another.

What does have presuppositions? A nice example of a system that has presuppositions is geometry. There, we have axioms, and from these axioms we can derive theorems. The axioms themselves are treated as givens. Some mathematicians have thought that these were intuitively obvious. Beginning in the nineteenth century, though, mathematicians began to use different axioms and so discovered that there are alternative geometries. Lines are parallel in Euclidean geometry, for example, but they curve either towards or away from each other in non-Euclidean geometries. Hegel clearly believes that philosophical systems shouldn't contain presuppositions in this sense. I suggest that he believes that his system lacks presuppositions because the concepts in his system mutually support each other.

However, what about the claim that his system is generated by thought thinking itself a priori? Here, the idea is that thought necessarily begins with Being and that we are then, as it were, off to the races. Wouldn't this be a system without presuppositions? No. Or at least no – when someone objects. For contentious critics might deny that Being can count as a concept. They might maintain that a concept must apply to some things and not to others, that it serves to demarcate some things from other things. As a result, these troublemakers would claim that Being, which seems to apply to every-thing – even perhaps to Nothing – is not a concept. These rascals would conclude that Hegel's entire system is unacceptable because its initial inaugurating move is illegitimate.

Now, surely the mighty Hegel could respond effectively to these people. He might argue, for example, that there is no compelling reason to accept their definition of a concept as applying only to some things but not to all things. The point, though, is that Hegel couldn't simply ignore this objection; doing that would be dogmatic, but instead he would need to *argue* against it. This argument, then, would in turn serve as the *presupposition* to his beginning with Being.

In what way is the *Phenomenology of Spirit* an introduction to the system? Following Forster's reading, it seems that it presents Hegel's system from three perspectives – shapes of consciousness, the sociological or institutional context of those shapes, and religion – as these have emerged historically in the West. The *Logic* tells this story again, but this time from the perspective of concepts. Hegel's *Logic* has three main sections: Being, Essence, and Concept or Notion. (Earlier translators use "notion" to translate the German word *Begriff* because that word has etymological ties with *nous*, the Greek word for "mind." But later translators thought that "notion" incorrectly suggested that Hegel is discussing something subjective or idiosyncratic. "Concept" is the word that is standard now.) In the first section, Being, Hegel shows that such concepts as Being, Nothing, etc., are internally contradictory and actually lead to their opposites. In Essence, we see the limitations of attempts to conceptualize things based on a distinction between appearances and underlying processes or principles. Finally, in Concept, Hegel resolves such dualisms as appearance and essence, contingency and necessity, form and matter. The essence of a thing, for example, consists in the multiple ways in which it can appear, such that its appearances are its essence. Again, contingency itself is seen to be necessary.

Is Hegel's *Logic* a category theory, a presentation of the ways in which we think? Or is it instead a metaphysics, telling us about the fundamental structure of reality. Both! One way to characterize the difference between Kant and Hegel would be to say that, while Kant distinguishes between how we cognize a thing (and so how it appears to us) from how it actually is, in-itself, Hegel believes that there is nothing behind or beneath the thing as it appears. So, how a thing appears *is* what it is, in-itself. Appearance can be deceiving, however, those contentious critics may object. True, but a deceiving appearance is shown to be such by its subsequent appearances. However, a deceiving appearance may always deceive, these critics may further gripe; it may never be revealed for what it actually is. Hegel's move at this point would be to shrug his shoulders with indifference and to ask what reason we could have, in such a supposed case, to believe that this appearance was deceiving. If it never appeared to be deceiving, then it is idle and baseless to suggest that, nevertheless, it still is deceiving. As with phrenology in the

Phenomenology of Spirit, the appearance would be entitled to punch anyone who impugned its good name.

In general, this is Hegel's response to modern forms of skepticism which suggest that we might, for all we can tell, be systematically and incorrigibly deceived by a demon, as Descartes fears, or by the Matrix, as certain Hollywood producers suggest. Hegel wouldn't argue that such scenarios are impossible. He does think that, unless we are given reasons to believe that we are being fooled by a demon or the Matrix, however, we don't need to consider this further. And since we are supposedly *systematically* and *incorrigibly* deceived, such reasons won't be forthcoming. So, ho-hum to that.

The point that is relevant here is that Hegel's *Logic* is both a category theory *and* a metaphysics. Describing how we think about things also tells us about the way things are. A discussion of how we think of things (Philosophy of Mind and Epistemology) is also a discussion of how things are (Ontology and Metaphysics).

Is Hegel telling us how we do think, in which case his *Logic* is a type of empirical psychology, or is he telling us how we ought to think, where he would be engaged in normative epistemology. Both! In the first instance, Hegel's *Phenomenology of Spirit* tells us historically how we have thought and the *Logic* narrates this tale at the level of concepts, and so it would seem that the first alternative is correct. But how we think itself contains a normative component regarding how we ought to think. When Hegel then finally arrives at the modern condition, describing how we now think, he is also saying how we think we ought to think.

To step back from Hegel's text for a moment, we can see that his approach is generally correct. If people believe something, they also believe that they are justified in believing it, that they have sufficient reasons. It would be quite odd for individuals to say that they believe one thing while conceding that reason and evidence would indicate the truth of some counter-claim. The point here is that we can maintain a distinction between how people think and how they ought to think only when we are considering *other* people. When we consider *ourselves*, however, how we think is also the way we think we ought to think. If we didn't think that we were thinking as we ought to think, then we wouldn't think what we think.

Hegel's *Logic*, then, is simultaneously a category theory, a metaphysics, an empirical psychology, and normative epistemology.

How are the transitions from moment to moment, within the *Logic*, generated? As we have seen, some philosophers claim that these transitions are logically necessary as thought thinks itself.

They further claim that both the content and the rules by which the process proceeds are generated in this very process. If the rules are themselves generated by this process, however, then it would seem impossible to adjudicate disputes between individuals who claim to arrive at different rules. There are alternative moments to those articulated by Hegel, moreover – moments that seem equally plausible to his. Confronted with the shilly-shallying between Being and Nothing, the ancient Greek sophist Gorgias might propose that, rather than resolving into Becoming, as Hegel has it, the next moment is the startling claim that only Nothing is. Alternatively, the Indian Buddhist Nāgārjuna could suggest that the next moment is Emptiness. Emptiness isn't an especially promising resolution at the level of empirical reality – where my cat is now happily purring as she lies across the keyboard, making typing difficult – but it is hard to object to it at the level of thought thinking itself. Again, Wittgenstein might suggest that the resolution is to be found in Silence or through dissolving the felt need for a *Logic* in the first place.

So, if not thought's self-determining determinations, then what? I suggest that the *Logic* is grounded in the history of Western thought and that the sequence of logical moments is the same as those in the *Phenomenology of Spirit*, only now at the level of concepts. The *Logic*'s "Being – Essence – Concept" corresponds to the *Phenomenology of Spirit*'s shapes of consciousness (Consciousness – Self-Consciousness – Reason). This in turn corresponds to the Spirit section (True Spirit – Spirit Alienated from Itself – Spirit Certain of Itself), which again corresponds to the Religion section (Natural Religion – Religion as Art – Revealed Religion).

It won't be possible to provide a discussion of all the moments in Hegel's *Logic*. Rather, I will provide brief descriptions of the most important ones. Readers often find the transitions difficult to follow. It will be easier to follow them, I believe, if you think of Hegel as generating his story backwards, beginning with the final moment, the absolute idea, and then asking what led to it. This way of approaching the text will be useful even if Hegel's *Logic* is generated purely a priori, with thought thinking itself. (I have already indicated why I believe that his interpretation isn't viable.)

After an Introduction, Hegel divides his *Logic* into three main sections, and each of these is, in turn, divided into three subsections. The three main sections are Being, Essence, and what is variously translated as the Concept, Comprehension, or Notion. What is the relation of these sections and subsections?

Let's begin by discussing the relations of the three main sections of the *Logic*: Being, Essence, and Concept. As a first approximation, Being is the moment where things are simply described, and taken actually to be, as they appear. This might be considered akin to phenomenology – Husserl's, not Hegel's – which describes objects as they appear to consciousness. This approach is limited, however, in that it can't account for why similar things are similar and it can't explain why things appear as they do. These failures result in a transition to the second main moment, Essence. Essence attempts to explain what appears in Being, the level of the descriptive, by postulating hidden internal and external forces that cause a thing to appear as it does. The furthest Essence gets, though, is recognizing that forces can act on each other, thereby modifying the effects of each. This notion of reciprocal interaction has not yet advanced to the insight that a thing can modify and affect itself. It also leaves unexplained *why*, as opposed to *how*, things would be caused to appear as they do. These difficulties are overcome at the level of the Concept. Here, it is recognized that there is a directional purpose to change and that things tend towards a goal. Simplifying, we could say that Essence tries to explain things by appealing to mechanical causation. Here, the analogy might be the interaction of billiard balls or, somewhat more sophisticatedly, the ways that planets gravitationally affect each other's orbits. At the level of the Concept, by contrast, things are explained by pointing to their purposes or goals. Moreover, these purposes are internal to the things rather than being externally imposed. The analogy here might be biological organisms. A stone may be used as a paperweight, an instance of external purpose, but the growth of a plant is internally purposive.

It is important to recognize that Being, Essence, and Concept are moments that not only successively replace but also include their predecessors. Essence, for example, attempts to explain why things appear as they do, and so it encompasses Being. The Concept, further, regards the explanations of Essence not as false, but rather merely as external and limited, at most explaining how an event happens but not indicating the inherent rationality that it happens so. At the level of the Concept, we can comprehend not only how the heart pumps blood, for example, but also why it does so. This is not to suggest that Hegel believes that there is a rational reason for every happening. Some things are entirely contingent. Far from necessity excluding contingency, however, contingency is itself necessary.

We are about to trudge through the *Logic*'s forest. So that we don't get lost, figure 1 shows an outline of its major trees; the boldface and italics may help to make things clearer. It will be helpful to refer back to this outline as I discuss these trees.

I'll now discuss the three subdivisions of **Being**: *Quality* (with its three divisions: Being, Determinate Being, and Being-for-Itself), *Quantity* (Pure Quantity, Quantum, Degree), and *Measure*.

Quality has to do, in the first instance, with a thing's characteristics, although we are not yet at a point where a distinction can be made between the characteristics a thing happens to have, which it has as a matter of contingent fact, and its defining characteristics. This is the level of immediate determinateness, where any change results in a transition to something different. Hegel begins with Being, as it is the most general concept, referring to everything and anything. The contrast to Being is Nothing. Since Being is a wholly general concept, however, we are unable to specify how Nothing differs from it. We intend for there to be a distinction between them but we can't say what the difference is.

This oscillating movement between Being and Nothing results in the concept of Determinate Being. Here, a being is defined by reference to another being. So, a thing *is* because it is*n't* something else. Its determinateness carries the sense that it ought to be that thing, while limiting it from being some other things. Insofar as it changes, it becomes something other than itself.

And so we reach Being-for-Itself. Because a thing becomes something else when it changes, there is a sense in which the change is canceled. This is so because to talk about a thing changing presupposes that something of that thing persists, such that we can meaningfully talk about that specific thing changing. If a thing becomes some other thing when it changes, however, that thing doesn't persist. Rather, one thing ceases to be and some other thing comes to be. As a result, we can't really say that one thing changes – or even that it changes into another thing; we can only say that one thing was and now another is. Since a thing is what it is by not being another thing, moreover, there is no reference point that allows us to say that a thing has become another thing. By becoming another thing, it no longer has another to contrast with it. A thing, then, continues to be because, in becoming something else, there is no longer a contrasting something else that allows us to say that it has become something else. Just so, however, there is no contrasting other to define it and so allow it to be at all. What is needed, then, is for a thing to be able to change, more or less, and still remain the

Being

> *Quality*
>
>> Being, Determinate Being, Being-for-Itself
>
> *Quantity*
>
>> Pure Quantity, Quantum, Degree
>
> *Measure*

Essence

> *Essence as Pure Categories*
>
>> Identity, Difference, Ground
>
> *Appearance (or Phenomenon)*
>
>> Existence, Appearance, Relation
>
> *Actuality (or Reality)*
>
>> Substance, Causality, Reciprocal Interaction

Concept

> *The Subjective Concept*
>
>> The Concept as Such, the Judgment, the Syllogism
>
> *The Object*
>
>> Mechanism, Chemism, Teleology
>
> *The Idea*
>
>> Life, Cognition, the Absolute Idea

Figure 1 Outline of Hegel's *Logic*

thing that it is, so that it can be recognized as a thing that has changed instead of an entirely different thing. And so, we transition from *Quality* to *Quantity*.

A thing's quality is what it is. To change the quality of a thing is to change that thing itself, so that it no longer is the thing that it was. Quantity, by contrast, is an indifferent determination. That is to say, the quantity of a thing can change without the thing becoming some other thing. This is a matter of Degree. There is, in the first instance, no limit to which a quantity may change. If it becomes infinitely small, though, it becomes zero. If it becomes infinitely large, this would be a state beyond which no further quantitative change would be possible. This process loops around, however, and so results in a qualitative change. Remove enough stones from a heap and you remove the heap too. Add enough, the heap becomes a hill . . . and then a mountain.

As readers might anticipate, the final subdivision of **Being**, *Measure*, involves being able to specify the amount of a quantum, so that we can say that there are, for example, more or fewer trees in a forest. Measure also involves, though, a notion of the appropriate or fitting amount. We have this sense when we speak, for instance, of taking the measure of a man. It is in this sense, moreover, that a sufficient change in the measure of a thing can change its quality, making it another thing. Too many stones taken from a heap causes the heap to be lost, leaving only some stones lying about. Too many stones added to a heap likewise causes the heap to be lost, resulting in a hill or, with even more stones, a mountain.

From *Measure*, the last subdivision of **Being**, we transition to **Essence**, the second main division of Hegel's *Logic*. In this moment, an inner essence is postulated to explain the appearance of a thing. Essence is divided into *Essence as Pure Categories*, *Appearance (or Phenomenon)*, and *Actuality (or Reality)*. Each of these has three subdivisions. *Essence as Pure Categories* is subdivided into Identity, Difference, and Ground. *Appearance* is subdivided into Existence, Appearance, and Relation. *Actuality* is subdivided into Substance, Causality, and Reciprocal Interaction.

We begin with the first moment of *Essence as Pure Categories*, Identity: that a thing is identical to itself, that A = A, and so a thing (A) can't simultaneously be itself (A) and its other (non-A). Then we move to the second moment, Difference, or Diversity, which is that no two things are wholly identical with each other. So, a thing either has a determination or it doesn't: A is either B or not-B and cannot be both B and not-B. There is no third, sometimes referred to as the principle of the excluded middle; either a statement or its negation is true. *Essence as Pure Categories'* third moment is Ground, according to which every thing has a sufficient reason or ground. It is its ground that makes a thing the thing that it is. This is still far too abstract, however, because we don't know how the ground of a thing can account for that thing's non-essential features, or, more seriously, how to distinguish its essential features from its non-essential features. Positing the ground, moreover, doesn't explain why the thing appears as it does. To anticipate, are some of its appearances being taken as its ground?

Here we transition to **Essence**'s second moment, *Appearance (or Phenomenon)*, where a thing's Existence (*Appearance*'s first division) is its standing forth, appearing, out of its ground. This standing forth is its appearance as a thing. The thing has properties which are different from each other and indifferent to each other. That is to say, one property can change without affecting the others. The thing, then, is its properties, as it can be specified only by means of its properties. Although a thing is its properties, it is nevertheless the unity of those properties. A thing is not a mere list of properties, as it were, but it is also what holds the properties together as items on the list. A contradiction has arisen. A thing is its properties, which are indifferent to each other, and a thing is the unity which holds its properties together *as* its properties. A thing is its properties, and it has its properties while being different from them.

At this point, we transition from *Essence as Pure Categories* to *Appearance*, moving from Ground (the last subdivision of *Essence as Pure Categories*) to Existence (the first subdivision under *Appearance*). Here, with Existence, it is recognized that there is nothing in the ground that isn't in the appearance, and nothing that appears that isn't also in the ground. Put otherwise, matter and form, appearance and ground, are mutually co-determining concepts, presupposing each other. This, then, gives rise to the third subdivision, Relation. We now see a distinction between whole and part. The whole is constituted by its parts and the parts are parts only by being parts of the whole. So, there is a mutual dependence of whole and part, neither having priority over the other. The whole, as the internally active form, is force. Force manifests itself as the whole's parts, and force is conditioned or solicited to manifest itself by what is external to it. Its manifestation depends upon solicitation, however, and it is only by having been manifested that its solicitation can have occurred. Thus, solicitation and being solicited also prove to be mutually co-determining notions. Thus, the whole must more properly be thought to include both what is internal and what is external, these being only different perspectives.

Here, we move to *Actuality (or Reality)*, **Essence**'s third major division. Readers will have observed that, although we advance through these concepts, certain themes or motifs continually reoccur. With Substance, the first division under Reality, essence is in-and-for-itself. That is to say, substance is not caused by anything external to it. Its accidents or properties are the ways in which substance manifests itself. The accidents are distinct from substance, yet they are also its determinations and, in their totality, constitute substance. They are actual insofar as they do manifest themselves, potential insofar as they are unmanifestly in substance. Because unmanifest accidents really do have the potential to become manifest, however, they are themselves actual. Indeed, the potentiality of substance, its ability to make itself manifest, is its actuality. So, potentiality isn't opposed to actuality because the potential is actual.

From here, we move to Causality, *Actuality*'s second moment. The cause seems, initially, to be distinct from the effect produced. Nevertheless, there is nothing in the effect that was not in the cause, and the cause is the cause that it is only because of the effect. That is to say, a cause without an effect would not be a cause, after all, and it would be a different cause if the effect was different. Since every effect has a cause, and since every cause is the effect of a previous cause, an infinite regress is generated. We break out of this infinite regress with the next concept, Reciprocal Interaction, which recognizes that cause and effect are mutually co-determining, that the cause is equally well an effect and the effect a cause.

At this point, Hegel interrupts the progression through the *Logic* to discuss Kant's antinomies. Kant, in his *Critique of Pure Reason*, examined four antinomies, or contradictions, that reason encounters when it attempts to go beyond that which is presented in experience and to know directly the things-in-themselves. More precisely, Kant claims that these antinomies occur when reason attempts to apply the categories of the understanding to things-in-themselves. Kant maintains that there are four such antinomies, in which apparently compelling arguments can be provided for each of the contradictory assertions. This signals, for Kant, an inherent limitation of reason. Reason can operate properly, he believes, only when dealing with possible objects of (sense) experience. When reason attempts to go beyond its proper bounds, when it attempts to apply itself to that which isn't a possible object of experience, it invariably and inevitably falls into contradictions. Because of this, Kant urges that reason must confine itself to experience and not attempt to go beyond that.

Hegel responds to this not by denying that reason encounters contradictions, but instead by insisting that those things which reason would think about are themselves contradictory. Kant has a misplaced tenderness for reality, in Hegel's estimation, believing that reality itself couldn't contain contradictions. For Hegel, by contrast, it isn't a limitation of reason that it encounters contradictions, nor is it a sign that reason has exceeded its proper bounds. Rather, it is reality itself that is contradictory, and these contradictions must be thought through by reason until they resolve themselves into a higher synthesis.

Hegel's discussion of the **Concept**, the last main section of the *Logic*, has three divisions: *the Subjective Concept, the Object*, and *the Idea*. Each of these, in turn, has three subdivisions. *The Subjective Concept* is subdivided into the Concept as Such, the Judgment, and the Syllogism. *The Object* is subdivided into Mechanism, Chemism, and Teleology. *The Idea* is subdivided into Life, Cognition, and the Absolute Idea. Now, there is a sense in which Hegel's *Logic* might be thought to conclude when he finishes his discussion of Essence. This is so because, in Being and Essence, he is concerned to investigate the application of thought to its object, or how that which is experienced and thought about is comprehended. This project is concluded in **Essence**.

With the **Concept**, Hegel turns to investigating not that which is thought about, experienced, and comprehended, but rather thought itself. So, the Concept as Such, the first division of *the Subjective Concept*, notes this transition: the focus is now on thought rather than on its object. But a Concept as Such can function as a concept, can indeed only be a concept, within a Judgment, where something is said about some thing. This is so because a concept functions *as* a concept only within a Judgment; it is only within a judgment that a concept becomes determinate or has a specific content. A Judgment, in turn, finds its proper place within a Syllogism, where Judgments are linked together in inferences. The Judgments contained within the Syllogism are not merely listed, but instead are articulated together so that two of them function as premises which establish a conclusion. One could link here to Robert Brandom's books *Making it Explicit* and *Articulating Reasons*. To possess a concept, an individual must be able to recognize what can properly be inferred from it as well as what it excludes. To have the concept *red*, for example, requires recognizing that it is a *color* and, as such, excludes *green* but not *large*.

As noted above, *the Object*, the second division of the **Concept**, is divided into Mechanism, Chemism, and Teleology. Mechanism attempts to explain things by means of particles, impacts, and inertia. Here, it is believed that objects alter their trajectory only as a result of an impact with some other object. On this view, all motion – more precisely, all change in trajectory – occurs only because of collisions. This is referred to, sometimes, as the billiard ball or marbles view of action. Chemism, the second moment, recognizes the limitations of Mechanism and supplements it with an account of chemical reactions. Teleology, in turn, supplements this with a notion of goal-directed purpose.

The Idea has three divisions: Life, Cognition, and the Absolute Idea. Life is purposeful, aiming at some ends. Cognition is Life's ability to comprehend its environment and then further to comprehend that very process of comprehension. The Absolute Idea, finally, is the comprehension of the entire sojourn through the *Logic*, and so it is also the comprehension of the *Logic* itself. As such, the Absolute Idea is analogous to the concluding chapter, Absolute Knowing, of the *Phenomenology of Spirit*.

From the *Logic*, we move to the *Philosophy of Nature*, as the other of thought. In the *Logic*, Hegel describes matters from a perspective internal to thought. Now, in the *Philosophy of Nature*, he will discuss that which initially appears to be external to thought. Hegel will show that what at first appears to be other than thought actually has a rational structure and so isn't, finally, *other* than thought.

5

Hegel's *Philosophy of Nature* and *Philosophy of Spirit*

Nature

Hegel's *Logic* concludes with the transition to Nature. Here, he will show that what at first appears to be other than and external to thought actually has a rational structure. As a result, it isn't ultimately *other* than thought. There is a sense in which readers might have anticipated this. Recall that Hegel argues, in the *Phenomenology of Spirit*, that the problem of knowing whether consciousness corresponds to the object is misconceived. Although initially it appears as if consciousness must somehow be brought into contact with an object that is outside of consciousness, Hegel urges that the object is already internal to consciousness insofar as the object is experienced (and an unexperienced object is nothing to consciousness). Readers might foresee, then, that nature won't and can't be thought's other.

Having seen that we could discuss the *Phenomenology of Spirit* and the *Logic* only by first considering what sorts of books they are, readers will anticipate that this pattern will be repeated a third time. Such clever readers! Yes, we must first talk about what sort of book the *Philosophy of Nature* is. To do that, though, we must again talk about the *Logic*.

To simplify things a bit, there are two contending interpretations of the *Logic*. The first interpretation sees it as developing in an entirely a priori manner, without any connection to the world. According to this interpretation, the *Logic* is solely the product of thought thinking itself.

When that is how the *Logic* is understood, there are two main ways in which the *Philosophy of Nature* can be interpreted. The first interpretation maintains that the categories of the *Philosophy of Nature* are articulated in the same manner as those of the *Logic*, wholly a priori, thought thinking itself. Again, on the assumption that the *Logic* is wholly a priori, the second interpretation of the *Philosophy of Nature* sees it as resulting from applying the categories of the *Logic* to nature – or, more accurately, this second interpretation says that the *Logic*'s categories are applied to the natural science of Hegel's time.

In the previous chapter, on Hegel's Logic, I indicated why I don't believe that any such interpretation of the *Logic* – as being generated wholly a priori by thought thinking itself – can ultimately succeed. There is no reason to repeat those considerations here. If the *Philosophy of Nature* could be interpreted along either of the two lines just mentioned, however, there would be this considerable advantage: it wouldn't ever need to be revised, at least in its basic categories. If the *Philosophy of Nature* is generated entirely by thought thinking itself a priori, then it would be independent of the development in the natural sciences. Alternatively, if it is the result of applying the categories of the *Logic* to the natural sciences, then the *applications* alone would need to be modified when there are substantial developments in the natural sciences, but the basic categories, imported from the *Logic*, wouldn't need to be altered. On the first version, then, there is no new work that ever needs to be done, while, on the second, it is only the *examples* that would need to be updated. And that could be left to graduate students.

As we saw in the previous chapter, however, there is another reading of the *Logic*. This reading sees the *Logic* as telling the story of Western history from the perspective of concepts. It reads the *Logic* as a fourth perspective on Western history, complementing the three presented in the *Phenomenology of Spirit*: first, the ideology of the West, what Hegel calls "shapes of consciousness"; second, the social institutions in which those ideologies are embedded; and, third, the religion and philosophy of the West. On this reading, the *Logic* doesn't develop a priori but rather is the a posteriori articulation of concepts that have emerged throughout the West's history. On this reading of the *Logic*, moreover, the *Philosophy of Nature* doesn't emerge as a further instance of thought thinking itself a priori.

Question: Even if the *Logic* a posteriori articulates the West's concepts, couldn't the *Philosophy of Nature* still be a consequence of applying the categories of the *Logic* to the natural sciences? There is one sense in which that is correct, as I will discuss in a moment, but it is mostly incorrect.

Rather, the natural sciences reveal the working of nature as well as whatever essential or constitutive features, kinds, or forms that nature possesses. What Hegel then does is to arrange these in a hierarchy of ascending forms, from the most basic to the most advanced, as they increasingly approximate Spirit. Nature never actually reaches Spirit. Why not? The primary reason is that he believes that there is only change, but no progress or development, in nature. The seasons follow each other, generations are born, reproduce, and die, but there is no progress. How does Hegel understand progress? Finally, as will be discussed more fully in later chapters, progress is the increasing realization of human freedom. Spirit emerges from nature and nature provides the material support, the physical conditions of the possibility of Spirit.

So, what is correct in the one-sided claim that Hegel applies the categories of the Logic to nature is the recognition that there is a parallelism between the *Logic* and the *Philosophy of Nature*. The *Logic* begins with the most basic concepts and subsequently articulates more advanced ones, while the *Philosophy of Nature* begins with the most elementary material forms and advances to those that are more complex.[1]

Hegel denies that there is any actual development in nature. He rejects evolution. Rather, he believes that the constitutive forms of nature are always present. No constitutive form of nature develops out of any other; and no such engenders another. He believes that there are actual transitions from one form to another only at the level of Spirit. Prior to that, in nature, forms are frozen in an eternal same old same old. So, although Hegel arranges the forms of nature in a hierarchy, there aren't any transitions at work.

Does nature arrange itself in a rational hierarchy that Hegel then discerns? Or does he impose this hierarchy on nature? It might seem that we must choose between these alternatives. However, I will suggest that both are correct.

Michael O. Hardimon urges that Hegel's project, in his *Philosophy of Right*, is one of reconciliation.[2] That is, Hegel argues that citizens of his contemporary Prussia can and should be reconciled to their society, that its basic institutions have a rational structure, such that its citizens may feel at home in their society. (Those who read the chapter on the *Philosophy of Right* will see that the story is actually more complicated.) Hardimon's account should be extended to all of Hegel's philosophy. That is to say, Hegel systematically seeks to persuade his readers that they can and should be reconciled to their world, that it is a home for them. When we turn to his *Philosophy of Nature*, then, he is concerned to persuade his readers that nature itself has a rational structure, that Spirit is not precariously situated in a universe that is indifferent or hostile to it, but that Spirit emerges from nature, where nature is Spirit's home. True, there is a fundamental rupture between nature and Spirit. Unlike nature, there are actual transitions of forms within Spirit. Moreover, Spirit becomes aware and self-aware of its sojourn. Ultimately, Spirit has a determining role in the trajectory of that journey. Nevertheless, nature provides the material conditions of Spirit.

In the first instance, Hegel arranges the constitutive forms of nature in a hierarchy, beginning with the most elementary and progressing until they are on the verge of Spirit's emergence and break from nature. And if someone wants to say that Spirit is nature that has become first conscious and then self-conscious, that wouldn't be wholly wrong. It seems Hegel constructs this story by working backwards, that the order of presentation is the opposite of the order in which these forms are initially articulated. To see this point, we might examine the table of contents of the *Philosophy of Nature*. If we begin with any item, we can see that the previous one must be present in order for that item to be possible. So, Hegel began with Spirit, working backwards by asking, at each moment, what must be in place in order for this moment to be possible. Arriving at the most basic of nature's constitutive forms, he was now in a position to narrate this by beginning with those most basic forms and from there to advance to the more complex ones.

There is an alternative interpretation, of course, according to which Hegel actually begins with nature's most basic constitutive forms and then discerns, somehow, which other forms come next in the series. We have seen versions of this interpretation in the previous chapters when discussing the *Phenomenology of Spirit* and the *Logic*. The problem with this version is the same as the problem with those. If the moments are initially generated retrospectively – by seeing where we are now and then asking how we got here – then a plausible story can be told about why those moments are in the narrative and why they are at the places where they are. If the narrative is actually supposed to be generated prospectively, however, then many other moments can be suggested as plausible successors to any specific moment – moments other than the one that Hegel identifies as that moment's successor. As a result, the assertion that each moment somehow requires or engenders one unique successor isn't credible. If this is what Hegel is doing, then Karl Popper's sneer that his dialectic is "the mystery method" would seem appropriate.[3]

So, Hegel is telling a retrospective story of how nature's constitutive forms can be organized in a hierarchy so that they successively converge upon and approximate Spirit. Neat! If this is what is happening, though, how can it also be plausibly maintained that *nature itself* has this rational structure? Shouldn't we instead conclude that the rational structure which Hegel claims to discern is nothing more than a projection onto a nature that is fundamentally non-rational or irrational? Isn't the hierarchy of nature's constitutive forms, then, analogous to the Rorschach test, onto which Hegel projects his fantasies of rationality?

Of course not!

To comprehend why Hegel discerns a rational structure actually present in nature – although ordering nature's constitutive forms into a rational hierarchy has been his own work – it is useful to take a slight detour, turning to the issue of realism in recent philosophy of science. Theoretical physics, for example, postulates the existence of objects – protons, electrons, quarks – that can't be directly observed. The question, then, is whether these objects actually exist (that is the position of scientific realism) or if, instead, they are merely useful fictions (instrumentalism). Scientific realism may be endorsed at this point by urging that the best evidence that such objects really do exist is that they play crucial roles in theoretical physics and that those theories would be blinkered without such objects. If such a line of reasoning is acceptable in that context, then it may be extended to defend Hegel. According to this extension, is the best reason for believing that nature actually has a rational structure that it plays a crucial role in Hegel's philosophy? Almost. Rather, it plays a crucial role in reconciling Hegel's readers to all spheres of the world as a home. Even nature is not finally estranged from or alien to Spirit but is instead the space from which Spirit emerges and the condition for Spirit's possibility. This allows us to comprehend our world as *ours*.

There is a considerable disadvantage to this reading, however. If Hegel has indeed taken the findings of the natural sciences of his day and then arranged them so as to exhibit a rational structure and a hierarchy of constitutive forms converging on Spirit – a hierarchy that will have become internal to nature – then this would require that his *Philosophy of Nature* be substantially revised whenever the paradigms of the natural sciences change. As Jacques Rancière writes, mutatis mutandis, "one does not correct the texts of ideological struggle when conditions of the struggle change: one writes new ones."[4] And this couldn't be left to overworked graduate students! This disadvantage is, from another perspective, an advantage. It means that, after Hegel, philosophy continues. Hegelian Philosophy!

As noted earlier, Hegel doesn't believe that the constitutive forms in nature actually transform into other forms. In that sense, he thinks that nature is frozen, static. Seasons change, to be sure, and the earth goes round the sun. But it is just a repeat of what has gone before – nothing new. And so Hegel rejects evolution. One reason, as just mentioned, is that he doesn't accept that natural forms transform into other forms.

Hegel hierarchically ranks the moments of the *Philosophy of Nature*, leading up to the transition to Spirit. It might seem as though each category in the *Philosophy of Nature* morphs into a successor in an attempt more adequately to approximate, or become, Spirit, and so to overcome the limitations that adhered to its predecessor. Nevertheless, Hegel views the moments of the *Philosophy of Nature* as frozen and unmoving. Although he has transitions from one level to another in the *Philosophy of Nature*, the constituents aren't able to modify themselves, or be modified, so as to make the transitions. At the zoo, we may go from the lemur cage to the monkey house, but the lemurs don't become monkeys (even if they get into the monkey house). While Nature as a whole may be seen as striving to become Spirit, with its moments ordered hierarchically, Hegel nevertheless maintains that its moments do not develop. They are what and as they are, always and forever.

Another reason that Hegel rejects evolution is that – writing before Charles Darwin's introduction of the idea of natural selection – he believes that there is no viable mechanism that would explain it. And, so, there is no progress in nature.

Accepting evolution would obviously change Hegel's *Philosophy of Nature*. It wouldn't require that the work be jettisoned but that it would need to be revised. A revised version would concede that biological constitutive forms do transform into other forms. And, insofar as the history of evolution is viewed retrospectively as leading to a species – us! – capable of comprehending this very process, then the revised version would also need to allow that there is progress in nature. And so, rather than there being a rupture from nature when Spirit emerges, there would be more of a transition. Not wholly so, though, as we are still the only species capable of comprehending the natural processes that made us possible.[5]

Hegel's *Philosophy of Nature* is divided into three major sections: Mathematics, Inorganic Physics, and Organic Physics. As we saw in the previous chapter, at the conclusion of the *Logic*, nature is posited as the other of reason. In the *Philosophy of Nature*, Hegel will show that nature is not finally other than reason but, rather, that nature itself has a rational structure. Moreover, nature is spirit, *Geist*, in its nascent state. With the last moment of *Philosophy of Nature*, the Animal Organism, we have advanced as far as possible within nature proper; the next moment takes us out of nature into spirit. Hegel will argue that the mathematical stage of nature is the most elementary and restricted. This moment is nevertheless important because it is here that we first see that nature does exhibit a rational structure. Hegel is quite critical of attempts to reduce nature, or its rational structure, to mathematics, seeing this as the most elementary aspect of nature as well as the most formal. At the level of Inorganic Physics, we have explanations in terms of mechanistic forces, where change happens as a result of one object impacting another. It is only when we reach the level of Organic Physics that nature begins, in a discernible way, to converge on spirit. Geological nature provides the context in which vegetarian nature can emerge and flourish. Vegetarian nature, in turn, is required for the emergence of the animal organism. The animal organism, of course, will be that from which spirit, embodied in humans, emerges.

I will now provide a brief summary of the chief points of Hegel's *Philosophy of Nature*. My goal here is not to write a commentary but, rather, to provide readers with an initial orientation. Like Hegel's *Phenomenology of Spirit* and *Logic*, his *Philosophy of Nature* is sufficiently complex that it is difficult to summarize without distortion. If this summary enables readers subsequently to recognize its distortions, it will have succeeded.

Hegel informs his readers that nature presents itself as the idea – which the *Logic* explicates – in the form of otherness. There is a subtle point being made here, one often missed. Nature is not ultimately the other of the idea, according to Hegel, but instead is the idea itself – although it initially appears as other to the idea. And so, at that moment, nature is other than the idea. But that moment will be sublated. There is a sense in which we might have anticipated this move. Hegel argues that nature is comprehensible because it has a rational structure, which it would have if it were ultimately alien to and other than the idea. The *Logic* has just presented the history of the West, but at a highly conceptual level. The *Philosophy of Nature* begins not by continuing from the Logic's conclusion, but rather by returning to its beginning. This time, however, it begins not at the level of concepts but, instead, at the level of the material embodiment of those concepts.

Although Hegel denies that there are any actual transitions within nature, he will present nature as though it were intent upon successively approximating, and thereby realizing, Spirit. Nature doesn't advance, only Spirit can do that. Nevertheless, it seems as though even the stones long to call out. Nature never progresses, it is the idea frozen.

For this reason, Hegel urges that nature isn't to be worshipped or exalted. Any aspect of spirit, however trivial or tedious, is already more advanced than the most majestic aspects of nature. The laws that nature obeys are external to it, whereas spirit finally gives itself the laws that it follows. As an example, we might note that an asteroid simply maintains a specific trajectory until something alters its course – Neptune's gravitational field, perhaps – whereas spirit will have decided where it is going and how it will get there.

Nature is the realm of necessity and contingency. What nature lacks, what spirit is, is freedom. As a result, nature can't move forward, it can't progress, although the moments of reason within it can be arranged in a succession of stages.

Nature is a living whole, Hegel maintains. At the level of nature, however, this is life that dies. However, nature is spirit in its nascent state. Nature and spirit are both the idea, but, with spirit, the idea is no longer life that dies but rather life that generates itself through death.

This leads to nature outside of itself (space and time, mathematics), nature's material existence (inorganic nature, physics), and nature as alive (organic nature, physiology).

Hegel begins with a discussion of Mathematics and then moves to Inorganic Physics. He discusses Mechanics, Elementary Physics (Elementary Particles, Elements, Elementary Process), and the Physics of Individuality (Shape, Particularization of Differences, Process of Isolation). He then transitions to the final section, Organic Physics, in which he discusses Geological Nature, Vegetarian Nature, and Animal Organism. The animal must die because it cannot fully embody its concept. This results in a transition to the *Philosophy of Spirit*.

Spirit

Hegel's *Philosophy of Spirit* is the concluding third part of his *Encyclopedia of the Philosophical Sciences;* the other two parts are the *Logic* and the *Philosophy of Nature.* The *Philosophy of Spirit* consists of Hegel's extremely condensed lecture notes as well as additional notes from several of his students. Hegel's notes were intended primarily to help his students follow his lectures. An analogy would be a set of PowerPoint slides. In his lectures, Hegel amplified and elucidated his notes, which would have been unintelligible without his lectures to explicate them. Fortunately for us, we have the notes of several of Hegel's students. They copied his lectures.

Here, we transition from an examination of nature, which is spirit's context and precondition, to spirit itself. What is spirit? Readers will not go too far wrong if they interpret spirit as human culture, which culminates in art, religion, and philosophy. Hegel's philosophy is one of reconciliation. In the *Philosophy of Nature*, he argued that nature is not, finally, alien to thought and that it exists in order to make spirit possible. Nevertheless, Hegel claims that there is no progress in nature. Spirit is only nascent, only implicit, in nature. Nature is neither conscious nor is it capable of self-direction. It is only at the level of spirit that progress occurs. Progress is towards increasing levels of freedom.

As even moderately attentive readers by now would expect, the *Philosophy of Spirit* is divided into three main sections: Subjective Spirit (which is further subdivided into Anthropology, Phenomenology, and Psychology), Objective Spirit (subdivided into Law, Conscience, and Morality), and Absolute Spirit (Art, Religion, and Philosophy). In this chapter, I will discuss Subjective Spirit in more detail than Objective Spirit or Absolute Spirit. The next three chapters are devoted to Hegel's lectures on the *Philosophy of Right* and the *Philosophy of History* (Objective Spirit) and to the *Aesthetics* and *Religion* (Absolute Spirit). These lectures substantially expand the positions he articulates in the discussion of Objective Spirit and Absolute Spirit. His discussions of phenomenology, as readers will recognize, recapitulate portions of the *Phenomenology of Spirit.*

Let's begin by again asking a seemingly naïve question: What is spirit? At the level of subjective spirit, it is at first the individual mind, which begins in infancy as the active response to what it selects as stimuli – and so, already here at this level, we see that spirit is never something merely passive or simply reactive – and it then develops into the consciousness of the adult. At the level of objective spirit, it is the social, legal, and cultural institutions and customs that provide the context and horizon for subjective spirit; at the level of absolute spirit, it is the self-reflective articulation of spirit itself, where spirit tells itself what it is. The intelligence that was externalized in Nature becomes internalized in Spirit.

There are two points to note here. First, although objective spirit comes after subjective spirit in Hegel's narrative, objective spirit must already be in place in order for there to be subjective spirit. Subjective spirit partially develops through education, but that requires that some processes of education, however rudimentary, should already be in place. So, while it might seem that we begin with subjective spirit and later arrive at objective spirit, objective spirit must already be firmly in place. Second, absolute spirit is the moment when spirit tells itself what it has become. What must not be overlooked is spirit's performative aspect. Absolute spirit becomes what it is in the act of telling itself this. It has the freedom to become itself and Spirit is its manifestation. What this means is that, in a sense, Hegel's *Philosophy of Spirit* must be read backwards. That is to say, it is only from the perspective of absolute spirit that objective spirit and then subjective spirit can be properly comprehended. Readers should by now be familiar with this strategy.

Subjective spirit is immediate or implicit (Anthropology), mediate or explicit (Phenomenology), defining itself in itself (Psychology). The awakening of consciousness.

Anthropology is the point where spirit initially emerges from nature. Here, we are dealing with life that is not yet conscious; we might say that its thought is still pre-conscious. Hegel refers to this as the Physical Soul. The soul, for Hegel, is that which is alive in matter, or, rather, matter animate. The soul is not only matter animate, as it seems to be for Aristotle; it also consists of psychic states. The soul doesn't distinguish between itself and others, or between itself and the external world (or objects in the external world). These distinctions emerge only at the level of spirit, not soul, in Phenomenology. Hegel notes the influence of climate on race and the characteristics he believes are associated with the various races. Some of what he says may make readers uncomfortable. What can be said on Hegel's behalf, though, is that he believes that climate is determinate, and so his views aren't racist. He doesn't believe that race is destiny. Put otherwise, he believes that, were a group to migrate to another climate, its racial characteristics would eventually change. This is Hegel's considered opinion. He may not always remember it. He has interesting discussions of childhood and sexuality, as well as of waking and dreaming. Of especial interest is that sexuality results in individuals losing, and thereby transcending, their individuality in another. Also, waking and dreaming are distinguished in that the ideas arising in dreams link to each other merely by association.

From here, Hegel discusses what he calls the Feeling Soul. He notes that the mother's physical and psychic connection with the fetus is deep, so that her experiences can be transmitted to the fetus. Friends are crucial in individuals becoming conscious, as friends allow individuals to see themselves reflected in others. Disease results from an imbalance within the body and health is re-established when that balance is restored. Surprisingly, Hegel accepts that some individuals have clairvoyance and the ability to use divining rods to locate water. These might seem rather fanciful. Nevertheless, they are well attested, and it is a mark of Hegel's faithfulness to empirical evidence that he doesn't reject them as superstitious nonsense. He also accepts that individuals can have portents of the future, but he regards this as predictive of what the future likely will be, not determinative of what it must be.

Hegel then discusses various forms of mental instability. These range from idiocy, distractedness, and rambling to actual insanity, dementia, and mania. The insane cut off connection with the common, rational world of others and substitute their private and idiosyncratic judgments for shared and public ones. It is not only that they arrive at views with which others disagree. They also base those views on grounds that others reject. Indeed, others often cannot comprehend how such considerations could function as grounds. Hegel thinks that the root causes of insanity are vanity and pride, and so he believes that every individual is potentially susceptible to insanity. To see his point, we might note that individuals who are paranoid schizophrenics likely make two epistemic errors. First, they believe that everything that happens is meaningful, that nothing is random or coincidental. Second, they also believe that everything relates to them. This second belief allows them to regard themselves as of immense importance, since everything that happens – even if it is malicious – occurs because of them. The insane may be cured through a regimen of work. The goal here is to involve them in the world and to establish the trust in others that they have lost.

Hegel next discusses the role of habit, noting that it emancipates individuals from mere feelings. Habit is a second nature.

Individuals can be taught, and can teach themselves, to habituate themselves. For example, individuals can learn to become relatively indifferent to the cold. Habit allows us to do many useful things without having to think about them – taking a stroll, for instance – freeing our minds to think about other things. Non-human animals can also develop habits but they don't decide to habituate themselves. Hegel believes that habit is indispensable for intellectual life. From here, we reach the level of the Actual Soul, where spirit becomes conscious and transitions from Anthropology to Phenomenology. It is important to note that, for Hegel, spirit doesn't emerge *naturally* from nature. That is to say, spirit cannot be adequately comprehended with the tools appropriate for inorganic nature or even biological entities. Rather, spirit must be comprehended with the tools appropriate for understanding society, politics, history, and culture.

Phenomenology is the level of consciousness proper. Here, spirit finally emerges and, unlike the soul, begins to distinguish itself from others (and from the world and its objects). It also begins to relate to them. Hegel moves from sensuous consciousness through sense perception to intellect. He then discusses self-consciousness, the truth of consciousness. Here, I am aware of an object as mine – that is, as the object that I am observing and conceptualizing – and so I become aware of myself as observing and conceptualizing. Hegel next discusses appetite, instinctive desire, self-conscious recognition, and universal self-consciousness, transitioning from there to Reason. These discussions parallel those in the *Phenomenology of Spirit*. In the struggle for recognition, self-knowledge as well as knowledge of the other is obtained. Intersubjectivity emerges because, for Hegel, knowledge of self and other are mutually conditioning. An individual never has knowledge of self immediately but only through knowledge of the other. Individuals discover who they are by seeing themselves reflected in the estimation of others. What needs to be added here is that this discovery is also constitutive. In the *Phenomenology of Spirit*, the struggle of recognition between lord and bondsman, master and slave, results in Stoicism. In the *Philosophy of Spirit*, by contrast, the struggle for recognition is sublated in recognition, in mutual love and friendship. This leads in turn to the concept of Right. In recognizing others, individuals also recognize them, and so recognize themselves, as persons who have rights.

From Phenomenology, Hegel transitions to Psychology. The Psychology is subdivided into three sections: Theoretical Spirit,

Practical Spirit, and Free Spirit. In the section on Theoretical Spirit, Hegel urges that spirit is a totality, a whole. Its parts, aspects, are what they are because of how they are articulated within the whole. And the whole results from that articulation. Neither part nor whole is primary. Rather, they are mutually co-defining and co-constituting. The goal here is for spirit to know itself and its world. Spirit must not only recognize what it has become, it must actively endorse and acknowledge that. It must own what it has become. Spirit must, as Robert Williams writes in his "Translator's Introduction," move from found to posited.[6] But what if, to raise a seemingly naïve objection, spirit doesn't want to own what it has become? What if spirit decides it doesn't like itself all that much? It would then be crucial, Hegel might respond, that spirit not merely accept what it has become while simultaneously being alienated from itself. If it did this, there would be a sense in which it has moved from found to posited. Only what would be posited would not be ownership and possession but alienation and estrangement. It would be imperative that spirit take steps to overcome its self-alienation (as it does in the *Phenomenology of Spirit*, Hegel could add).

Hegel next discusses the Imagination and Memory. He maintains that we think in names, not images. Names are signs that can become detached from the objects to which they initially referred. Hegel's example is "lion." It is not necessary to have a mental picture of a lion to use this word in a meaningful sentence. This is the case for all names. Ultimately, they have the content that spirit confers upon them rather than the content that they initially had. Here, we have another instance of Hegel's move from found to posited. Names are initially encountered as having a particular content. Children initially learn "lion" by having someone show them a lion or a picture of one. When they have learned "lion," however, they can then think and talk about lions without having to picture or imagine a lion.

This is why Hegel believes that mechanical memory is crucial, where poems, say, are learned by rote, without learning the meaning of the words. Children in elementary school may memorize poetry which they can't yet comprehend, for example, or a college student may be able to recite in Sanskrit the first chapter of the *Bhagavad Gītā* without knowing at all what it means, merely by overhearing a roommate, who had to memorize it for a Sanskrit class, repeat that chapter aloud many times. Alternatively, the meaning of a phrase or word can dissolve when it is incessantly repeated. Memorizing what is not understood may seem a wretched waste of time, but Hegel sees that ability as evidencing spirit's power over everything that is given or found.[7] Here, spirit can hold together, in thought, what is meaningless to it. It can, moreover, confer meaning on it. Indeed, this is the point of the move from found to posit. Spirit can hold together meaninglessness.

This is why Hegel compares spirit to a pit. It is a receptacle which holds all things together. Spirit is not an entity but a nothingness that contains everything. Unlike the contents of ordinary pits, which consist only of what has been thrown into them, the contents of the pit that is spirit are generated by it. Things only have the meanings they do, finally, because those meanings have been conferred upon them by spirit.

We can see Hegel's discussion of Practical Spirit as a movement beyond both Aristotle and Kant. The difficulty with Kant's ethics, according to Hegel, is that the categorical imperative is purely formal and so, with a bit of ingenuity, can be made compatible with anything. Hegel also thinks that nothing important is ever done without passion, and so the attempt by Kantian ethics to separate reason from inclinations is flawed. In order for the categorical imperative to do any actual work, it must have content that comes from the specific social and cultural worlds in which persons are embedded. Aristotle's ethics, by contrast, does appeal to the social, but it treats that as something entirely natural. It doesn't recognize that the social is something that humans have created and that it has developed historically.

Hegel's discussion of Objective Spirit in the *Encyclopedia* is more fully elaborated in the *Elements of the Philosophy of Right* and the *Philosophy of History*. Likewise, his discussions of art and revealed religion (Christianity) in the section on Absolute Spirit are developed in the *Aesthetics: Lectures on Fine Art* and the *Lectures on the Philosophy of Religion*. We will investigate those texts in the next three chapters. Here, we still need to investigate Hegel's discussion of philosophy.

The astonishing thing about Hegel's discussion of philosophy is how short it is – barely ten pages. He claims that philosophy is the unity of art and religion. Art expresses the concept – roughly, the narrative that we tell ourselves about who we are – in a sensuous medium. Religion expresses the concept in representational or picture thinking, myth. Philosophy alone is able to express it adequately at the level of conceptual thinking. Philosophy transcends art and religion, to be sure, but it also incorporates and subsumes them. It provides the retrospective account of how we arrived where we are.

Hegel defends philosophy against the charge of being pantheistic. If pantheism is the view that God is immediately to be identified with objects in the world, then no one has ever advocated such a view. In the *Bhagavad Gītā*, as Hegel interprets this text, Kṛṣṇa claims to be supreme among everything, not identical with everything. Hegel believes that Hinduism is split between a determinationless unity (that is, a monism where there is only identity but no difference) and a profusion of particularity (an incoherent pluralism that is incapable of articulating how anything could be one thing), with no way to link unity and particularity. As a result, Hinduism is as much a monotheism as it is a polytheism, but it cannot coherently think these together. Hegel urges that the monotheism of Islam is an advance, as here there is a spiritual unity which is an elevation above the finite. But this results in an acosmism, a view that so emphasizes God that the world itself is lost from sight. The focus is entirely on the infinite, and so excludes finite particulars, such as planets, persons, and peas; as a result, this acosmic infinity cannot include the infinite and the finite. To return to the language of the *Phenomenology of Spirit*, we have substance but not yet subject. The required additional step is to move to subject, spirit, a concrete unity that consists in the recognition that substance is also subject.

Philosophy is the self-thinking idea. Hegel concludes by discussing three syllogisms, three ways in which philosophy could be articulated. In the first, we have his actual procedure: logic, nature, mind. Here, logic constitutes the ground or presupposition, mind is the result, and nature is the middle term that links logic and mind. The second syllogism is nature, mind, logic. And the final one is mind, logic, nature. This strongly suggests that any of these sequences could express the Hegelian philosophy. It also suggests that interpretations that emphasize only the necessity of Hegel's actual procedure – logic, nature, mind – are one-sided.

In the next chapter, on the *Elements of the Philosophy of Right*, we will begin a more detailed discussion of Objective Spirit.

6

Hegel's *Philosophy of Right*

It is a commonplace in discussions of Hegel's philosophy to suggest that his later writings are substantially more conservative than his earlier ones. I will urge that this is incorrect and that there is no convincing evidence to support the claim that Hegel becomes more conservative as he ages. One of the most important passages that are cited in support of the claim that the later Hegel is conservative occurs in the Preface to his *Philosophy of Right*. There, he says that Philosophy always arrives too late to give advice about what should be done. His claim is that Philosophy is entirely retrospective, and so it is only when an era is coming to a close that Philosophy can discern that era's fundamental characteristics. The owl of Minerva – Philosophy – only flies at dusk.

Although Hegel does say these things, they are belied by his actual practice in the *Philosophy of Right*. This disjunct between words and act isn't a lapse, I suggest. Rather, the claims that Hegel makes in the Preface are intended for the Prussian censors, to reassure them that there is nothing in the *Philosophy of Right* that could cause them concern. Let's discuss this in a bit more detail.

There is an epistemological problem. Hegel says that Philosophy can comprehend an age only in retrospect, when it has exhibited all of its potentials. Presumably, Hegel would have to say then, regarding his *Philosophy of Right*, that he is able to write his book because his own era has now fully actualized itself. But how could he know this?! He would need already to be firmly established in a new era so that he could then look back and discern the relevant features of the old. This isn't the case, however, as he is describing features of his own era. (Actually, this is what Hegel, in the Preface, *says* he is doing. We will see in a moment that things are both more complicated and more interesting.)

So, Hegel is describing his own time. As he would be the first to admit, he doesn't have clairvoyance and cannot summon the future. As a consequence, he is in no position to know whether he stands at the cusp of one era's ending and the beginning of another or whether, for example, he is smack in the middle of an era. That is, Hegel could only identify his form of life as living or as dying if he could know whether it actually will live or die; even if it initially appears to be dying, it may nevertheless have the internal resources to recover. He could have opinions, of course, but opinions are exactly what he wants to disbar from Philosophy.

Then there is the Beautiful Soul. You will recall this character from the *Phenomenology of Spirit*. The beautiful soul believes that the world is so thoroughly corrupt and corrupting that any interaction with the world will result in the corruption of its soul. As a consequence, the beautiful soul looks on the world with at best benign neglect, more frequently with contemptuous indifference, but it does nothing to ameliorate conditions. As we saw in the *Phenomenology of Spirit*, Hegel doesn't regard the beautiful soul as an innocent in a wicked world, which is how the beautiful soul would describe itself, but rather considers it as the source of the very evil it perceives. It is the beautiful soul's own surreptitious and disavowed intervention that describes the world as so hopelessly evil that any attempt to make things better will only corrupt the agent, rather than seeing the world as pretty good but potentially better.

Now, it is most implausible that Hegel would have forgotten about the beautiful soul. This is exactly what he would have had to do, however, in order to describe his own age as already over, such that it is always already too late for Philosophy to intervene. Claiming this would itself be an intervention.

Moreover, many of the features that Hegel attributes to a rational state are ones the Prussian state of his day lacks. As Michael O. Hardimon notes, these include "a constitutional monarchy, a representative bicameral assembly, and public jury trials."[1] Further, Jay Drydyk notes that Hegel describes his rational state as practicing "a universal right to capitalization," whereby male citizens would receive a substantial sum of money from the government upon coming into their majority, even though capitalization doesn't exist in Hegel's Prussia.[2] And, while he doesn't explicitly state that the monarch can't veto legislation, that Hegel doesn't explicitly include this among the monarch's powers strongly suggests that the monarch lacks this ability.

Hence, Hegel's Preface must be seen as written for the Prussian censors. In fact, his *Philosophy of Right* is an intervention that aims to transform the Prussian state by implicitly contrasting it with the rational state he describes. Here description functions also as prescription. Hegel aims to let the owl of Minerva fly at noon.

As we know by now, Hegel likes to punctuate things by threes. It comes as no surprise, then, that the *Philosophy of Right* is divided into Family, Civil Society, and State. Here are some highlights.

Hegel believes that the basis of the family is the love between a man and a woman. As a man of his time, the family he describes is the so-called nuclear family, heterosexual. It would be possible to update Hegel a bit, queer him up, and I have tried my hand at that elsewhere.[3] Here, I play it straight. Although Hegel's family is nuclear and heterosexual, it would be a mistake to dismiss this as too conservative to be taken seriously. Rather, it's innovative! In claiming that the family should be based on the love of a man and woman, Hegel allows marriages arranged by families, but he adds that the families should consider the affections of their children. Hegel's family is instead based on the claims of individuality. He believes that the institutions of marriage and the family are ways in which natural sex is transformed into something cultural. There is this too. In light of the vulnerable economic conditions of women in Hegel's day, and unfortunately largely still prevalent today, linking sex to marriage functions as a mechanism by which women won't solely be responsible for the care and cost of raising children.

Hegel thinks that the husband will be the wage earner in a family and the wife will be responsible for the house. While this is unimaginative and tedious, there is no reason to believe that Hegel – the text, if not the man – would be opposed to women also having jobs and careers. Care would need to be taken so that children have quality and quantity time with their parents and so that husbands contribute to the housework, but these could be managed.

Hegel believes that children need to be educated. He is primarily concerned that the boys be educated, but he also says that girls should be educated based on their aptitude. Although he no doubt anticipates that girls will generally have less aptitude than boys, he nevertheless must be open to an equality here.

Family property is the property of the family. That is to say, Hegel doesn't believe that the husband may sell this property against the family's wishes. One might well expect that this would be codified in law. The main intent of this is to protect the family from a husband's idiosyncratic or arbitrary behavior. Hegel rejects primogeniture, the practice of the first-born son inheriting all of the family property.

Hegel believes that what characterizes the family is love and that love is what unites the family. In the family, each person is loved and accepted because that person is a member of the family. In order to develop an individuality, however, a person must also be valued for his or her talents and accomplishments. This occurs in the sphere of civil society. Only males need to leave the family and enter civil society, Hegel believes, while females naturally belong to the family. This appeal to nature to justify what is clearly cultural is surprising in Hegel. No doubt, he deserves some kicks here. The most that can be said in his defense is that this aspect of his thought is an expression of the conditions of his time. It is also surprising that Hegel seems to have no historical sense of the ways in which the family of his time is a product of social and economic conditions. More kicks, perhaps. There is this, though. It is Hegel who decisively underscores the importance of history – crucially arguing, for example, that reason itself develops historically – and so our ability to criticize him is itself a debt we owe to him. We can pull Hegel's ears only because we stand on his shoulders.

Civil society is the sphere of economic relations. Hegel is greatly impressed by Adam Smith's analysis, in *The Wealth of Nations*, of the emerging industrial age and capitalism. Like Smith, Hegel believes that this economic system is inherently unstable, tending to produce fabulous wealth for a few individuals, grinding poverty for most, cycling between frenzied economic activity and depressions. To curb these, Hegel introduces regulating mechanisms, some at the level of civil society itself, others at the level of the state. (The family also might have a modest role here. Because the family is based on *love*, its members who are active in civil society may be somewhat less tempted to believe that are no other legitimate goals beyond the acquisition of wealth.)

In Hegel's civil society, workers are organized into guilds based on their crafts. Those wishing to hire, say, carpenters would do so through a guild, and so guilds also have some resemblance to modern labor unions. Carpenters would not compete against each other for the lowest wages and benefits. The guild sets entry requirements for membership, provides for education and apprenticeship programs to teach new members the requisite skills and competencies, and also maintains insurance programs for unemployment, illnesses, deaths, and accidents. Many of the social safety nets now associated with the so-called welfare state are located within the guilds.

Civil society is a sphere of mutual needs where individuals begin to comprehend their interdependence with others. Although this sphere isn't fully rational – this will occur only when it is complemented by the state – there is a substantial element of rationality in it. Its rationality is one-sided, however. The aim of civil society is the economic prosperity of its component parts, not the general welfare or the common good. So, a specific guild is concerned to promote its own interests and will care about the interests of other guilds or society in general only insofar as those are aspects of promoting its own interests.

Civic organizations, such as clubs, are also part of civil society. These organizations point their members towards concerns that transcend the acquisition of wealth and bring disparate individuals together who nevertheless have some shared interests, such as Indian cooking, stamp collecting, or singing.

The state is composed of the police and judiciary, the legislature, and the monarchy. About the first group, all that needs to be said here is that courts would try criminal and civil cases, but they have no power to overturn or modify legislation. This is so because Hegel's state doesn't have a constitution, and so there is nothing beyond enacted legislation to which citizens could appeal. It might be thought that this would allow the abuse of minorities, but Hegel would respond that this is prevented by structural features of his system discussed below. The legislature has two houses. Somewhat like the British system, one house is composed of landed gentry and hereditary nobles, the other of elected representatives. Hegel believes that a system where legislators represent constituents based on geographical location will be experienced as estranging and alienating because the constituents won't see that their interests are being represented. This is so because geography is a poor selector of shared interests. Instead, legislators represent constituents based on their guild membership. The carpenters, for example, would elect legislators to represent their interests in the legislature, and so they would recognize that their interests are represented by their legislators. Since Hegel has most women in the home and so not belonging to any guild, this system of representation would require some modifications to be workable and acceptable. Such enhancements, however, would be eminently feasible.

The monarchy. It is crucial to recognize that when Hegel is discussing the monarchy he usually isn't talking about the monarch. His system is a constitutional monarchy (but Hegel has an unwritten constitution) where one man, the monarch, represents and embodies the state and so, on behalf of the state itself, signs legislation into law. Other than representing the state at official functions and pardoning criminals of their punishment in exceptional circumstances, signing his name is all that he does! The monarch can't veto or propose legislation. He can sign his name only to legislation that has been passed by the legislature. It is because of his severely curtailed powers that Hegel believes that it doesn't matter if the monarch is an idiot, as long as he can sign his name. The position of monarch is hereditary. This would be a cause for worry and concern, of course, if the monarch were required to do anything substantial other than signing his name to legislation.

The monarch himself is only one component of the monarchy. The important part is what Hegel refers to as the universal class. This is a group of bureaucrats who manage the affairs of the state. Hegel envisions these persons as civil servants who are hired and promoted based solely on their ability, merit, and accomplishments. They aren't allowed to own property or to invest in businesses, and so their interests, as individuals and as a group, will be the same as those of society as a whole. Put otherwise, their particular good can be furthered only by promoting the common good. Their advancement depends on that of society as a whole. This is why they constitute a *universal* class. Unlike other classes that seek to promote their own good in relative indifference to the common good, the universal class is *universal* because it advances the good of the entire society.

It is the universal class that introduces legislation. The legislature can vote only to accept or reject the proposed legislation. There is a sense, then, in which Hegel's system has checks and balances. The universal class introduces legislation but can't enact it. The legislature enacts legislation but can't introduce or modify it. The monarch must sign legislation enacted by the legislature. The debates and speeches of the legislators are reported in the newspapers, since this allows people both to see that their interests are being represented and to become educated in the affairs of the state, learning about the views and interests of other guilds, and so to develop a concern for society as a whole.

However, Hegel also advocates censorship of the press. It might seem initially that this is objectionable, but in fact all governments have, and must have, restrictions regarding what can be reported. It is a feature of Hegel's system, not grounds for complaint, that he is explicit about this. He maintains that there must be a presumption of truth in reporting, such that those making warrantless or defamatory claims would be liable. He also insists that the state and its representatives must be referred to with respect.

It is important to note that Hegel, in contrast to many others in his day who asserted that only Christians should be citizens, believes that Jews should be citizens of a nation. His argument is that Jews are humans and that what qualifies persons for citizenship is their humanity, not religion.

Kant has a retributive justification for punishment, while Jeremy Bentham and John Stuart Mill believe that punishment is justified because it promotes the best consequences. Hegel's theory is closer to Kant's. He says that punishment negates the crime. He doesn't mean that the crime never happened if it is punished. Rather, when individuals commit crimes, they implicitly announce that they are not accountable to their society's moral and legal conventions. Indeed, there is a sense in which, in committing crimes, individuals are attempting implicitly to make crime itself the law. (This last point is best illustrated in societies where, perhaps due to civil war, a general collapse of the legal structure occurs. What order then exists is solely the result of force. Warlords provide a good example of this, where intimidation and extortion replace the rule of law.) Punishment demonstrates that society can, nevertheless, hold criminals accountable. Since their crimes implicitly place them outside of their society, punishment is also a mechanism whereby they may be reintegrated.

Kant, in his essay on cosmopolitanism, argues that a single world-state is rational, and so individuals and currently existing states have a moral obligation to promote – or at least to do nothing to interfere with – its realization.[4] Hegel rejects the idea of a single world-state, urging instead that the currently existing system of nation-states is rational. He believes that Kant is invoking an empty "ought" in asserting that there ought to be a world-state, an "ought" that has no connection to actually existing circumstances. He could also note that Kant seems to be involved in a performative contradiction. On the one hand, Kant claims that the world-state and its governing institutions must emerge through a process of rational deliberation. On the other hand, however, he claims that the world-state should be a republican monarchy. It seems, then, that Kant believes that he can know in advance what the result of *rational* deliberation ought to be, which would make *deliberation* superfluous.

Hegel also rejects the suggestion that there should be a federation of states that would impose restrictions on the activities of states and so make wars and acts of aggression less common. He notes that the more powerful states in any such federation would be in a position to impose their will on its weaker members. There would be nothing to prevent states from resorting to force, moreover, when they believed that this would further their interests. As a consequence, although a federation of states may initially appear to be an improvement over the present plurality of nation-states, it is not actually so.

Hegel is notorious for having allegedly justified war. To consider this adequately, we need to step back for a moment. We have seen before, especially in our discussions of his *Phenomenology of Spirit* and *Logic*, that Hegel doesn't believe that any position is wholly mistaken. Rather, he maintains that false positions are one-sided, having some aspect of the truth but wrongly believing that this aspect represents the whole truth. Similarly, he would maintain that no human practice or institution is wholly irrational – that it contains some element of rationality. Back to Hegel on war: he isn't justifying war per se. Rather, he is claiming that there is an element of rationality in war. So, what's rational about war?

Hegel recognizes that – unlike the members of the universal class, police, legislators, judiciary, et al. – most people aren't directly employed by the state but instead will be involved in commerce in civil society. Others will remain in the family (he has in mind stay-at-home housewives, but we can include househusbands too). While the bureaucrats in the universal class will be concerned for society as a whole, persons in the family will be concerned primarily for their own family (or perhaps their family, some relatives, and nearby neighbors), and those in civil society will be concerned with their own financial activities. During war, however, the state interrupts and interferes with all of this, demanding that citizens make sacrifices to support the war effort. In this way, persons actively realize that they are members of a society and that there is a common good that transcends their own particular goods. They thereby think of themselves as citizens, rather than only as members of a family or guild, and so recognize that they and their fellow citizens constitute a *we* instead of being separate *I*'s.

About colonialism. True, Hegel allows for this. However, he seems to regard it as a mechanism for responding to extraordinary situations – crop failures, for example – rather than as a policy for normal times. As Gabriel Paquette recognizes, for Hegel, "colonization cannot operate without constraint, and only functions effectively as a safety valve amidst acute turmoil."[5] He advocates establishing colonies where there are no or few people, and he does not suggest that indigenous natives be displaced. He also argues, instancing America's experience with Great Britain, that the home countries and colonies are benefited most when the colonies are politically independent.

Finally, a word about conscientious objection. Hegel doesn't recognize the legitimacy of appeals to conscience, as he realizes that any idiocy or enormity can be defended by such appeals. Nevertheless, he believes that states may allow those who oppose war on grounds of conscience to perform an alternative service.

In the next chapter, on the *Philosophy of History*, we will continue our discussion of Objective Spirit.

7

Hegel's *Philosophy of History*

Hegel claims that there are three main ways to write history: original, reflective, and philosophic. Original history is contemporaneous with the events it describes and is based on eye-witness accounts. Memoirs belong to this genre. Reflective history is written at a later time and age than the events it describes, where the culture of the historian is different than that of the era narrated. Frequently, moreover, there is an attempt to place that era within a larger historical context, discussing the events that made it possible as well as the era's subsequent influence. Most histories are written in this genre. So, this leaves philosophic history. What's that?

Before considering this question directly, it will be useful to consider that Hegel's overall strategy in his *Philosophy of Nature* and his *Philosophy of Right*, discussed in previous chapters, is to reconcile his readers to, respectively, nature and society (especially the state), to show that they are at home in their world. He does this in the *Philosophy of Nature* by taking the science of his day and telling a story such that nature can be seen to exhibit a rational structure. This is also the strategy he employs in the *Philosophy of Right*, although there we saw that the rational state that Hegel describes doesn't fully match any existing society and that he is attempting as much to motivate his readers to enact the reforms necessary in order to make their society rational as he is to reconcile them to it. This is also what Hegel does in his *Philosophy of History*. He will tell the story of (mainly Western) history so that his readers will see that it too exhibits a rational structure. That is to say, he will tell his readers how they have arrived at the present conjuncture, and he will do so in such a way as to show that both the conjuncture itself and the trajectory of events that led to it are rational. This is history in the philosophic mode.

As we saw in the previous chapters, some interpreters of Hegel's philosophy believe that the categories of the *Logic* are generated wholly a priori. Some of those interpreters then maintain that those of the *Philosophy of Nature*, the *Philosophy of Right*, the *Philosophy of History*, the *Lectures on Aesthetics*, and the *Lectures on Religion* are also generated a priori; others claim that the categories of the *Logic* are applied to empirical material in each of those domains. I have already presented arguments that the *Logic* itself is an a posteriori account, presenting the history of the development of the categories of Western thought, and so there is no need to repeat them here. Nevertheless, readers should be aware that these interpretive questions emerge at every level of Hegel's philosophy.

When discussing philosophic history, Hegel doesn't mean by "history" a mere chronicle of things that happened. For him, history must involve progress and development. There could be no history of fashion, in Hegel's sense of "history," because such a history would be only a report of change, not progress. (This might not be correct, though. If a history of fashion also discusses how fashion both reflects and influences its social context, then changing fashions in women's clothes, for example, whereby they become less restrictive and confining, could indeed be progressive and so linked to history in Hegel's sense.)

Hegel thinks that there is a deep connection between what actually happened and the remembering of those events in writing. He claims that it is no accident that the German word for "history," *Geschichte*, has both meanings, as this indicates that historical narration emerges simultaneously with the occurring of historical events. What actually happened becomes a function of what we take to have happened, such that any suggestion that things may have occurred differently necessarily involves a counter-narrative. Michel Foucault was correct to worry, by the way, about "the extent to which our anti-Hegelianism is possibly one of his tricks directed against us, at the end of which he stands, motionless, waiting for us."[1] Foucault is closest to Hegel at the precise moment he believes he has taken his leave of Hegel. Historical events are not matters of myths or legends, or of fabulous things said, but instead are events for which documented evidence is available. History is not simply a sequence of events, according to Hegel, but rather it is the narrative of the progressive realization of freedom. That history is progressive is linked to self-consciousness and self-determination. Humans continually understand more fully their social institutions and themselves as their own creations, not as natural or divine givens.

Hegel believes that history is possible only after there is a state. It is only then, he believes, that written chronicles are kept which allow historical events to be distinguished from legends and myths. Hegel categorizes the intertwining of the narration of actual events with legends as "prehistory." He is not claiming that everything which prehistory says occurred did not happen. Without written records, however, it is impossible to distinguish events from legend. Equally important, it is only within a state that freedom can be realized. The modern state provides for subjective freedoms – including individuals having their rights respected by others and having rights against the state. Hegel believes in what Isaiah Berlin refers to as positive liberty. That is to say, freedom in its fullest sense is not primarily the freedom of caprice – individuals' freedom to do as they please – but instead a society where individuals recognize their desires as rational and the laws as embodying this rationality. This requires, of course, that individuals respect the rights of others. Hegel also believes that, for freedom to be actual rather than merely formal, the appropriate social institutions must be in place to allow persons to realize their freedom.

Hegel's narrative of the progressive realization of freedom's flourishing can be described briefly. As we have seen, there are three major periods of world history. In the Oriental World – by this, Hegel refers mainly to areas in the so-called Far and Near East – persons comprehend only that *one person*, the pharaoh or the emperor, is free. In the world of ancient Greece and Rome, people realize that *some persons*, mainly wealthy citizens, are free. However, freedom isn't extended to such persons as slaves, guest workers, traders, and farmers – and these persons may constitute the majority of the population. Finally, in the Germanic World – by "Germanic" Hegel refers to Western Europe, including Britain and Ireland – people now realize that *all persons* are free. In writing this, Hegel is not making the obviously false claim that all persons are actually free. He is instead making a normative claim that all persons are recognized as having a right to freedom.

As just seen, Hegel says that the story of the progressive realization of freedom begins with one individual who is free, moves to some being free, and concludes with all persons being free. Nevertheless, it is crucial to recognize that he doesn't mean this in a purely qualitative sense. As we move from the one, to some, to all, the very conception of freedom – of what freedom consists in and what it requires – changes.

Although there is much to deplore and little to praise in modern colonialism, it actually illustrates Hegel's claims. Even though the colonizers were exploiting the peoples they dominated, they nevertheless recognized that those people had a right to freedom and so felt compelled to rationalize their shenanigans as being in the best interest of the persons they were exploiting. In the Oriental and Greco-Roman Worlds, by contrast, there was no felt need so to rationalize the exploitation of others. Nor were these rationalizations merely lies told to deceive the exploited. The colonizers themselves believed their own rationalizations. Such individuals as Gandhi could argue that the British should "quit India," for example, by taking these rationalizations seriously and insisting that the British live up to them.

It may already be obvious that the notion of freedom itself fundamentally changes throughout history. In the Oriental World, the freedom of the pharaoh is a matter of caprice and whim. More than anyone else, he can do what he wishes to do. His wishes are mere givens, however, and largely don't have a rational structure. Freedom in the modern world, by contrast, involves concepts of human and citizen rights, including rights against the state.

The cunning of reason. At various points, Hegel describes reason as working behind people's backs, manipulating their actions so that, despite their intentions, these people actually further the progressive realization of freedom. He describes this in theological terms, and so unwary readers might believe that he maintains that there is a really existing entity – Reason, or God – who acts to further human freedom. Having already briefly discussed Hegel's views about religion in the *Phenomenology of Spirit*, however, it is clear that such a fanciful account as God using persons to promote freedom can't be his considered view. So, what does Hegel think?

Hegel believes that human actions frequently have unintended by-products and that these can produce consequences which ultimately undermine the intended results of the agents. Julius Caesar and Napoleon may have had as their primary goals self-aggrandizement. Nevertheless, the results of their actions eventually furthered human freedom. This is a tale that can be told only in hindsight, of course, after those unintended by-products have emerged. So, the cunning of reason is an effect produced by telling the history of human freedom, not itself a causal force, although the unintended by-products are.

World-historic individuals. Hegel believes that individuals such as Caesar and Napoleon produce major changes in world history. As already mentioned, furthering freedom is frequently an unintended by-product of their actions.

As seen above, Hegel divides world history into three periods, Oriental, Greco-Roman, and Germanic – put otherwise, into one, some, all. Since we have arrived in the Germanic World, which implicitly recognizes that all persons are entitled to be free, does this mean that history is over? This is certainly the conclusion of many interpreters. Raymond Plant, Alexandre Kojève, Francis Fukuyama, and Barry Cooper all claim that, for Hegel, history is over.[2] In a sense, they are obviously correct: history has ended. Having recognized that *all* persons are entitled to freedom, there is no place to go beyond all. In another and more important sense, however, they are clearly mistaken. For this *all* can be (and, since Hegel's own time, has been) expanded, in terms of both its scope and its content. Let's consider its scope first.

Some of Hegel's texts seem to suggest that he himself would have wished to restrict the *all*'s scope so that it applied only to men, although his other writings suggest that he knew better. In any case, as a descriptive and empirical claim about the political and moral sensibilities of his time, many of his more enlightened contemporaries would have wanted so to restrict this *all*. Since then, fortunately, it has expanded to include women as well as racial and ethnic minorities. It is in the process of expanding further, to embrace those who are physically or mentally challenged and queers (such as transgendered, lesbians, gays, and others). Stateless people, refugees, persons without citizenship, immigrants (legal and illegal), homeless individuals, exiles, enemy combatants, displaced persons – in short, all those whom Giorgio Agamben refers to as the *homo sacer* – are obvious points where the expansion of the *all* hasn't been complete or consistent.[3] Without claiming to summon the future, moreover, we might legitimately speculate that this *all* will eventually expand to take in such non-human creatures as parrots, dolphins, chimpanzees, and other apes. This would transform the very concept of freedom in such a way that it could be intelligibly extended to animals, of course, but that is what already occurred in the progression from one is free, to some are free, to all are free. When persons realize that they must alter their practices so that those practices are consistent with their concept of freedom – when earlier persons recognized no such inconsistency – their concept of freedom has also been revised.

The content of this *all* has expanded too. Many of the rights articulated in the United Nations' International Bill of Human Rights – adequate water, nutrition, housing, health care, education, and clothing – wouldn't have been imagined to be rights by many of Hegel's contemporaries.

There is no reason to believe that the content of the *all* won't continue to expand, and so the concept of freedom transformed, in some cases perhaps in ways so far unimagined.

Perhaps, though, the point about the end of history isn't that the scope and content of the *all* can't be further expanded. Might such interpreters as Plant, Kojève, Fukuyama, and Cooper instead be suggesting that there seems to be no point in further expanding the *all*? Although the goal of obtaining maximum liberty and justice is noble, they might urge, Hegel's society seems to have no goal beyond that. In response, this may be correct, but it is no objection. Individuals would still be free to pursue art, religion, and philosophy, even if society itself has no further goals.

Isaiah Berlin distinguishes between two concepts of liberty.[4] Negative liberty is the freedom from external constraints, the ability to do as one wishes without others interfering. Positive liberty, on the other hand, insists that freedom involves rationality. If a person is acting irrationally, that individual may have negative liberty but lacks positive liberty. Berlin endorses negative liberty but not positive liberty because he worries that injustices and cruelties may be inflected on people in order to force them to be free. Hegel would accept both senses of liberty but would insist that persons are free to do what they want only insofar as their desires are rational.

Hegel is also crucially concerned that freedom be actual rather than merely formal. It does little good and may actually do harm, he would maintain, to say that people have a right to education if there are no schools for them to attend, if they can't afford tuition and books, if they are so impoverished that they must forego education in order to support themselves and their dependants, or if they are too malnourished to pay attention (here the old joke about being too poor to pay attention becomes instead a bitter irony).

Hegel does not believe that the citizens of a state need to share an ethnicity. Indeed, he maintains that Greece and Rome flourished as they did because of their ethnic diversity.[5]

Defending Hegel from objections. Occasionally it is claimed that Hegel is Eurocentric, imperialist, etc., to maintain, as he does, that some societies have realized freedom more than others. These critics actually agree with Hegel, however, and are confused when they object to his claim. They would agree that things would have been morally better if the countries that engaged in exploitative colonialism hadn't done so. A Britain that had done its utmost to work with Indians to promote their interests would have been morally superior to the Britain that actually existed. To concede this, however, is just to agree with Hegel's claim that some societies have realized human freedom more than others. This isn't to assert, of course, that this means that Hegel's views are wholly correct, though it is to say that whatever differences remain are family squabbles.

But Hegel says that Africa and India have no history! Sigh . . . yes, so he does. It may be that he can be legitimately criticized here. If so, however, the grounds for criticism are considerably more subtle than most of his critics recognize. His opinion would be different if he were now asked about how things stand, when the time since his day to the present is considered. To begin a partial defense of Hegel, when he claims that Africa and India have no history, he is writing in the nineteenth century. He speculates that "America is . . . the land of the future, where, in the ages that lie before us, the burden of the World's History shall reveal itself – perhaps in a contest between North and South America."[6] During the twentieth century, America was that land of the future. It is likely that Hegel would now doubt that there is an immanent contest between North and South America, however, and that he would instead suggest that, in the twenty-first century, India is the land of the future and that the contest will be between India and China.[7]

Hegel's critics frequently overlook that, when he talks about history, he means the progressive realization of human freedom. When he denies that Africa and India have histories, he is saying that there has been no progressive realization of freedom in those places. His critics often charge that he overlooks or is ignorant of substantial cities or civilizations that existed in Africa and India. This is irrelevant, however; the question is not whether there were cities or civilizations in Africa and India but instead whether there was a progressive realization of freedom there. Sometimes it is noted that the Indian emperor Akbar (1542–1605) spoke about the importance of freedom. What needs to be asked, of course, is what it means for an emperor to talk about freedom. What content does that have? In any event, while Akbar may have left a legacy to which persons can now return and employ, his innovations didn't outlast him.

Robert Bernasconi has claimed that Hegel's depictions of Africa and his characterizations of its people are racist.[8] However, Hegel claims that the chief reason that Africa has no history is because of its enervating climate. This has nothing to do with race. Hegel would say, moreover, that, if any other society had been in Africa, it would have had relevantly similar experiences. That there are various connections between sub-Saharan Africa and the rest of the world, another point that Bernasconi brings forth to undermine Hegel's views, no more invalidates Hegel's discussion of the former than connections between, say, Canada and the rest of the world would disallow characterizations of Canada. Indeed, were Bernasconi's proposal followed, it would prohibit characterizations of any place whatsoever.

Hegel believes that India lacks a history because its caste system prohibited any substantial realization of human freedom. Again, there is nothing racial about this. Hegel would maintain that freedom in any society with such a caste system would equally have been inhibited.

What would be required to falsify Hegel's claim that Africa and India had no history? One would either have to show that Hegel is mistaken in claiming that there is no substantial "one, some, all are free" trajectory in Africa or India. It is not impossible that evidence for this will be forthcoming, of course, but this line of argument doesn't appear promising. Alternatively, it might be argued that conditions in Africa or India crucially affected the history of the West. (Again, it must be remembered that the history under consideration is the progressive realization of freedom, not any other developments.) So, back to Akbar. Salman Rushdie's novel *The Enchantress of Florence* presents a counterfactual history in which Akbar's policies of religious tolerance and promotion of inter-faith dialogue directly influences the Italian Renaissance.[9] (In *The Theology of Unity*, Muhammad 'Abduh plausibly argues that the values and ideas crucial to the Reformation, and subsequently to the Enlightenment, are derived from Islam.[10]) If something like this were shown to be true of Africa or India, then it could be argued that either does have a history. Hegel himself might still stubbornly maintain that one or other still lacks a history, but he would at least need to concede that Africa or India has influenced world history.

Hegel claims that, like the sun, human freedom begins in the East and sojourns to the West. However, he further maintains that, unlike the sun, freedom doesn't circumnavigate the globe.[11] There are compelling reasons to maintain not only that India has seen freedom circle the world but that it is the land of the future. Writing in the nineteenth century, as noted above, Hegel speculates that America is the land of the future. Writing in the twenty-first century, India seems to be future's land. It is the world's largest democracy. The opportunities and challenges India faces, with so many different traditions, religions, languages, cultures, and dialects – and only to mention its tradition of non-harming, *ahimsa*, vegetarianism – strongly suggest that this is where freedom will next express itself. Although Hegel himself must be criticized in claiming that freedom can never circumnavigate the globe, the larger point is that it is his own philosophy of history that articulates the trajectory that goes beyond his own more parochial views. South Africa's struggles to transcend apartheid also indicate that freedom has circled the world. Indeed, there are now reasons to expect that the West will need to look to the East for freedom's rising.

In the next chapter, on the *Aesthetics: Lectures on Fine Art* and the *Lectures on the Philosophy of Religion*, we will discuss Absolute Spirit.

8

Hegel's Lectures on Philosophy and Religion

Aesthetics

Hegel claims that art is the concept expressed in a sensuous medium. The average person is likely to think, on first hearing this, that this is splendid, while wondering what it means. Let's start with the *concept*.

To simplify things a bit, but not too much, we can say that, for Hegel, the concept is the story that we tell ourselves about our world, both social and natural, and our place in it. This is also the story of who we are, of how we came to be the people we are, and – perhaps most important – of who we aspire to become. Hegel maintains that there is only one concept. Initially, this seems odd. Why couldn't there be many concepts? Or at least two? If we think of the concept as a narrative, however, then the reason is straightforward. Let's imagine for a moment, for the sake of argument, that there were two narratives. How might that happen? Well, we could imagine encountering persons with whom we have had no previous contact. They have their narrative, presumably, and we have ours. Now that we have met them, the new we (that is, us and them) will tell a story that links our two narratives. That narrative, then, will encompass both. And so, Hegel is correct when he claims that there is only one concept.

We could rewrite Hegel's claim about art by saying that it is the narrative expressed in a sensuous medium. Our next step is to comprehend what is meant by a *sensuous medium*.

Let's work backwards for a moment. Hegel will maintain, finally, that this narrative is fully expressed only in the language of philosophy. Philosophy uses concepts that adequately and accurately articulate what is at issue. One level down from philosophy, so to speak, is religion, which expresses the same narrative, but this time in myth. (True, "myth" doesn't quite capture the meaning of Hegel's *Vorstellung*, but translating it as "representational thinking" or "picture thinking" isn't any more helpful; Hegel wanted philosophy to speak German, but let's see if it can speak English too.) Art expresses the narrative, this time two levels down, but now in a medium such as architecture, sculpture, painting, music, or poetry. Each of those is progressively more conceptual – more like a narrative. The *Iliad* can tell us more about who the Greeks understood themselves to be than the Parthenon can, although there is also a sense which – once we learn how the Greeks understood themselves by reading the *Iliad*, *Odyssey*, etc. – we can see that the Parthenon is trying to articulate that too – in stone. But, while the interpretive road between the Parthenon and the *Iliad* may be a two-way street, most of the traffic goes from the latter to the former. That is, we comprehend the Parthenon mainly in light of the *Iliad*.

As we saw in the chapter on his *Philosophy of History*, Hegel divides history into three periods: the Oriental World (where it is recognized that one person is free), the Greco-Roman World (where it is recognized that some are free), and the Germanic World (which recognizes that all are entitled to freedom). These three periods correspond to the three periods into which Hegel divides the history of art: symbolic, classical, and romantic. The symbolic is characterized primarily by architecture. It attempts to express the concept by looking for exemplars in the natural world. The connections, however, are arbitrary. A lion might express courage, for example. The classical looks to sculpture and to the human form itself. The romantic period is characterized by painting and poetry. Especially in poetry, Hegel explains, art develops as far as it can while still remaining art. When it develops further, it passes over into religion. Poetry is the most developed form of art because it is the most conceptual. Poetry could consist not only of the rhymed verse that we initially think of as poetry but also of novels.

There are two points here that are important. First, for Hegel, art is cognitive. That is, art is saying something, or at least attempting to say something, that can be expressed conceptually. This is in contrast to other views on art which see it as primarily a matter of emotions, either as an expression of the artist's feelings or as seeking to provoke an emotional response in the audience. The concept expressed by art, according to Hegel, is different because it is an expression of the self-understanding of a culture or an era. In this sense, Hegel's view is neither a theory of authorial intention, where a work of art means what its creator intends, nor a form of reader response, where a work's meaning is how its contemporary audience understands it.

The second point to note is that Hegel believes that art has a developmental *history*. The history of art is no mere chronicle of change but, rather, the story of art's successively more adequate attempts to articulate the concept. Hegel also believes that advances in art are consequences of perceived inadequacies in its previous forms. Experiencing the limitations of articulating the concept in architecture, for example, persons turn to sculpture and later to painting.

As Hegel claims that philosophy is an age expressed in thought, so art is that age expressed in a sensuous medium, and religion – as we will soon see – is that age expressed in myth.

A couple of other points are worth noting. First, when a form of art is superseded, it isn't abandoned but continues to be practiced. Perhaps the most obvious example of this is architecture. Although other forms of art subsequently emerged which more adequately express the concept, we are not now all living outdoors. Second, although art at its highest level passes over into religion, and religion into philosophy, all three develop together.

What about Hegel's celebrated, or notorious, thesis regarding the end of art? What does it mean? And what reasons might support it? As noted a moment ago, Hegel believes that art at its highest level, romantic art, can't progress any further. Insofar as progress then occurs, art is transformed into religion. So, it seems that Hegel believes that art ends with the romantic period – not that persons will stop producing art or cease admiring, enjoying, and collecting it. Rather, his point is that art is incapable of any further *conceptual* development after the romantic period. There, it expresses the concept as adequately as it is capable of doing. Were Hegel to be presented with supposed counter-examples, whereby art articulates the concept in ways that go beyond that of romantic art, his strategy would likely be to urge that these are really instances of romantic art, after all, or that they have passed over into religion.

Very well, critics might reply, but what about various forms of non-representational art, twelve-tone composition, postmodern art? Surely these are not romantic, the critics would press, nor is it plausible to claim that they are not art but religion. Don't these forms of art then express the concept in ways that go beyond romantic art without thereby ceasing to be art? Doesn't this disprove Hegel's end-of-art thesis? And doesn't this finally mean that we have finally found one point where we can say unequivocally that Hegel is wrong?!

No, of course not. As attentive readers will already have anticipated, Hegel is always right. And, even when he is wrong, his philosophy provides the resources to correct him. Unlike his comments in the *Philosophy of History* – about freedom, unlike the sun, not circumnavigating the globe – where we had to employ the trajectory of his philosophy to correct his provincial claims, here we can argue that he is correct. How so? To return to the *Philosophy of History* for a moment, we saw that there is a sense in which history is over when we arrive in the Germanic World. That is to say, once we realize that *all* persons are entitled to freedom, there is nowhere to go beyond all. Game's over! In a sense. However, we also saw that there is another sense in which history continues, because both the scope and the content of the *all* can expand. Hold that thought. We will return to it shortly.

Although the romantic is an advance beyond the classical, Hegel maintains that the classical expresses its own age more completely than the romantic does. How can this be? The classical expresses the harmony, wholeness, and sense of completeness to which its age aspires. This aspiration couldn't be realized, however, because there were internal tensions, contradictions, within that society that it lacked the resources to reconcile or overcome. We saw this with *Antigone*. Antigone appeals to the laws of the family, Creon to the laws of the state. Both are correct, in a sense, but each is also partial and one-sided. And so, their conflict is tragic. Classical art exhibits what its age is – not so much in fact, but in aspiration. To use terminology that is foreign to Hegel, classical art renders perfectly not the actually existing circumstances of its age but, rather, the ideology of its age – an ideology that exists both to legitimate and make bearable those circumstances.

When we come to the romantic period, though, we discover a lack of such a perfect rendering of its era. Why? Because the harmony, completeness, totality to which the classical period aspired has been abandoned. The tensions that the earlier period couldn't reconcile or overcome are now accepted and negotiated by being placed into a ranked hierarchy whereby, for example, the claims of the state trump the claims of the family. Romantic art itself expresses such tensions within itself, and so it simultaneously advances beyond the classical while also being less perfect.

So, back to non-representational art, twelve-tone composition, etc. Since these are innovations that extend art beyond what was available in Hegel's day, it is tempting to conclude that his end-of-art thesis must be rejected. And, insofar as these are viewed as actual advances rather than as regressions or just more of the same old same old, then again there is a strong temptation to say that the end-of-art thesis must be rejected. Okay, we can smoke, drink, and do drugs, if we must, but we should certainly resist temptation. I suggest that we regard these innovations and advancements in art not as going beyond romantic art but, rather, as extending its scope and content. This is so because the world which these arts express – our world – is fundamentally similar to Hegel's. In a sense, Hegel is our contemporary. We have no more been able to overcome the tensions that exist in our society than people in Hegel's day were able to transcend theirs. Like them, we have largely abandoned any prospect of overcoming those tensions, or even believing that such overcoming would be desirable. Instead, we accept that the tensions cannot be transcended but only negotiated. And our art expresses this.

Religion

As is the case with world history and art, for Hegel, religion has a developmental history. Earlier forms of religion are experienced as inadequate and give way to progressively more developed forms. This culminates in Protestant Christianity, the revealed or consummate religion. A point that must be noted, which may already be apparent to readers, is that religions which are superseded don't cease to exist, for the most part, but instead continue. So, Hegel places Hinduism at an early stage, for example, but today it still has more than a billion followers. Another point, perhaps also evident, is that, although art passes over into religion at its highest point of development, in romantic art, art and religion emerge and develop together. As a consequence, I suggest that Hegel's claims regarding art transforming into religion be seen not only as asserting a historical or chronological thesis, but also as an articulation of a logical or conceptual thesis about the relation of art and religion. The sensuous medium in which the concept is expressed in art becomes progressively less sensuous until it reaches a point where the medium is thought itself – thought that nonetheless is embedded in myth, in the case of religion, not the myth-free thinking of philosophy.

What is mythical about religion? As we saw in the previous chapter, "myth" is not quite an accurate translation of Hegel's *Vorstellung*, but "representational thinking" or "picture thinking," or sticking with the German, don't seem to be obvious improvements. They avoid the misleading connotations associated with "myth" – such as that we are dealing with stories that are primarily fanciful and false – but they avoid those connotations by themselves not carrying any clear sense. So, let's stick with "myth" and ask what characterizes it. What primarily characterizes it, for Hegel, is the belief that there is some distance between the divine and the human.

Hegel is often criticized for what is perceived as his provincialism in claiming that Christianity is the highest form of religion – and not just Christianity in general, but Lutheran Protestantism. What about Roman Catholicism or, casting the net wider, Islam, Buddhism, or Hinduism? What makes Christianity better than these? In order to respond to these sensible questions, I need simultaneously to simplify to the extreme and enter into interpretive stormy waters. But first, some context. After Hegel's death in 1831, his followers divide into two opposing groups: the Right and the Left Hegelians. The former are religiously and politically more conservative, interpreting Hegel as supporting the status quo Prussian monarchy and as being an orthodox Lutheran, while the latter believe him to be more liberal. As readers might expect, both factions missed the full truth, being partial and one-sided in their comprehension and appropriation of Hegel.

To explain Hegel's view within the language of myth, he believes that the distance between humans and God is reflected back into God. God's incarnation as Jesus is intended to overcome both distances: God from humanity as well as God from Himself. Hegel sees the incarnation as the pivotal moment in human history. It results, in Christianity, in a new emphasis on the individual, including the rights that individuals possess merely by virtue of their being human. The movement in world history from the Greco-Roman World's comprehension that *some* (citizens) are entitled to freedom to the Germanic World's realization that *all* are so entitled is directly occasioned by the incarnation and subsequent development of Christianity. So, in this sense, then, Hegel himself isn't a Left Hegelian. He doesn't believe that the incarnation tells us something that is timelessly true of all persons, informing and illustrating for us the divine spark within each of us. That's Gnosticism, not Hegel. Rather, he thinks that the incarnation is an absolutely unique event. It only happened once and, indeed, it could only happen once. In Jesus, the Christ, God becomes fully human. The Right Hegelians are vindicated but, as we are about to see, in a way that would deeply disturb them. In more traditional forms of Christianity, God is thought to be a trinity of persons: God the Father, Son, and Holy Spirit. And so, when Jesus is crucified, the Son dies, but the other two do not. Moreover, the Son doesn't cease to exist but instead – according to the Church's various confessions of faith – goes to hell to set the captives there free. Hegel's own view is much darker than this, although also, in a sense, more liberatory. Although he doesn't repudiate the trinity, his view is that God becomes fully incarnated in Jesus, with no remainder or leftover. The God who created the universe now becomes a human who, empirically, is no different or more remarkable than anyone else. When Jesus dies, God dies too – and ceases to exist! In a sense, then, atheism is true. But, while atheists believe that God never existed, for Hegel, He once did. This isn't the end of the story, however, because there is a resurrection. What rises is not Jesus. His body is still in some forgotten grave. Instead, what arises is the believing community that worships God as well as whose members mutually and lovingly support each other. And so, there is a sense in which God continues to exist. There's no afterlife, however, other than the memories that remain.

I said a moment ago that Hegel's vision is quite dark. This is so because, with God's death, we lose any moral realism as this is usually understood. For atheists often still believe that, although there is no God, nevertheless there exists some moral absolutes, that we are accountable to _____ – and here one may fill in the blank with a variety of things: morality, the world, the human community, family, the nation. Even Jean-Paul Sartre, that intrepid existentialist, blinked from accepting the full consequences of his atheism by saying that, although individuals decide what their ethics are, their choices are necessarily universal and so apply to all persons. This residual Kantianism can have no place in a consistent atheism, of course, which rather would have to maintain that we are accountable only to those things to which we hold ourselves accountable – and only for as long as we do so. Do I need to add that God's death also represents the loss of any purpose beyond those that we fix for ourselves?

Hegel consistently portrays himself as an orthodox Lutheran. Is there any justification for this? Indeed there is. It is possible to regard Hegel as extending certain ideas already advanced by Luther – although Luther himself might be startled and displeased to see his ideas extended in this way. Luther believes that God is revealed only through Jesus Christ. What God may be like apart from this, or what God's essence might be, is wholly unknowable and unfathomable. It is only a slight extension of this idea – "slight," of course, from a certain perspective – to say that God wholly incarnates himself in Jesus Christ so that, when he dies, God dies too. In Luther's view, there is more than the suggestion that behind what God reveals to us in Jesus Christ remains the inscrutable mystery of God as He really is. The question to be put to Luther, though, is: "Given that all that can be known of and about God is what is revealed in Jesus Christ, why should we believe that there is any remainder left over?" Hegel would urge that there is no such reason. As a result, his claim that God wholly empties Himself into Jesus can be regarded as extending Luther's own view, and so Hegel can plausibly maintain that he is an orthodox Lutheran.

Earlier I said that a consistent atheism would need to purge itself of any residual Kantianism which would maintain that we are accountable to anything beyond ourselves. Schelling thinks this too, of course, but he finds it terrifying, referring to it as the *abyss* of freedom. We are so free that we can even choose to destroy ourselves. This gives Schelling the willies. Although Hegel seems to have had his dark depressive moments, the chief theme that emerges from his philosophy is an optimism that could be described as cheerful – even gay.[1] Yes, he admits that history can be seen as a slaughter bench. Yes, he concedes that happy periods don't leave a mark on history because these are the times when nothing much happens. Still, he looks to the future not with fear, trepidation, or loathing, but rather with a sense of eager expectation. Why is this? Why can he seemingly shrug his shoulders at the freedom which Schelling regards as a frightening abyss? Is he stupid? No, he's just again following Luther.

Luther maintains that there are two kingdoms: the kingdom of heaven and the kingdom of earth. However – and here is where Luther is startlingly radical – far from the kingdom of heaven having a claim on us, Jesus Christ frees us to be fully agents in the earthly kingdom. Surprising as this may be, Luther doesn't believe that God tells us what to do. Instead, He leaves things up to us. And, since God trusts us, we ought to have confidence in ourselves.

Hegel follows this theme. We can regard the future with expectation, not dread, because it will be our own creation. And we should trust ourselves.

At this point, we must return to a point discussed already in the chapters on Hegel's *Philosophy of History* and *Philosophy of Right*: his philosophy is not primarily descriptive but rather constitutes an intervention. To be cheerful in facing the future is to believe that we can and will do what is required in order that the future, which will have been our own creation, will be something to be proud of. If we have any doubts about this, which we may, then we must act now so that the future, when it arrives – when what is now future becomes present – will be welcomed. Where, because we are free to do anything, Schelling gazes into an abyss that inspires vertigo, Hegel is hopeful and cheery.

It follows from Hegel's account that religion is subservient to the state. What counts as religion and which of its expressions are acceptable is something for the state to decide. To put it crudely, perhaps, but not inaccurately, the state says to God: if you want to live here, you must obey our laws, follow our customs, and behave yourself. But what of freedom of religion? All sensible people agree that the state can prohibit expressions of what are claimed to be religious: human sacrifice and cannibalism would be obvious examples. What about religion's prophetic witness to the state, speaking truth to power? Religion certainly can play that role, perhaps must play it, but again it is the state which will have decided which expressions of prophecy will have been acceptable. This is so, even when prophesy results in changes in the state's structures or policies. In the concluding chapter, we will see what happens after Hegel.

9

After Hegel

In this chapter, I discuss how Hegel's philosophy continues after his death in 1831. Before I begin doing that, though, I would like to say a few words about interpretation. First, a distinction can be made between two differing approaches to a historical figure. The first would believe that there is a single correct meaning of that person's text and that the goal of interpretation is to discover that meaning. Often, that meaning is said to consist in the author's intentions. Here, the goal is to discover what the author was attempting to communicate. Occasionally, meaning is instead said to consist in the contemporary readers' response. In this case the goal is to discover not what the author intended but, rather, how the author's text was understood by his or her contemporaries. Both of these assume that there is a single correct interpretation and that the goal is to discover it. In marked contrast stands another approach, which claims that a text has multiple and contradictory interpretations. This approach abandons the view that a text has a single correct meaning. Indeed, on this approach, an interpretation of a text becomes an aspect of the text itself. On this approach, the correct interpretation of a text, if we can still speak of such a thing, would consist in the history of its interpretations. Since there could be conflicting histories, however, there is no prospect that there could be a single correct meaning. This approach is the one that I follow. Rather than seeking the truth of Hegel's texts, we will watch what becomes of them after Hegel. It could be expanded to include, in addition to explicit interpretations – as in Roland Barthes' essay "From Work to Text" – whatever is

occasioned by the text.[1] These can be both positive responses that
continue the text in another discursive domain and negative
responses that oppose or check the text. Here, all texts become,
finally, aspects of one text.

After Hegel's death, those influenced by him split into two
groups, the so-called Right Hegelians and the Left Hegelians (also
referred to as the Young Hegelians). The Right Hegelians interpret
Hegel as an orthodox Lutheran and as a political conservative
whose philosophy defends the status quo. The Left Hegelians, by
contrast, read him as an atheist and as implicitly challenging the
status quo. The truth is somewhere in the middle, of course, but is
closer to the Left Hegelians.

Partially to oppose Hegel's influence, especially in its Left Hegelian version, Friedrich Wilhelm Joseph Schelling (1775–1854) lec-
tured at the University of Berlin after Hegel's death. According to
Schelling, Hegel's philosophy is merely a thought experiment where
concepts are generated without any connection to empirical reality.
To this, Schelling opposes his own "Positive Philosophy," which
begins with the fact of existence. He believes that reason can determine, a priori, the essential properties that a thing would have *if* it
existed, and he concedes that Hegel's philosophy can tell us this.
However, he claims that reason cannot know whether that thing
exists. To know that something exists requires a sensuous representation (*Vorstellung*), whereby that thing is presented to thought
through, for example, sense experience. On this interpretation,
Hegel generates his *Logic* entirely conceptually, without any contact
with empirical reality, by linking concepts to each other. Although
there are contemporary scholars who interpret Hegel in this way, I
have urged that his *Logic* is grounded in the history of Western
thought, and so it does have the empirical component that Schelling
believes is lacking.

Søren Aabye Kierkegaard (1813–1855) attended Schelling's lectures, and his criticisms of Hegel are frequently based in Schelling's
interpretation. Kierkegaard believes that Hegel emphasizes the universal at the expense of the individual, so that the individual is
wholly lost. He seeks to reverse this by focusing on the individual.
The problem with this approach, from a Hegelian perspective, is
that the individual is only such within a greater whole and that
privileging either the individual or the greater whole is a one-sided
distortion that misses how they mutually determine each other.
Kierkegaard also seeks to return to an authentic Christianity with
an immediate relation to God, and so he opposes Hegel's attempt

to comprehend Christianity as a historical religion that emerges through a historical development.

Ludwig Andreas von Feuerbach (1804–1872) could be seen as standing for everything that Kierkegaard opposes. A Left Hegelian, Feuerbach claims that what Hegel shows is that humans have created God by projecting onto that construct all of their ennobling qualities, leaving humanity's less desirable characteristics to themselves. The present task, Feuerbach believes, is for humans to realize that humanity itself is the only God there is or that would be needed. Since states and churches have often supported their oppressive dictates by asserting that these are God's will, Feuerbach holds that recognizing that humanity is itself divine will be socially and politically liberating. This is fully compatible with Hegelianism, Feuerbach maintains, urging that what was hidden and implicit in Hegel is now manifest and explicit in his own philosophy.

Karl Heinrich Marx (1818–1883) breaks with the Young Hegelians because he believes that they follow what he regards as Hegel's error of believing that ideas cause social and political change. Material conditions, primarily economic conditions, cause change, Marx holds, and ideas follow those changes. Ideas don't just appear but instead arise when people think about something. And what people think about, in the first instance, is their own lived conditions. Even when they imagine alternatives, what they imagine is rooted in their conditions. (People who live in a desert might imaginatively long for a better place where there is plenty of water, but that won't figure in the imaginings of those who live next to a lake.) Marx believes that the Young Hegelians fail to recognize that religious beliefs are grounded in social conditions and that those beliefs can be fundamentally altered, not through critique, but only through changing the social conditions which support them. Whereas Hegel believes that modern society is an articulated whole – consisting of the family, civil society, and the state – Marx claims that society is split into two factions, the bourgeoisie and the proletariat. To simplify, the former are the capitalists, those who own property to rent and the means of production such as factories; the latter are those who must sell their labor power to survive. These two factions have opposed interests – what benefits one, harms the other – and so Marx denies that modern society is a whole or that there is a *common* good. Recent scholarship has suggested that Hegel's views are closer to those of Marx than the latter realized. Hegel also allows a considerable role to social forces. Nevertheless, he believes that persons can rationally endorse the basic institutions of modern society, whereas Marx believes that those institutions benefit only the bourgeoisie and so need to be abolished. There is this to be said for Marx's view: Hegel claims that the modern state can be rationally endorsed, yet he also recognizes that its economic system generates poverty and envisions no mechanism to correct this; he can only suggest that the poor beg. It may be that the economic policies of John Maynard Keynes (1883–1946) would be sufficient to overcome this problem in capitalism. But we might agree with Marx that no system that creates an impoverished class is rational.

Although Marx disagrees with Hegel's assessment of capitalism and the modern state, he does adopt Hegel's logic of relations and his teleological approach to history. As we have seen, Hegel believes that things are what they are because of their relations to other things. So, when Marx analyzes capitalism, he comprehends it as a system of relations. Capitalists and workers act the way they do because of the demands of the economic system in which they are embedded. It is not necessarily that individual capitalists are greedy people who want to pay their workers subsistence wages, for example; rather, capitalists are forced to do this to maintain their profit margins, and they will be driven out of business by their competitors if they don't.

Marx also seems to believe not only that the economic systems that preceded capitalism, such as feudalism, were necessary in order for capitalism to emerge but also that capitalism was inevitable. He suggests, moreover, that capitalism's demise is necessary too. I have argued that Hegel's own concept of necessity is entirely retrospective. Given a specific shape of consciousness, its predecessors are necessary in the sense that, had they been different, that specific shape would be different too. This concept of necessity is compatible with its contingency. That a specific shape exists entails that its predecessors occurred. They might not have happened, though, and then that shape wouldn't exist. Marx, however, seems to believe that the preconditions were necessary if capitalism were to occur but also that those preconditions were themselves necessary. While Hegel maintains that we can see retrospectively that history has been the progressive realization of freedom, Marx claims that there is a prospective necessity to the emergence of capitalism.

Friedrich Wilhelm Nietzsche (1844–1900) may be seen as implicitly correcting Marx's misinterpretation of Hegel's teleology and as returning to a position that is closer to Hegel's own. Nietzsche does not recognize that this is close to Hegel's position, however, and so he believes that he is rejecting Hegel. Let me talk first about an aspect of Nietzsche's thought that has not yet reached the level that Hegel obtained and then about another aspect that is compatible with Hegel's.

Nietzsche argues at various places that humans may be incapable of obtaining the truth about nature. Instead, he urges, humans have acquired useful beliefs. There is no reason to assume, though, that a belief's being useful entails that it is true. This skepticism that humans are capable of obtaining truth is frequently lauded by persons influenced by postmodernism, believing that it is an adequate response to the arrogance of Western imperialism and scientism. Nietzsche's approach, if generalized, would introduce again Kant's distinction between things as we experience them and things as they actually are in themselves apart from our experience of them. The arrogant could happily concede that how things really are in themselves may be ultimately unknowable while still asserting scientism as correct for things as they are experienced. Hegel, following Fichte, is correct to reject the distinction between things as they are in themselves and things as they are experienced, maintaining instead that we actually experience things as they are in themselves.

Where Nietzsche is compatible with Hegel is in his genealogical approach. Things have histories, Nietzsche urges, and what a thing is now may have little relation to its antecedents. He argues that modern morality, for example, isn't ahistorical. Instead, what it developed from is scarcely recognizable as morality. The heroes of Homer's *Iliad* and *Odyssey* follow what Nietzsche designates as master morality. This is a code of conduct that differentiates them, as masters, from others. The chief imperative is that each hero should strive to be superior to all other heroes. Whereas modern morality is thought to be universal, specifying rights and responsibilities that apply to all human beings, master morality is class or caste based, applying only to specific individuals. What Nietzsche refers to as slave morality, which he identifies with Judaism and Christianity, arises among those classes that are socially inferior to the members of master morality. Slave morality arises from resentment towards the perceived ill-treatment received from the heroes. Whereas a hero strives to exalt himself – master morality is masculine – over other heroes, the members of slave morality believe that no one should be superior to anyone else. Nietzsche argues that modern morality is grounded in slave morality, that its professed concern for the equality of all persons actually masks a hatred of any pre-eminence in others.

Such a story is, in broad outline, compatible with Hegel's view of history. As we have seen in Hegel's account of freedom – where the Oriental World knows that one (the pharaoh) is free, the Greco-Roman World that some (citizens) are free, and the Germanic World that all are free – freedom initially is tyranny and caprice. The Oriental World's comprehension of freedom is the pharaoh's ability to follow impulse, not his acting on rational considerations. So, Hegel would not be hostile to Nietzsche's suggestion that modern institutions developed from earlier forms that we now regard as politically and morally unacceptable. Where they differ is the consequences they draw from this. Hegel and Nietzsche both agree that a thing can develop beyond its origin and so can become some other thing. Nevertheless, Nietzsche seems to think that he is revealing the truth of modern morality, displaying what it really is, when he tracks it back to slave morality's resentful rebellion against master morality. By contrast, Hegel would say that whether modern morality deserves our endorsement is a question of what it currently is, not what its ancestors were.

Although it is not as famous as British Idealism, which I will discuss in a moment, there was also American Hegelianism. There were the Ohio Hegelians – Peter Kaufmann (1800–1869), August Willich (1810–1878), John Bernhard Stallo (1823–1900), and Moncure Daniel Conway (1832–1907) – as well as the St Louis Hegelians – Henry Conrad Brokmeyer (1828–1906), William Torrey Harris (1835–1909), Thomas Davidson (1840–1900), and Denton Snider (1841–1925). While there were many similarities and connections between these persons and the American Transcendentalists, the Hegelians believed that the Transcendentalists focused attention unduly on the individual and so missed the importance of society. Although their views are different enough that they can't be considered a school, these Hegelians attempted to interpret America's history in light of Hegel's philosophy, seeing the Civil War, for example, in light of the lord/bondsman section of the *Phenomenology of Spirit*. Unfortunately, these Hegelians had little direct influence on subsequent philosophy in America. I should also mention Josiah Royce (1855–1916), an idealist who taught at Harvard University for many years. Rejecting Hegel's absolute, as he interpreted it, Royce developed a concept of an absolute knower who encompasses all knowledge and error of the past and present, who exists in time, who develops through time, and who is best understood through the category of "person." Royce believed that it is only within a community that there can be individuals – a view that is influenced by Hegel, although it misses that Hegel denies that communities are logically prior to individuals, maintaining instead that both are mutually co-determining – and Royce developed a notion of the "beloved community" whose members would be committed fully to loyalty and truth.

The American pragmatist and naturalist John Dewey (1859–1952) could be seen as a Hegelian who accepted Hegel's account of society and history, while rejecting Hegel's absolute as he interpreted it. Like Hegel, Dewey argued that individuals and society are mutually self-constituting, and so he rejected any attempt to reduce one to the other. Dewey also believed that knowledge must be understood in terms of what a given society counts as knowledge rather than transhistorical or ahistorical standards. However, he did not accept the concept of an absolute, and he denied that there is necessarily progress in history. Whether there is progress depends on what sort of society people create for themselves.

The leading exponents of British Hegelianism, also known as British Idealism, were Edward Caird (1835–1908), Thomas Hill Green (1836–1882), William Wallace (1844–1897), Francis Herbert Bradley (1846–1924), Bernard Bosanquet (1848–1923), John Henry Muirhead (1855–1940), John McTaggart (1866–1925), Harold Henry Joachim (1868–1938), Robin George Collingwood (1889–1943), and Geoffrey Reginald Gilchrist Mure (1893–1979). They believed that the Absolute is an all-encompassing system that is simultaneously epistemological and metaphysical, and not only that reason can reveal the Absolute, but that reason is the Absolute. Rejecting dualism, they adopted a monism where thought and the object of thought are ultimately identical. These philosophers were influenced by Kant and Schelling as much as they were by Hegel, and so this movement is best referred to as British Idealism. As may be clear from this brief description, the Absolute of British Idealism is closer to Schelling's than to Hegel's. Whereas Hegel sought to articulate an Absolute that would preserve difference within an overarching identity, British Idealism placed so much emphasis on identity as to risk losing difference.

This is important in understanding the rejection of Hegelianism by Bertrand Russell (1872–1970) and George Edward Moore (1873–1958). It is often believed that Analytic Philosophy began by decisively refuting Hegel's philosophy. Insofar as Analytic Philosophy refuted anything, it was British Idealism, not Hegel. What is generally overlooked is that the position from which Analytic Philosophers criticized British Idealism was a version of Platonism, according to which true propositions are facts that have a real existence that is independent of thought. This position was later substantially modified. Analytic Philosophers generally didn't return to the earlier criticism of British Idealism to see whether it could it be cogently reformulated from the modified position.

There are three points to make here. First, a philosophy's influence can be positive or negative. That is, subsequent thinkers may believe that a philosophy was correct, or at least proceeding in the correct direction, and so they may seek to extend it further. Alternatively, thinkers may believe that a philosophy was mistaken and so argue against it. Early Analytic Philosophy is influenced by British Idealism – and so, indirectly, by Hegel – in this second, negative, way. Nevertheless, negative influence can decisively shape the direction taken by an opposing philosophy. It is unlikely that Analytic Philosophers would have developed their version of Platonism, for example, had they not been concerned to overthrow British Idealism. Second, when a philosophy has been criticized on the basis of premises which are subsequently abandoned or modified, then the criticism must be reformulated or withdrawn. This might seem an obvious point, but it is surprising how often it is overlooked. In the case of Analytic Philosophy's criticisms of British Idealism, this oversight almost certainly occurred because Analytic Philosophers weren't in sympathy with British Idealism, as they understood it, and so weren't seeking to defend it. Rather, they had already decided that it wasn't acceptable, and so it didn't occur to them that the earlier criticisms were now inadequate. Finally, students were told and accepted that British Idealism wasn't viable, and so British Idealism wasn't rehabilitated. Only in recent years has this changed, as Analytic Philosophy itself has become part of the history of philosophy.

Moreover, now there is Analytic Hegelianism! Wilfrid Stalker Sellars (1912–1989) was one of the giants of Analytic Philosophy, and, unlike others, he had no hostility to the history of philosophy in general or to German Idealism in particular. One point at which Sellars's thought touched Hegel's philosophy was in his rejection of what he referred to as "the myth of the given," unconceptualized presences or bare facts, which Russell denoted as "knowledge by acquaintance" as opposed to "knowledge by description." Sellars denied that individuals can have immediate knowledge – knowledge unmediated by concepts – of external objects, internal sensations, or logical axioms. In this, he was in agreement with one of the main themes of the section on "Sense-Certainty" in Hegel's *Phenomenology of Spirit*. Sellars also was Hegelian in recognizing that what appear to be our most basic beliefs and experiences – that we have minds and thoughts, for example – have actually emerged historically.

Influenced by Sellars, John Henry McDowell (b. 1942) and Robert Brandom (b. 1950) are the main Analytic Hegelians. McDowell is more concerned to articulate the implications of the rejection of any perceptual given. Following Sellars, who followed Hegel, McDowell rejects the Kantian distinction between intuition and concept. It is not that first there is experience that is then conceptualized. Rather, what is experienced is experienced as conceptualized. We don't first have an experience and then apply a concept to recognize that it is a chair that is the object of our experience – to give a simple example – instead, we directly experience the chair as a chair. The conceptual encompasses and permeates the experiential; the "logical space of reasons" is unbounded. So, our perspective is "sideways on." While I must confess that I don't fully understand that metaphor, it is clear that, for McDowell, there is no point where the process of giving reasons is based on something that is itself not a reason (such as unconceptualized sense experience). Even when we appeal to experience, that experience is conceptual.

Brandom seeks to make explicit the consequences of rejecting any logical given. Linking his discussion to Hegel's views on recognition, Brandom argues that the practice of giving reasons is social. Which considerations could count as reasons are determined by the community, and so the practice of giving reasons has a normative component. We recognize that someone knows something, Brandom urges, when that person is able to make relevant inferences. So, we accept that a child knows what chartreuse is – while a non-human animal does not know this, even if the animal can reliably detect chartreuse – if the child comprehends that chartreuse is a color, that it's not a sound, that an object that's completely chartreuse can't also be red, and so forth. Brandom sees his own project as broadly Hegelian – making explicit the rules and norms we implicitly follow.

There are two points where Analytic Hegelianism is not yet fully Hegelian. First, as Tom Rockmore (b. 1942) notes,[2] Analytic Hegelianism does not comprehend the importance of history, focusing attention on the present logical space of reasons with its accompanying normativity without acknowledging that these have developed. This both causes it to overlook the ways in which the logical space of reasons and normativity are historical achievements and leads to its downplaying the extent to which the logical space of reasons is a contested space, where dissensus occurs as often as consensus. Finally, this leads to its missing the issues of power which Foucault underscored. Giving reasons is a normative practice, as Analytic Hegelianism perceives. However, those who consistently violate those norms are regarded as insane or cranks – which they may be, but they also may be visionaries or prophets, developing new ways of thinking that follow new norms of reasoning. The norms that we follow are frequently in tension, if not contradiction, with each other. The practice of making explicit is not neutral, then, but instead is an active even if surreptitious intervention. By asserting that certain norms are actually the ones that we implicitly follow, while ignoring or marginalizing others, the practice of making norms explicit also prescribes those norms. (This practice may be acceptable as a rhetorical strategy of persuasion; however, if philosophers believe that they are merely engaged in a process of making explicit what we already do, then they may be endorsing an ideology and overlooking potentially emancipatory alternatives to it.) These limitations aren't incorrigible, as Rockmore worries, but they are points where Analytic Hegelianism remains one-sided.

Second, Analytic Hegelianism advances a non-metaphysical interpretation of Hegel's philosophy. That is, it foregrounds Hegel's discussions on normativity – social, logical, and ethical – but neglects or denies the metaphysical aspects of his philosophy. There seem to be two main reasons for this. First, Analytic Hegelianism isn't especially interested in metaphysics. Fair enough, but this risks missing the ways in which Hegel's views on normativity are grounded in his metaphysics. It is not that the former can't be studied, but that it can't be fully comprehended without the latter. Second, Analytic Hegelianism believes that Hegel's metaphysics is too fantastic to be credible. It must be conceded that Hegel's metaphysics departs significantly from untutored common sense on a number of issues – but no more than such philosophically respectable metaphysics as the eliminative materialism of Paul Churchland (b. 1942) and Patricia Smith Churchland (b. 1943), the modal realism of David Kellogg Lewis (1941–2001), or the panpsychism of Galen John Strawson (b. 1952). Moreover, Hegel's own views can frequently be described as extensions or radicalizations of contemporary Anglo-American philosophy. When Hegel's metaphysical views are neglected because they are believed to be too fantastic, it is often because people haven't fully acknowledged how fantastic contemporary metaphysics can be.

Reading the plays and epigrams of Oscar Wilde (1854–1900), it is obvious that he learned the art of dialectical reversal from Hegel. The positing of the presuppositions that Wilde attributes to the Prodigal Son in *De Profundis*, the greatest letter ever written, is thoroughly Hegelian. Wilde's *Soul of Man under Socialism* is a continuation of Hegel's *Philosophy of Right*.

Vladimir Ilyich Lenin (1870–1924) may be considered the first Hegelian Marxist. In his Conspectus of Hegel's *Science of Logic*, Lenin abandoned his earlier reflection theory of knowledge, according to which knowledge consists in a reflective correspondence with the external world, and recognizes the importance of the knower's own knowing activities in the constitution of what is known.[3] He further recognized that "real" and "ideal" are concepts that are mutually co-determining and that his own previous view that they were in strict opposition was unwarranted. Lenin argued that social change occurs because of a society's internal contradictions. More fundamentally, he learned from Hegel the importance of positing the presuppositions. That is, rather than waiting for the right moment to engage in revolutionary activity, Lenin recognized that revolutionary activity would generate the right moment for it to have occurred. György Lukács (1885–1971) continued Lenin's line of argument. Lukács rejected theories of economic determinism, claiming rather that it is the notion of totality, seeing how things are constituted because of their relations to each other and to the whole of which they are members, that is essential to Marxism.

The Frankfurt School consisted of German thinkers who argued that Marxism alone was inadequate to explain why workers supported fascism and that Marxist categories needed to be supplemented by those of Freud. Herbert Marcuse (1898–1979) argued that Hegel's own philosophical method, if not his specific views, were rightly seen as preparing the way for Marx.[4] Marcuse was especially concerned to refute the claim that Hegel's philosophy is allied with fascism or authoritarianism. Rather, what is crucial to Hegel, Marcuse urged, is dialectical thinking – the ability to negate and challenge presently existing conditions. Theodor W. Adorno (1903–1969) further claimed that Hegel's dialectical method should terminate in its negative moment and not continue to a synthesis. Simplifying to the extreme, Adorno believed that capitalism (thesis) could be critiqued and contested and its internal contradictions exposed (antithesis), but that any proposed synthesis would actually be a rearticulation of the thesis in other terms. This is so because the concepts employed to develop a synthesis would be those developed under capitalist conditions, and so those concepts would still implicitly presuppose those conditions. Still simplifying, Jürgen Habermas (b. 1929) argues that Hegel lacks the resources to reconcile the many diverse tendencies of modern thought and society. According to Habermas, Hegel merely asserts that reason will reconcile these tendencies – indeed, that they have already been reconciled and that all that is required is the recognition of that reconciliation – but that his notion of reason is not sufficiently communicative and dialogic. The beginning of a dialogue with Habermas would be to respond that Hegel's philosophy actually is dialogic. It not only describes previous dialogues and reports their outcomes, it also engages in advocacy which readers can either endorse or contest.

Martin Heidegger (1889–1976) is often contrasted with Hegel in a way that is not useful. Hegel's concept of Being in the *Logic* is the emptiest of concepts, indistinguishable from nothing, while Heidegger's Being is the richest of concepts. True, but the analogue in Hegel's philosophy to Heidegger's Being is Spirit, *Geist* (or, if someone insists on staying with the *Logic*, the Absolute Idea).

Heidegger charged that Hegel's concept of time is inauthentic. It is a mere sequence of nows rather than originary, lived, and experienced temporality. Heidegger argued that the felt experience of temporality is primary, while thinking of time in terms of hours and days – where the content of one day varies from that of another, but the time of one day is identical to that of another – is parasitic on felt experience. A quick way to see Heidegger's point would be to take the example of calendars, where certain dates – Christmas, Diwali, Eid al-Fitr, Hanukah, Independence Day – have a special significance, recollecting and repeating a previous date. And a quick response would be that Heidegger's interpretation unduly emphasized Hegel's analysis of time in his *Philosophy of Nature* and paid insufficient attention to the *Phenomenology of Spirit*.

Heidegger also claimed that Hegel already presupposes Absolute Knowing at the beginning of the *Phenomenology of Spirit*. There is a sense in which Heidegger was correct. In narrating the journey of Spirit, Hegel knows where it will arrive. He knows because his narration is retrospective. Looking to the past, Hegel tells his readers how Spirit has developed historically to become what it is. The real question is not whether Hegel knows where Spirit will arrive, and where it will go to get there, but rather whether Spirit's journey is predetermined. In this book, I have argued that it isn't. Looking back at Spirit's sojourn, its every moment was necessary in the sense that, given where Spirit is now, it would have been elsewhere if any of its moments would have been different. However, if each of its moments were contingent, Spirit might have arrived somewhere else.

Alexandre Kojève (1902–1968) argued that the key to Hegel's *Phenomenology of Spirit* was the discussion of the master–slave, or lord–bondsman, struggle. Influenced by Marxism, Kojève argued that all other sections of this text are re-enactments of that struggle. He interpreted this as an argument that history is on the side of the slave. The master seeks recognition from the slave. However, since the master regards the slave not as a person but as a sort of tool or machine that does the master's bidding, the master cannot receive from the slave the recognition that the master desires. The slave, by contrast, is able to alter the external environment through his own labor. As a consequence, the slave can receive recognition by seeing the products of his labor as his will externalized. While the master depends on the slave's labor – and futilely seeks the slave's recognition – the slave doesn't need the master. Kojève viewed the *Phenomenology of Spirit* and history itself as the chronicle of the slave's progressive efforts to become free of the master. He interpreted Hegel as holding that the future is necessarily progressive – that is, until history ends. Kojève held that the end of history would occur when the Germanic World was realized and all persons were free. At that point, history would be over in the sense that there would be no further emancipatory progress, although there might be technological improvements.

Simone de Beauvoir (1908–1986) saw Hegel's discussions of the struggle between the master and slave, or lord and bondsman, and of mutual recognition as analogous to the relation between Man and Woman, where Man is the master (the absolute Subject) and Woman is the slave (the inessential Other). While the slave can successfully revolt and overthrow the master, according to de Beauvoir, Woman cannot rebel against Man. Frantz Fanon (1925–1961) used Hegel's master–slave dialectic, White Master/Black Slave, to comprehend Western colonialism, racism, and violence. Whereas Hegel's slave ultimately finds recognition through the products of his own labor and so does not need the master's recognition, for Fanon, the Black Slave continues to need the White Master's recognition. Jean-Paul Sartre (1905–1980) believed that the relation of master and slave describes human relations in general. Individuals fall into self-deception by denying that they are free to decide what they want to be. They try to turn themselves into things to escape the anxiety that freedom entails. They also attempt to treat others as things and so master them.

Although there are significant differences between the so-called poststructuralist philosophers – Emmanuel Levinas (1906–1995), Louis Pierre Althusser (1918–1990), Jean-François Lyotard (1924–1998), Jacques Derrida (1930–2004), Gilles Deleuze (1925–1995), and Michel Foucault (1926–1984) – all of them were negatively influenced by Hegel. Rather than discuss each in detail, I will instead speak about their general criticisms of Hegel's philosophy. Poststructuralism is influenced by Kojève's interpretation of Hegel. That is, the Hegel it rejects is Kojève's Hegel. Poststructuralism believes that Hegel advocated a necessary teleology towards a future in which all persons are free. Hegel's freedom, it urges, is the freedom for people to be consumers in a capitalist society. Such a society is inseparable from – indeed, depends on – imperialism and exploitation. Rather than being the pinnacle of civilization, this is precisely what needs to be overcome. Poststructuralism also rejects a representational democracy where some people – legislators and judges – speak for others while the others must remain silent. Such a politics inhibits thought and favors the repetition of slogans and platitudes. Although influenced by Marx, Poststructuralism believes that Marx's criticisms of capitalism unwittingly accept the capitalist ideology, and so, rather than being a genuine alternative to capitalism, Marxism is instead a species of it. Marx believes that history is the story of class struggle, to be sure, while capitalism claims that it is the tale of progressive social betterment and economic prosperity for increasing numbers of persons. Nevertheless, Marx agrees with the capitalist ideology that capitalism is an inevitable and progressive development rather than recognizing that it is in many regards a by-product of contingent events which were themselves only contingently related. (The Enclosure Laws in Britain, which threw many people off of the lands that they had traditionally used for farming, for example, coincided with the beginnings of factories; the industrial revolution required masses of people prepared to work for subsistence labor, and these people were only available because of the Enclosure Laws.) Marx doesn't recognize the possibilities of societies that bypass capitalism rather than being an arrested stage in its development. A genuine alternative to capitalism can't be developed through a process of internal criticism,

Poststructuralism insists, but can be created only by effectively ignoring capitalism.

More radically, Poststructuralism denies that humans have an essence, a fixed set of characteristics that would, if not determine, constrain the possibilities of transcending present social institutions as well as political and ethical beliefs. Instead, it maintains that humans are always in a process of becoming and that this becoming (or these becomings) need not be constrained by the past. What humans are becoming cannot be known in advance of its appearance; there is no pre-established trajectory. Nor is there a goal or stopping point of becoming. The emphasis of Poststructuralism here is more on the becomings of individuals than on humanity. This position is sometimes referred to as "anti-humanism," rejecting a humanism that would advocate a certain vision of rights and ethics based on a supposed human nature. So, anti-humanism is anti-human, where humans are thought to have an essence, but not necessarily anti-humane. Poststructuralism also believes that Hegel intended to advance a philosophy that would encompass not only all other philosophies but all human endeavors. Not only does Hegel aim at totality, Poststructuralism charges, but he is guilty of totalitarianism. Everything must be in its proper dialectical pigeon-hole, where – to mix metaphors – it plays its assigned role and obediently repeats the lines Hegel has written for it. Naturally, there are truncheons and gags for the recalcitrant. Finally, Poststructuralism alleges that Hegel's dialectical method is a cheat. He does not achieve totality and closure by legitimately following his method but instead merely asserts that the absolute has been reached: game over!

Hegel is a Post-poststructuralist! That is to say, Poststructuralism hasn't superseded his philosophy. Rather, it hasn't yet reached his level – or so I will suggest. It is correct that Hegel accepts a form of capitalism. However, his version has substantial government regulation and intervention. As a consequence, it is not laissez-faire. It is also correct that Hegel has no effective solution to the poverty that, as he recognized, capitalism itself creates; Frank Ruda's book *Hegel's Rabble*[5] is crucial reading. It seems likely that the economic policies proposed by John Maynard Keynes (1883–1946) would significantly eliminate poverty and, if so, Hegel's capitalism would be acceptable. It is also correct that Hegel defends a version of representational democracy. As discussed in the chapter on his *Elements of the Philosophy of Right*, though, legislators are elected by members of the Estates (which are relevantly similar to trade guilds), and they can only enact or reject legislation that is proposed by the civil servants working in the monarchy; note that the monarchy can only propose but not enact legislation. By having persons vote for legislators based on their membership in Estates, Hegel intends to overcome the alienation that results when individuals vote for legislators based on their geographical location. In the latter case, but – Hegel intends – not the former, individuals may believe that their votes don't really matter, and they may not feel that the legislators actually represent their interests. In this way, legislators don't speak for the members of the Estates but rather are the voices through which those members speak.

Can genuine alternatives emerge through a process of internal criticism? Perhaps not. Internal criticism can show that something is contradictory or that it fails by its own criteria for success. By itself, this does not indicate what to do next. Showing that two propositions are contradictory, for example, does not tell us which to retain and which to reject. Score for Poststructuralism? Not yet. Creating a radical sui generis alternative is easier said than done, especially if Poststructuralism asserts that even to recognize problems with, say, an economic system is already to be caught in its terrain. It is more plausible to believe that a genuine alternative emerges through a process of successive tinkering and improvising, much of this through trial and error, so that the later stages bear little resemblance to earlier ones.

About teleology. One of Poststructuralism's major gripes is against Hegel's view that there is a necessary progression in history. As I have argued previously, Hegel's necessity is retrospective and so it is entirely compatible with – indeed, requires – contingency. Poststructuralism rejects not Hegel, but Kojève's Hegel. This links to Poststructuralism's anti-humanism. Hegel would agree that humans don't have an essence. They do, he would add, have a history, and this history is the progressive realization of freedom. Retrospectively, we can tell a narrative that culminates in the present age, where it is realized that all humans are free. So, Hegel would affirm Poststructuralism's claim that the rights and duties can't be based on human nature, as humanism asserts. Whereas Poststructuralism finds this a reason to be suspicious of rights and duties, Hegel instead grounds them in mutual recognition. Persons have rights and duties – moreover, persons have the status of persons – because they are so recognized by others and, in turn, so recognize others.

It may surprise some readers to learn that Martin Luther King Jr (1929–1968) was influenced by Hegel's philosophy. It surprised me too, although, in retrospect, it is obvious.[6] King accepted Hegel's view that history is the progressive realization of human freedom. He further agreed with Hegel that a level of freedom, once achieved, could never be lost. It is arguable that it is Hegel's philosophy of history, as much as the Gospels, that inspired King to believe that "the arc of the moral universe is long but it bends toward justice" and that the struggle for civil rights would ultimately be victorious. King also accepted Hegel's claim that truth exists in a synthesis of opposing views, not in the one-sidedness of a thesis or its antithesis.

After the end of the Soviet Union, and influenced by Kojève, Francis Fukuyama wrote an article[7] in which he argued that history had ended. By this, he meant that Western capitalism coupled with the welfare state represented an unsurpassable level. He claimed that the downfall of the Soviet Union demonstrated that the communist alternative wasn't viable. It is still possible to make Western liberal welfare capitalism more just and efficient. However, there isn't any alternative that would be more just and efficient. Insofar as history is understood as Hegel understood it, as the progressive realization of human freedom, then history has ended – or so claimed Fukuyama. Although it is now fashionable to say that Fukuyama was naïvely incorrect, many people implicitly agree with him – not necessarily in what they say but in how they live. They live as though the present system is permanent. It seems clear, however, that we are in for some drastic changes. Several factors point this way. First, so-called first-world countries are dependent on oil, a non-renewable resource; plastics and gasoline are produced from oil. The oil companies may yet discover some more deposits, but eventually those too will dry up. When that happens, and it will happen soon rather than later, things will have to change radically. Second, there is global warming. If this process isn't reversed soon – and it may already be too late – the world's climate will change dramatically. Third, the middle class is shrinking, and there is an increasing distance between the few who are wealthy and the many who live near or below the subsistence level. Fourth, money is playing a greater role in elections, and there is more voter apathy, causing candidates to take more extreme views. No doubt readers could suggest other factors. Together, they strongly suggest that Western liberal welfare capitalism isn't sustainable. Could Fukuyama respond, claiming that history is over in the sense that there can be no further progress, even though the level achieved can't be maintained and so conditions will likely deteriorate and eventually restabilize at a lower level of progress? Perhaps, but he would part company with Hegel here. Hegel believed that once a level of freedom is achieved, it can never be lost. He wouldn't have agreed that a social and economic system could be the highest possible and also be unsustainable.

Slavoj Žižek (b. 1949) explicates Hegel's philosophy by playing it off of three other domains: popular culture (especially cinema), the psychoanalysis of Jacques Marie Émile Lacan (1901–1981), and Althusser's Marxism. He argues that the only way that the Left can advance is through a fundamental thinking through Hegel. Žižek does not call for a return to Hegel's philosophy but rather that Hegel's intervention should be repeated in the present context.

Judith Butler (b 1956) wrote her first book on the twentieth-century French reception of Hegel. The influence of Hegel is most evident, though, in her book *Gender Trouble*. There, she argues that gender isn't natural but rather is constructed through its performative enactment. Once this is recognized, persons can take on, and thereby constitute, new and hitherto unimagined genders. This creativity is not only valuable in itself, it is also useful in overcoming the dominance of men over women. Dominance becomes more problematic to maintain when there aren't only two genders but potentially many, and when it is recognized that persons become men and women by playing those roles. So, why stick with those? Take a walk on the *Geist* side!

We have come a long way together, dear readers. We have scaled the Himalayas of Hegel's thought. We have stood on Philosophy's roof. You could see your house from there. No surprise; you have made Philosophy your home! Your patience, fortitude, and courage are deeply appreciated. You never grumbled or complained. Okay, maybe once or twice, but I didn't hear.

You now have the resources to study Hegel on your own and to become, if you wish, a Hegel scholar. All you need to do is read Hegel. If that is still too challenging, read some of the books listed in "Suggestions for Further Reading."

And if, peradventure, you suspect that you already were able to read Hegel on your own and didn't need this book . . . well, then it served its purpose. Dorothy always had the power to go back to Kansas. Toto too? Toto too.[8]

Notes

Chapter 1 Introduction

1 David Carroll, "Rephrasing the Political with Kant and Lyotard: From Aesthetic to Political Judgments," *Diacritics* 14/3 (1984), p. 79.
2 Ibid.
3 Bertolt Brecht, *Flüchtlingsgespräche* (Frankfurt am Main: Suhrkamp, 1968), p. 111.

Chapter 3 Hegel's *Phenomenology of Spirit*

1 Michael N. Forster, *Hegel's Idea of a Phenomenology of Spirit* (Chicago: University of Chicago Press, 1998).
2 Charles Taylor, *Hegel* (Cambridge: Cambridge University Press, 1975).
3 G. W. F. Hegel, *The Phenomenology of Mind*, trans. J. B. Baillie (London: S. Sonnenschein, 1910); *Phenomenology of Spirit*, trans. Arnold V. Miller (Oxford: Clarendon Press, 1977).
4 Alexandre Kojève, *Introduction to the Reading of Hegel: Lecture on the Phenomenology of Spirit*, trans. James H. Nichols Jr (Ithaca: Cornell University Press, 1986).
5 Andy Clark and David J. Chalmers, "The Extended Mind," *Analysis* 58/1 (1998): 7–19.
6 Ibid., p. 8: "If, as we confront some task, a part of the world functions as a process which, were it to go on in the head, we would have no hesitation in accepting as part of the cognitive process, then that part of the world is (for that time) part of the cognitive process."
7 For complementary discussions of externalized memory, see Allen Newell and Herbert A. Simon, *Human Problem Solving* (Edgewood

Cliffs, NJ: Prentice Hall, 1972); and David E. Rumlehart, Paul Smolensky, James L. McClelland, and Geoffrey E. Hinton, "Schemata and Sequential Thought Processes in PDP Models," *Parallel Distributed Processing: Explorations in the Microstructure of Cognition*, Vol. 2: *Psychological and Biological Models*, ed. David E. Rumelhart and James L. McClelland (Cambridge, MA: MIT Press, 1986), pp. 7–57. Also, compare Frits Staal, *The Fidelity to Oral Tradition and the Origins of Science* (Amsterdam: North-Holland, 1986), pp. 37–8:

> I believe that it would be profitable for Western psychologists who are studying memory to learn Sanskrit. This would enable them to go to India and study the mnemonic techniques and practices of those increasingly rare traditional *paṇḍits* that are in popular parlance referred to as "walking encyclopedias." It would be interesting to enquire into a phenomenon that I can only explain by introducing the notion of "collective memory": I am referring to a practice that is common among Vedic reciters and chanters. Vedic brahmins always prefer to recite in pairs; for two do not only know more than one; two that recite together know more than the same two reciting separately . . . reciting together does not only increase the confidence of the chanters; it also leads to the recovery of a larger portion of the oral tradition than could ever be recovered by single performers.

8 Edwin Hutchins, *Cognition in the Wild* (Cambridge, MA: MIT Press, 1995); Karin Knorr Cetina, *Epistemic Cultures: How the Sciences Make Knowledge* (Cambridge, MA: Harvard University Press, 1999); Lynn Hankinson Nelson, *Who Knows: From Quine to a Feminist Empiricism* (Philadelphia: Temple University Press, 1990).
9 Hutchins, *Cognition in the Wild*, p. xiv.
10 Nelson, *Who Knows*, p. 313.
11 Forster, *Hegel's Idea of a Phenomenology of Spirit*, p. 186.
12 Rather than appealing to something else, these individuals could instead simply assert that they know that the authority is correct. In this case, they would fall into dogmatism instead of generating an infinite regress.
13 Compare Taylor, *Hegel*, p. vii: "The enterprise can easily go awry in one of two opposite ways. Either one can end up being terribly clear and sounding very reasonable at the cost of distorting, even bowdlerizing Hegel. Or one can remain faithful but impenetrable, so that in the end readers will turn with relief to the text in order to understand the commentary."
14 Kenley R. Dove, "Hegel's Phenomenological Method," in *The Phenomenology of Spirit Reader: Critical and Interpretive Essays*, ed. Jon Stewart (Albany: State University of New York Press, 1998), pp. 52–75.
15 Bertrand Russell, "Knowledge by Acquaintance and Knowledge by Description," *Mysticism and Logic and Other Essays* (London: George Allen & Unwin, 1918), pp. 209–32.

16 Saul Kripke, *Naming and Necessity* (Cambridge, MA: Harvard University Press, 1980).

17 Ludwig Wittgenstein, *Philosophical Investigations*, trans. G. E. M. Anscombe (Oxford: Blackwell, 1967).

18 In Plato's *Meno*, Socrates maintains that individuals implicitly know the forms and that he is attempting to have them remember those forms. Nevertheless, he proceeds as though this knowledge could have been almost wholly forgotten. Alternatively, the view that individuals implicity know the forms could be developed so that social practices and institutions would be examined in order to make explicit that implicit knowledge. This approach would then need to explain how different cultures – as well as any specific culture – could have conflicting practices, since those practices are supposedly based on implicit knowledge of the forms.

19 For a discussion of relevant logics, see Stephen Read, *Relevant Logic: A Philosophical Examination of Inference* (New York: Blackwell, 1988).

20 For the history of paraconsistent logics and discussions of formalized paraconsistent systems, see Graham Priest, Richard Routley, and Jean Norman, eds, *Paraconsistent Logic: Essays on the Inconsistent* (Munich: Philosophia, 1989).

21 Kojève, *Introduction to the Reading of Hegel: Lecture on the Phenomenology of Spirit*.

22 Compare Richard A. Lynch, "Mutual Recognition and the Dialectic of Master and Slave: Reading Hegel against Kojève," *International Philosophical Quarterly* 41/1 (2001): 33–48; and Patrick Riley, "Introduction to the Reading of Alexandre Kojève," *Political Theory* 9/1 (1981): 5–48.

23 Albert Camus (1913–1960), in his novel *La Chute* (*The Fall*, published in 1956), writes: "Après un certain âge tout homme est responsable de son visage" ["After a certain age, every man has the face he deserves"]. No particular age is mentioned. A final entry in the notebooks of George Orwell (1903–1950) is very similar: "At 50, everyone has the face he deserves."

24 Alasdair MacIntyre, "Hegel on Faces and Skulls," in *The Phenomenology of Spirit Reader: Critical and Interpretive Essays*, pp. 213–24.

25 See Robert B. Pippin, *Hegel's Practical Philosophy: Rational Agency as Ethical Life* (New York: Cambridge University Press, 2008).

26 Neel Mukherjee, *Past Continuous* (New Delhi: Picador India, 2008).

27 Donald Phillip Verene, *Hegel's Absolute: An Introduction to Reading the Phenomenology of Spirit* (Albany: State University of New York Press, 2007).

28 Compare Stanley Fish, "The Unbearable Ugliness of Volvos," *There's No Such Thing as Free Speech, and it's a Good Thing, Too* (New York: Oxford University Press, 1994), pp. 273–9.

29 See Isabelle C. DeMarte and J. M. Fritzman, "Diderot's Uncle, Hegel; Or *Rameau's Nephew* as a Branch of *The Phenomenology of Spirit*," *1650–1850* 14 (2007): pp. 177–220.

30 Slavoj Žižek, *The Sublime Object of Ideology* (London: Verso, 1989), p. 216.
31 Paul Redding, *Analytic Philosophy and the Return of Hegelian Thought* (New York: Cambridge University Press, 2007), pp. 28–9.
32 *Oxford English Dictionary*, 2nd edn, *sub verbo* "memory theatre." For a discussion of such mnemonic devices, see Frances A. Yates, *The Art of Memory* (Chicago: University of Chicago Press, 1966).

Chapter 4   Hegel's *Logic*

1   Keith Lehrer, *Theory of Knowledge*, 2nd edn (Boulder, CO: Westview Press, 2000).

Chapter 5   Hegel's *Philosophy of Nature* and *Philosophy of Spirit*

1   For a further discussion, see J. M. Fritzman, "Hegel's Philosophy – in Putnam's Vat?," *Polish Journal of Philosophy* 5/2 (2011): 7–25.
2   Michael O. Hardimon, *Hegel's Social Philosophy: The Project of Reconciliation* (New York: Cambridge University Press, 1994).
3   K. R. Popper, *The Open Society and its Enemies*, Vol. 2: *The High Tide of Prophecy: Hegel, Marx, and the Aftermath* (Princeton, NJ: Princeton University Press, 1966), p. 28.
4   Jacques Rancière, "On the Theory of Ideology – Althusser's Politics," in *A Radical Philosophy Reader*, ed. Roy Edgley and Richard Osborne (London: Verso, 1985), p. 136.
5   For a further discussion, see J. M. Fritzman and Molly Gibson, "Schelling, Hegel, and Evolutionary Progress," *Perspectives on Science* 20/1 (2012): 105–28.
6   G. W. F. Hegel, *Lectures on the Philosophy of Spirit 1827–1828*, trans. Robert R. Williams (New York: Oxford University Press, 2007), pp. 29–30.
7   Compare Frits Staal, *The Fidelity to Oral Tradition and the Origins of Science* (Amsterdam: North-Holland, 1986), pp. 31–2:

> A prerequisite for the traditional study of ritual is that the student knows his own Veda by heart. He must know it thoroughly, from beginning to end. When given any couple of words, he must be able to continue the recitation from there. If he is good or takes pleasure in games, he can recite it backward; recite every other word; do with the words anything that a computer can be programmed to do; single out or count their occurrences, group them together according to certain criteria; in brief, perform the kinds of exercise of which the *vikṛti* "modifications" are simple examples. On this foundation he can learn to change the traditional order that he has committed to memory; and here we witness

the beginning of those extraordinary exercises that are the bread and butter – or rice and ghee – of Vedic ritual. Most of these make no sense in terms of meaning (for the meaning has never been learnt), and often little sense even in terms of form; because many of them were, at the outset and at least in part, either due to intuitions that are no longer recoverable, or simply due to chance. Once put together, these exercises can be learnt. There may be elements that facilitate their study, for example, the occurrence of certain words; such as the word for dawn – *uṣas* – that the pupil will be familiar with even if he need not know what it means. Or "Agni," for that matter; much more common and familiar; yet to the young scholar who is beginning to find his way in the ritual maze, primarily nothing but a sound.

Chapter 6   Hegel's *Philosophy of Right*

1   Michael O. Hardimon, *Hegel's Social Philosophy: The Project of Reconciliation* (New York: Cambridge University Press, 1994), p. 58.
2   Jay Drydyk, "Capitalism, Socialism, and Civil Society," *The Monist* 74/3 (1991): 464. Compare Bruce A. Ackerman and Anne Alstott, *The Stakeholder Society* (New Haven, CT: Yale University Press, 1999); Andrew L. Friedman and Samantha Miles, *Stakeholders: Theory and Practice* (Oxford: Oxford University Press, 2006).
3   J. M. Fritzman, "Queer Eye for the *Geist* Guy: Hegel's Gay Science," *International Studies in Philosophy*, 40/1 (2008): 49–63.
4   Immanuel Kant, "Idea for a Universal History with a Cosmopolitan Purpose," in *Kant: Political Writings*, trans. H. B. Nisbet, 2nd edn (Cambridge: Cambridge University Press, 1991), pp. 41–53.
5   Gabriel Paquette, "Hegel's Analysis of Colonialism and its Roots in Scottish Political Economy," *Clio* 32/4 (2003): 423.

Chapter 7   Hegel's *Philosophy of History*

1   Michel Foucault, "Orders of Discourse: Inaugural Lecture Delivered at the Collège de France," trans. Rupert Swyer, *Social Science Information* 10/2 (1971): 28.
2   Raymond Plant, "Is There a Future in the Philosophy of History?," in *Hegel's Philosophy of Action*, ed. Lawrence S. Stepelevich and David Lamb (Atlantic Highlands, NJ: Humanities Press, 1983), pp. 93–102; Alexandre Kojève, *Introduction to the Reading of Hegel: Lecture on the Phenomenology of Spirit*, trans. James H. Nichols Jr (Ithaca, NY: Cornell University Press, 1986); Francis Fukuyama, *The End of History and the Last Man* (New York: Free Press, 1992); Barry Cooper, *The End of History: An Essay on Modern Hegelianism* (Toronto: University of Toronto Press, 1984).
3   Giorgio Agamben, *Homo Sacer: Sovereign Power and Bare Life*, trans. Daniel Heller-Roazen (Stanford, CA: Stanford University Press, 1998).

4   Isaiah Berlin, *Liberty*, ed. Henry Hardy (New York: Oxford University Press, 2002).

5   See G. W. F. Hegel, *The Philosophy of History*, trans. J. Sibree (New York: Dover, 1956), pp. 225–7 and 341–2.

6   Ibid., p. 86.

7   See J. M. Fritzman, "Geist in Mumbai: Hegel with Rushdie," *Janus Head* 11/1(2009): 99–118; Gina Altamura and J. M. Fritzman, "Hegel's Pyjamas: Refashioning World-History in Light of Postcolonial Criticism," in *Philosophical Frontiers: Essays and Emerging Thoughts*, ed. Richard H. Corrigan and Mary E. Farrell (Gloucester: Progressive Frontiers Press, 2009), pp. 91–120 (originally pubd in *Philosophical Frontiers* 3/1 (2008): 87–117.

8   Robert Bernasconi, "Hegel at the Court of the Ashanti," in *Hegel after Derrida*, ed. Stuart Barnett (London: Routledge, 1998), pp. 41–63.

9   Salman Rushdie, *The Enchantress of Florence: A Novel* (New York: Random House, 2008).

10   See Muhammad 'Abduh, *The Theology of Unity* (London: George Allen & Unwin, 1966), pp. 148–50.

11   Hegel, *The Philosophy of History*, pp. 103–4.

Chapter 8   Hegel's Lectures on Philosophy and Religion

1   See J. M. Fritzman, "Queer Eye for the *Geist* Guy: Hegel's Gay Science," *International Studies in Philosophy* 40/1 (2008): 49–63.

Chapter 9   After Hegel

1   Roland Barthes, "From Work to Text," in *Image, Music, Text*, trans. Stephen Heath (New York: Hill & Wang, 1977), pp. 155–78.

2   Tom Rockmore, *Hegel, Idealism, and Analytic Philosophy* (New Haven, CT: Yale University Press, 2005).

3   Vladimir Ilyich Lenin, "Conspectus of Hegel's Book *The Science of Logic*," in *Lenin's Collected Works*, Vol. 38, trans. Clemence Dutt, 4th edn (Moscow: Progress, 1976), pp. 85–241.

4   Herbert Marcuse, *Reason and Revolution: Hegel and the Rise of Social Theory*, 2nd edn (Boston: Beacon Press, 1960).

5   Frank Ruda, *Hegel's Rabble: An Investigation into Hegel's Philosophy of Right* (New York: Continuum, 2011).

6   See John Ansbro, "Martin Luther King's Debt to Hegel," *The Owl of Minerva* 26/1 (1994): 98–100.

7   Francis Fukuyama, "The End of History?," *The National Interest*, Summer 1989, later expanded into a book, *The End of History and the Last Man* (New York: Free Press, 1992).

8 See Gina Altamura and J. M. Fritzman, "Very Good, But Not So Mysterious: Hegel, Rushdie, and the Dialectics of Oz," in *The Wizard of Oz and Philosophy*, ed. Randall E. Auxier and Phillip S. Seng (Chicago: Open Court, 2008), pp. 33–48.

Suggestions for Further Reading

Hegel's Texts in English Translation

Aesthetics: Lectures on Fine Art, trans. T. M. Knox, 2 vols (Oxford: Clarendon Press, 1975).

The Difference between Fichte's and Schelling's System of Philosophy, trans. H. S. Harris and Walter Cerf (Albany: State University of New York Press, 1977).

Early Theological Writings, trans. T. M. Knox (Philadelphia: University of Pennsylvania Press, 1981).

Elements of the Philosophy of Right, trans. H. B. Nisbet (New York: Cambridge University Press, 1991).

The Encyclopedia Logic (with the Zusätze): Part I of the Encyclopedia of Philosophical Sciences with the Zusätze, trans. T. F. Geraets, W. A. Suchting, and H. S. Harris (Indianapolis: Hackett, 1991).

Encyclopedia of the Philosophical Sciences in Basic Outline, Part I: *Science of Logic*, trans. Klaus Brinkmann and Daniel O. Dahlstrom (New York: Cambridge University Press, 2010).

G. W. F. Hegel: Theologian of the Spirit, trans. Peter Crafts Hodgson (Minneapolis: Fortress Press, 1997).

G. W. F. Hegel: Political Writings, trans. H. B. Nisbet (New York: Cambridge University Press, 1999).

Hegel and the Human Spirit: A Translation of the Jena Lectures on the Philosophy of Spirit (1805–1806) with Commentary, trans. Leo Rauch (Detroit: Wayne State University Press, 1983).

Hegel on Hamann, trans. Lisa Marie Anderson (Evanston: Northwestern University Press, 2008).

Hegel: The Letters, trans. Clark Butler and Christiane Seiler (Bloomington: Indiana University Press, 1984).

Hegel's Dialectic of Desire and Recognition: Texts and Commentary, ed. John O'Neill (Albany: State University of New York Press, 1996).

Hegel's Introduction to Aesthetics: Being the Introduction to the Berlin Aesthetics Lectures of the 1820s, trans. T. M. Knox (Oxford: Clarendon Press, 1979).

Hegel's Lectures of the History of Philosophy, trans. E. S. Haldane and Frances H. Simson, 3 vols (New York: Humanities Press, 1955).

Hegel's Phenomenology of Self-Consciousness: Text and Commentary, trans. Leo Rauch and David Sherman (New York: State University of New York Press, 1999).

Hegel's Phenomenology of Spirit, trans. Arnold V. Miller (Oxford: Clarendon Press, 1977).

Hegel's Philosophy of Mind: Being Part Three of the Encyclopaedia of the Philosophical Sciences (1830), trans. A. V. Miller (Oxford: Clarendon Press, 1971).

Hegel's Philosophy of Mind: Translated from the 1830 Edition, Together with the Zusätze, trans. W. Wallace and A. V. Miller, with revisions and commentary by M. J. Inwood (New York: Oxford University Press, 2007).

Hegel's Philosophy of Nature, trans. M. J. Petry, 3 vols (London: George Allen & Unwin, 1970).

Hegel's Philosophy of Right, with Marx's Commentary: A Handbook for Students, ed. Howard P. Kainz (The Hague: Martinus Nijhoff, 1974).

Hegel's Philosophy of Subjective Spirit, trans. M. J. Petry, 3 vols (Dordrecht: D. Reidel, 1977).

Hegel's Political Writings, trans. T. M. Knox (Oxford: Clarendon Press, 1964).

Hegel's Preface to the Phenomenology of Spirit, trans. and with a running commentary by Yirmiyahu Yovel (Princeton, NJ: Princeton University Press, 2005).

Heidelberg Writings: Journal Publications, trans. Brady Bowman and Allen Speight (New York: Oxford University Press, 2009).

Introduction to The Philosophy of History, trans. Leo Rauch (Indianapolis: Hackett, 1988).

The Jena System, 1804–5: Logic and Metaphysics, trans. John W. Burbidge and George di Giovanni (Kingston: McGill–Queen's University Press, 1986).

Lectures on Logic: Berlin, 1831, trans. Clark Butler (Bloomington: Indiana University Press, 2008).

Lectures on the History of Philosophy 1825–6, Vol. I: Introduction and Oriental Philosophy, trans. Robert F. Brown (New York: Oxford University Press, 2009).

Lectures on the History of Philosophy, Vol. 3, trans. E. S. Haldane and Frances H. Simson (New York: Humanities Press, 1955).

Lectures on the Philosophy of Religion: The Lectures of 1827, trans. R. F. Brown, P. C. Hodgson, and J. M. Stewart (Berkeley: University of California Press, 1988).

Lectures on the Philosophy of Spirit 1827–1828, trans. Robert R. Williams (New York: Oxford University Press, 2007).

Lectures on the Philosophy of World History, Vol. I: *Manuscripts of the Introduction and the Lectures of 1822–1823*, trans. Robert F. Brown and Peter C. Hodgson (New York: Oxford University Press, 2011).

Lectures on the Proofs of the Existence of God, trans. Peter C. Hodgson (Oxford: Clarendon Press, 2007).

Natural Law: The Scientific Ways of Treating Natural Law, its Place in Moral Philosophy, and its Relation to the Positive Sciences of Law, trans. T. M. Knox (Philadelphia: University of Pennsylvania Press, 1975).

On the Episode of the Mahābhārata Known by the Name Bhagavad-Gītā by Wilhelm von Humboldt, trans. Herbert Herring (New Delhi: Indian Council of Philosophical Research, 1995).

Outlines of the Philosophy of Right, trans. T. M. Knox, rev., ed., and introduced by Stephen Houlgate (New York: Oxford University Press, 2008).

The Phenomenology of Mind, trans. J. B. Baillie (London: S. Sonnenschein, 1910).

The Philosophy of History, trans. J. Sibree (New York: Dover, 1956).

Philosophy of Right, trans. S. W. Dyde (Kitchener, Ontario: Batoche, 2001).

The Philosophy of Right, trans. Alan White (Newburyport, MA: Focus, 2002).

Philosophy of Subjective Spirit, Vol. 1, trans. M. J. Petry (Dordrecht: D. Reidel, 1978).

Science of Logic, trans. A. V. Miller (New York: Humanities Press, 1969).

The Science of Logic, trans. George di Giovanni (New York: Cambridge University Press, 2010).

Spirit: Chapter Six of Hegel's Phenomenology of Spirit, ed. Daniel E. Shannon, trans. the Hegel Translation Group (Indianapolis: Hackett, 2001).

System of Ethical Life (1802/1803) and First Philosophy of Spirit (Part III of the System of Speculative Philosophy 1803/1804), trans. H. S. Harris and T. M. Knox (Albany: State University of New York Press, 1979).

Three Essays, 1793–1795: The Tübingen Essay, Berne Fragments, the Life of Jesus, trans. Peter Fuss and John Dobbins (Notre Dame, IN: University of Notre Dame Press, 1984).

A Selection of Secondary Literature

Titles in **boldface** are recommended to those new to Hegel's philosophy.

General

Adorno, Theodor W., *Hegel: Three Studies*, trans. Shierry Weber Nicholsen (Cambridge, MA: MIT Press, 1993).

Althusser, Louis, *The Spectre of Hegel: Early Writings*, trans. G. M. Goshgarian (New York: Verso, 1997).

Amour, Leslie, *Being and Idea: Developments of Some Themes in Spinoza and Hegel* (Hildesheim: G. Olms, 1992).

Anderson, Sybol Cook, *Hegel's Theory of Recognition: From Oppression to Ethical Liberal Modernity* (New York: Continuum, 2009).

Barnett, Stuart, ed., *Hegel after Derrida* (London: Routledge, 1998).

Bates, Jennifer Ann, *Hegel and Shakespeare on Moral Imagination* (Albany: State University of New York Press, 2010).

Baur, Michael, and John Russon, eds, *Hegel and the Tradition: Essays in Honour of H. S. Harris* (Toronto: University of Toronto Press, 1997).

Beiser, Frederick C., ed., *The Cambridge Companion to Hegel* (New York: Cambridge University Press, 1993).

Beiser, Frederick C., ed., *The Cambridge Companion to Hegel and Nineteenth-Century Philosophy* (New York: Cambridge University Press, 2008).

Beiser, Frederick C., *Hegel* (New York: Routledge, 2006).

Berthold-Bond, Daniel, *The Ethics of Authorship: Communication, Seduction, and Death in Hegel and Kierkegaard* (New York: Fordham University Press, 2011).

Berthold-Bond, Daniel, *Hegel's Grand Synthesis: A Study of Being, Thought, and History*, (Albany: State University of New York Press, 1989).

Brinkmann, Klaus, *Idealism without Limits: Hegel and the Problem of Objectivity* (New York: Springer, 2011).

Bristow, William F., *Hegel and the Transformation of Philosophical Critique* (New York: Oxford University Press, 2007).

Brown, Alison Leigh, *On Hegel* (Belmont, CA: Wadsworth/Thompson Learning, 2001).

Burbidge, John W., *Historical Dictionary of Hegelian Philosophy* (Lanham, MD: Scarecrow Press, 2001).

Butler, Clark, *G. W. F. Hegel* (Boston: Twayne, 1977).

Caird, Edward, *Hegel* (Hamden, CT: Archon Books, 1968).

Ciavatta, David V., *Spirit, the Family, and the Unconscious in Hegel's Philosophy* (Albany: State University of New York Press, 2009).

Cobben, Paul, *The Paradigm of Recognition: Freedom as Overcoming the Fear of Death* (Leiden: Brill, 2012).

Collins, Ardis B., ed., *Hegel on the Modern World* (Albany: State University of New York Press, 1995).

Croce, Benedetto, *What is Living and What is Dead of the Philosophy of Hegel*, trans. Douglas Ainslie (Kitchener, Ontario: Batoche, 2001).

Cullen, Bernard, ed., *Hegel Today* (Brookfield, VT: Avebury, 1988).

Dallmayr, Fred R., *G. W. F. Hegel: Modernity and Politics* (Newbury Park, CA: Sage, 1993).

de Boer, Karin, *Thinking in the Light of Time: Heidegger's Encounter with Hegel* (Albany: State University of New York Press, 2000).

de Laurentiis, Allegra, and Jeffrey Edwards, eds, *The Bloomsbury Companion to Hegel* (London: Bloomsbury, 2013).

Deligiorgi, Katerina, ed., *Hegel: New Directions* (Chesham, Bucks.: Acumen, 2006).

Denker, Alfred, and Michael Vater, eds, *Hegel's Phenomenology of Spirit: New Critical Essays* (Amherst, NY: Humanity Books, 2003).

Desmond, William, *Beyond Hegel and Dialectic: Speculation, Cult, and Comedy* (Albany: State University of New York Press, 1992).

Desmond William, ed., *Hegel and His Critics: Philosophy in the Aftermath of Hegel* (Albany: State University of New York Press, 1989).

Dickey, Laurence Winant, *Hegel: Religion, Economics, and the Politics of Spirit, 1770–1807* (New York: Cambridge University Press, 1987).

Dudley, Will, *Hegel, Nietzsche, and Philosophy: Thinking Freedom* (New York: Cambridge University Press, 2002).

Duffy, Simon, *The Logic of Expression: Quality, Quantity, and Intensity in Spinoza, Hegel, and Deleuze* (Burlington, VT: Ashgate, 2006).

Elder, Crawford, *Appropriating Hegel* (Aberdeen: Aberdeen University Press, 1981).

Engelhardt, H. Tristram, Jr, and Terry Pinkard, eds, *Hegel Reconsidered: Beyond Metaphysics and the Authoritian State* (Dordrecht: Kluwer Academic, 1994).

Feldman, Karen S., *Binding Words: Conscience and Rhetoric in Hobbes, Hegel, and Heidegger* (Evanston, IL: Northwestern University Press, 2006).

Ferrarin, Alfredo, *Hegel and Aristotle* (New York: Cambridge University Press, 2001).

Findlay, J. N., *Hegel: A Re-Examination* (New York: Macmillan, 1958).

Flay, Joseph C., *Hegel's Quest for Certainty* (Albany: State University of New York Press, 1984).

Förster, Eckart, *The Twenty-Five Years of Philosophy: A Systematic Reconstruction*, trans. Brady Bowman (Cambridge, MA: Harvard University Press, 2012).

Forster, Michael N., *Hegel and Skepticism* (Cambridge, MA: Harvard University Press, 1989).

Gadamer, Hans Georg, *Hegel's Dialectic: Five Hermeneutical Studies*, trans. P. Christopher Smith (New Haven, CT: Yale University Press, 1976).

Gauthier, Jeffrey A., *Hegel and Feminist Social Criticism* (Albany: State University of New York Press, 1997).

Hamacher, Werner, *Pleroma: Reading in Hegel*, trans. Nicholas Walker and Simon Jarvis (Stanford, CA: Stanford University Press, 1998).

Honneth, Axel, *The I in We: Studies in the Theory of Recognition*, trans. Joseph Ganahl (Malden, MA: Polity, 2012).

Houlgate, Stephen, *Freedom, Truth and History: An Introduction to Hegel's Philosophy* (London: Routledge, 1991).

Houlgate, Stephen, *Hegel, Nietzsche, and the Criticism of Metaphysics* (New York: Cambridge University Press, 1986).

Hutchings, Kimberly, *Hegel and Feminist Philosophy* (Malden, MA: Blackwell, 2003).

Hutchings, Kimberly, and Tuija Pulkkinen, eds, *Hegel's Philosophy and Feminist Thought: Beyond Antigone?* (New York: Palgrave Macmillan, 2010).

Hyppolite, Jean, *Studies on Marx and Hegel*, trans. John O'Neill (New York: Basic Books, 1969).

Inwood, M. J., *Hegel* (London: Routledge & Kegan Paul, 1983).

Inwood, M. J., *A Hegel Dictionary* (Oxford: Blackwell, 1992).

Jurist, Elliot L., *Beyond Hegel and Nietzsche: Philosophy, Culture, and Agency* (Cambridge, MA: MIT Press, 2000).

Kainz, Howard P., *An Introduction to Hegel: The Stages of Modern Philosophy* (Athens: Ohio University Press, 1996).

Kaufmann, Walter Arnold, *Hegel: Reinterpretation, Texts, and Commentary* (Garden City, NY: Doubleday, 1965).

Kelly, Sean M., *Individuation and the Absolute: Hegel, Jung, and the Path toward Wholeness* (New York: Paulist Press, 1993).

Kolb, David, *The Critique of Pure Modernity: Hegel, Heidegger, and After* (Chicago: University of Chicago Press, 1986).

Lamb, David, ed., *Hegel and Modern Philosophy* (London: Croom Helm, 1987).

Lamb, David, *Hegel: From Foundation to System* (The Hague: Martinus Nijhoff, 1980).

Lamb, David, *Language and Perception in Hegel and Wittgenstein* (New York: St Martin's Press, 1980).

Lauer, Quentin, *Hegel's Idea of Philosophy: With a New Translation of Hegel's Introduction to the History of Philosophy* (New York: Fordham University Press, 1983).

Lewis, Thomas A., *Freedom and Tradition in Hegel: Reconsidering Anthropology, Ethics, and Religion* (Notre Dame, IN: University of Notre Dame Press, 2005).

Lewis, Thomas A., *Religion, Modernity, and Politics in Hegel* (New York: Oxford University Press, 2011).

Longuenesse, Béatrice, *Hegel's Critique of Metaphysics* (New York: Cambridge University Press, 2007).

Losurdo, Domenico, *Hegel and the Freedom of Moderns*, trans. Marella Morris and Jon Morris (Durham, NC: Duke University Press, 2004).

Lucas, George R., Jr, *Hegel and Whitehead: Contemporary Perspectives on Systematic Philosophy* (Albany: State University of New York Press, 1986).

Lukács, György, *The Young Hegel: Studies in the Relations between Dialectics and Economics*, trans. Rodney Livingstone (Cambridge, MA: MIT Press, 1976).

MacDonald, Sara, *Finding Freedom: Hegel's Philosophy and the Emancipation of Women* (Montreal: McGill–Queen's University Press, 2008).

Macherey, Pierre, *Hegel or Spinoza*, trans. Susan M. Ruddick (Minneapolis: University of Minnesota Press, 2011).

MacIntyre, Alasdair, ed., *Hegel: A Collection of Critical Essays* (Notre Dame, IN: University of Notre Dame Press, 1976).

Mackintosh, Robert, *Hegel and Hegelianism* (Bristol: Thoemmes Antiquarian Books, 1990).

Magee, Glenn Alexander, *Hegel and the Hermetic Tradition* (Ithaca, NY: Cornell University Press, 2001).

Magee, Glenn Alexander, *The Hegel Dictionary* (London: Continuum, 2010).

Magnus, Kathleen Dow, *Hegel and the Symbolic Mediation of Spirit* (Albany: State University of New York Press, 2001).

Maker, William, *Philosophy without Foundations: Rethinking Hegel* (Albany: State University of New York Press, 1994).

Malabou, Catherine, *The Future of Hegel: Plasticity, Temporality, and Dialectic,* trans. Lisabeth During (New York: Routledge, 2005).

Matarrese, Craig B., *Starting with Hegel* (New York: Continuum, 2010).

McCumber, John, *The Company of Words: Hegel, Language, and Systematic Philosophy* (Evanston, IL: Northwestern University Press, 1993).

Mills, Patricia Jagentowicz Mill, ed., *Feminist Interpretations of Hegel* (University Park: Pennsylvania State University Press, 1996).

Mure, Geoffrey Reginald Gilchrist, *An Introduction to Hegel* (Oxford: Clarendon Press, 1940).

Myers, Henry Alonzo, *The Spinoza–Hegel Paradox: A Study of the Choice between Traditional Idealism and Systematic Pluralism* (Ithaca, NY: Cornell University Press, 1944).

Nuzzo, Angelica, ed., *Hegel and the Analytic Tradition* (New York: Continuum, 2010).

Pinkard, Terry P., *Hegel's Naturalism: Mind, Nature, and the Final Ends of Life* (New York: Oxford University Press, 2012).

Pippin, Robert B., *Hegel's Idealism: The Satisfactions of Self-Consciousness* (New York: Cambridge University Press, 1989).

Pippin, Robert B., *Idealism as Modernism: Hegelian Variations* (New York: Cambridge University Press, 1997).

Plant, Raymond, *Hegel* (Bloomington: Indiana University Press, 1973).

Rae, Gavin, *Realizing Freedom: Hegel, Sartre, and the Alienation of Human Being* (New York: Palgrave Macmillan, 2011).

Redding, Paul, *Analytic Philosophy and the Return of Hegelian Thought* (New York: Cambridge University Press, 2007).

Rockmore, Tom, *Before and after Hegel: A Historical Introduction to Hegel's Thought* (Berkeley: University of California Press, 1993).

Rockmore, Tom, *Hegel, Idealism, and Analytic Philosophy* (New Haven, CT: Yale University Press, 2005).

Rose, Gillian, *Hegel Contra Sociology* (London: Athlone Press, 1981).

Rosen, Stanley, *G. W. F. Hegel: An Introduction to the Science of Wisdom* (New Haven, CT: Yale University Press, 1974).

Rotenstreich, Nathan, *From Substance to Subject: Studies in Hegel* (The Hague: Martinus Nijhoff, 1974).

Sedgwick, Sally, *Hegel's Critique of Kant: From Dichotomy to Identity* (New York: Oxford University Press, 2012).

Simpson, Peter, *Hegel's Transcendental Induction* (Albany: State University of New York Press, 1998).

Singer, Peter, *Hegel: A Very Short Introduction* (New York: Oxford University Press, 2001).

Smith, John H., *The Spirit and its Letter: Traces of Rhetoric in Hegel's Philosophy of Bildung* (Ithaca, NY: Cornell University Press, 1988).

Soll, Ivan, *An Introduction to Hegel's Metaphysics* (Chicago: University of Chicago Press, 1969).

Somers-Hall, Henry, *Hegel, Deleuze, and the Critique of Representation: Dialectics of Negation and Difference* (Albany: State University of New York Press, 2012).

Speight, Allen, *Hegel, Literature and the Problem of Agency* (New York: Cambridge University Press, 2001).

Speight, Allen, *The Philosophy of Hegel* (Stocksfield, Northumberland: Acumen, 2008).

Stace, W. T., *The Philosophy of Hegel: A Systematic Exposition* (New York: Dover, 1955).

Steinkraus, Warren E., ed., *New Studies in Hegel's Philosophy* (New York: Holt, Rinehart & Winston, 1971).

Stern, Robert, ed., *G. W. F. Hegel: Critical Assessments* (London: Routledge, 1993).

Stern, Robert, *Hegel, Kant and the Structure of the Object* (New York: Routledge, 1990).

Stewart, Jon, ed., *The Hegel Myths and Legends* (Evanston, IL: Northwestern University Press, 1996).

Stirling, James Hutchison, *The Secret of Hegel: Being the Hegelian System in Origin, Principle, Form, and Matter* (Edinburgh: Oliver & Boyd, 1898).

Surber, Jere Paul, ed., *Hegel and Language* (Albany: State University of New York Press, 2006).

Taylor, Charles, *Hegel* (Cambridge: Cambridge University Press, 1975).

Taylor, Mark C., *Journeys to Selfhood: Hegel and Kierkegaard* (New York: Fordham University Press, 2000).

Tubbs, Nigel, *Education in Hegel* (New York: Continuum, 2008).

Vernon, Jim, *Hegel's Philosophy of Language* (New York: Continuum, 2007).

Viyagappa, Ignatius, *G. W. F. Hegel's Concept of Indian Philosophy* (Rome: Università Gregoriana, 1980).

Wallace, Robert M., *Hegel's Philosophy of Reality, Freedom, and God* (New York: Cambridge University Press, 2005).

Weiss, Frederick Gustav, ed., *Beyond Epistemology: New Studies in the Philosophy of Hegel* (The Hague: Martinus Nijhoff, 1974).

White, Alan, *Absolute knowledge: Hegel and the Problem of Metaphysics* (Athens: Ohio University Press, 1983).

Williams, Robert R., *Hegel's Ethics of Recognition* (Berkeley: University of California Press, 1997).

Williams, Robert R., *Recognition: Fichte and Hegel on the Other* (Albany: State University of New York Press, 1992).

Williams, Robert R., *Tragedy, Recognition, and the Death of God: Studies in Hegel and Nietzsche* (Oxford: Oxford University Press, 2012).

Winfield, Richard Dien, *Overcoming Foundations: Studies in Systematic Philosophy* (New York: Columbia University Press, 1989).

Yovel, Yirmiahu, *Dark Riddle: Hegel, Nietzsche, and the Jews* (University Park: Pennsylvania State University Press, 1998).

Žižek, Slavoj, *Less than Nothing: Hegel and the Shadow of Dialectical Materialism* (New York: Verso, 2012).

Žižek, Slavoj, *Tarrying with the Negative: Kant, Hegel, and the Critique of Ideology* (Durham, NC: Duke University Press, 1993).

Žižek, Slavoj, Clayton Crockett, and Creston Davis, eds, *Hegel and the Infinite: Religion, Politics, and Dialectic* (New York: Columbia University Press, 2011).

Biographies

Althaus, Horst, *Hegel: An Intellectual Biography*, trans. Michael Tarsh (Cambridge: Polity, 2000).

d'Hondt, Jacques, *Hegel in his Time*, trans. John Burbidge, Nelson Roland, and Judith Lavasseur (Peterborough, Ontario: Broadview Press, 1988).

Harris, H. S., *Hegel's Development: Night Thoughts (Jena 1801–1806)* (New York: Oxford University Press, 1983).

Harris, H. S., *Hegel's Development: Toward the Sunlight, 1770–1801* (Oxford: Clarendon Press, 1972).

Pinkard, Terry P., *Hegel: A Biography* (New York: Cambridge University Press, 2000).

Phenomenology of Spirit

Cutrofello, Andrew, *The Owl at Dawn: A Sequel to Hegel's Phenomenology of Spirit* (Albany: State University of New York Press, 1995).

Forster, Michael N., *Hegel's Idea of a Phenomenology of Spirit* (Chicago: University of Chicago Press, 1998).

Harris, H. S., *Hegel's Ladder*, 2 vols (Indianapolis: Hackett, 1997).

Hyppolite, Jean, *Genesis and Structure of Hegel's Phenomenology of Spirit*, trans. Samuel Cherniak and John Heckman (Evanston, IL: Northwestern University Press, 1974).

Jameson, Fredric, *The Hegel Variations: On the Phenomenology of Spirit* (New York: Verso, 2010).

Kainz, Howard P., *Hegel's Phenomenology*, Part I: *Analysis and Commentary* (Athens: Ohio University Press, 1988).

Kainz, Howard P., *Hegel's Phenomenology*, Part II: *The Evolution of Ethical and Religious Consciousness to the Absolute Standpoint* (Athens: Ohio University Press, 1983).

Kojève, Alexandre, *Introduction to the Reading of Hegel: Lecture on the Phenomenology of Spirit*, trans. James H. Nichols, Jr (Ithaca, NY: Cornell University Press, 1986).

Loewenberg, Jacob, *Hegel's Phenomenology: Dialogues on the Life of the Mind* (La Salle, IL: Open Court, 1965).

Moyar, Dean, and Michael Quante, eds, *Hegel's Phenomenology of Spirit: A Critical Guide* (New York: Cambridge University Press, 2008).

Pahl, Katrin, *Tropes of Transport: Hegel and Emotion* (Evanston, IL: Northwestern University Press, 2012).

Pinkard, Terry, *Hegel's Phenomenology: The Sociality of Reason* (Cambridge: Cambridge University Press, 1998).

Pippin, Robert B., *Hegel on Self-Consciousness: Desire and Death in the Phenomenology of Spirit* (Princeton, NJ: Princeton University Press, 2011).

Rockmore, Tom, *Cognition: An Introduction to Hegel's Phenomenology of Spirit* (Berkeley: University of California Press, 1997).

Russon, John Edward, *Reading Hegel's Phenomenology* (Bloomington: Indiana University Press, 2004).

Russon, John Edward, *The Self and its Body in Hegel's Phenomenology of Spirit* (Toronto: University of Toronto Press, 1997).

Shklar, Judith N., *Freedom and Independence: A Study of the Political Ideas of Hegel's Phenomenology of Mind* (New York: Cambridge University Press, 1976).

Smith, John H., *The Spirit and its Letter: Traces of Rhetoric in Hegel's Philosophy of Bildung* (Ithaca, NY: Cornell University Press, 1988).

Solomon, Robert, *In the Spirit of Hegel: A Study of G. W. F. Hegel's Phenomenology of Spirit* (New York: Oxford University Press, 1983).

Stewart, Jon, ed., *The Phenomenology of Spirit Reader: Critical and Interpretive Essays* (Albany: State University of New York Press, 1998).

Verene, Donald Phillip, *Hegel's Absolute: An Introduction to Reading the Phenomenology of Spirit* (Albany: State University of New York Press, 2007).

Verene, Donald Phillip, *Hegel's Recollection: A Study of the Images in the Phenomenology of Spirit* (Albany: State University of New York Press, 1985).

Westphal, Kenneth R., ed., *The Blackwell Guide to Hegel's Phenomenology of Spirit* (Malden, MA: Wiley-Blackwell, 2009).

Westphal, Kenneth R., *Hegel's Epistemological Realism: A Study of the Aim and Method of Hegel's Phenomenology of Spirit* (Dordrecht: Kluwer Academic, 1989).

Westphal, Merold, ed., *Method and Speculation in Hegel's Phenomenology* (Atlantic Highlands, NJ: Humanities Press, 1982).

Logic

Baillie, J. B., *The Origin and Significance of Hegel's Logic: A General Introduction to Hegel's System* (Kitchener, Ontario: Batoche, 1999).

Bencivenga, Ermanno, *Hegel's Dialectical Logic* (New York: Oxford University Press, 2000).

Burbidge, John, *On Hegel's Logic: Fragments of a Commentary* (Atlantic Highlands, NJ: Humanities Press, 1981).

Butler, Clark, *The Dialectical Method: A Treatise Hegel Never Wrote* (Amherst, NY: Humanity Books, 2011).

Butler, Clark, *Hegel's Logic: Between Dialectic and History* (Evanston, IL: Northwestern University Press, 1996).

de Boer, Karin, *On Hegel: The Sway of the Negative* (New York: Palgrave Macmillan, 2010).

di Giovanni, George, *Essays on Hegel's Logic* (Albany: State University of New York Press, 1990).

Harris, Errol E., *An Interpretation of the Logic of Hegel* (Lanham, MD: University Press of America, 1983).

Hibben, John Grier, *Hegel's Logic: An Essay in Interpretation* (Kitchener, Ontario: Batoche, 2000).

Hyppolite, Jean, *Logic and Existence*, trans. Leonard Lawlor and Amit Sen (Albany: State University of New York Press, 1997).

Lauer, Quentin, *Essays in Hegelian Dialectic* (New York: Fordham University Press, 1977).

Lenin, Vladimir Ilyich, "Conspectus of Hegel's Book *The Science of Logic*," *Lenin's Collected Works*, Vol 38, 4th edn, trans. Clemence Dutt (Moscow: Progress, 1976), pp. 85–241.

Limnatis, Nectarios G., ed., *The Dimensions of Hegel's Dialectic* (New York: Continuum, 2010).

McTaggart, John McTaggart Ellis, *Studies in the Hegelian Dialectic* (Kitchener, Ontario: Batoche, 1999).

Mure, Geoffrey Reginald Gilchrist, *A Study of Hegel's Logic* (Oxford: Clarendon Press, 1950).

Pinkard, Terry, *Hegel's Dialectic: The Explanation of Possibility* (Philadelphia: Temple University Press, 1988).

Winfield, Richard Dien, *Hegel's Science of Logic: A Critical Rethinking in Thirty Lectures* (Lanham, MD: Rowman & Littlefield, 2012).

Philosophy of Nature

Cohen, Robert S., and Marx W. Wartofsky, eds, *Hegel and the Sciences* (Dordrecht: D. Reidel, 1984).

Hahn, Songsuk Susan, *Contradiction in Motion: Hegel's Organic Conception of Life and Value* (Ithaca, NY: Cornell University Press, 2007).

Houlgate, Stephen, ed., *Hegel and the Philosophy of Nature* (Albany: State University of New York Press, 1998).

Petry, Michael John, ed., *Hegel and Newtonianism* (Dordrecht: Kluwer Academic, 1993).

Stone, Alison, *Petrified Intelligence: Nature in Hegel's Philosophy* (Albany: State University of New York Press, 2005).

Philosophy of Spirit

Berthold-Bond, Daniel, *Hegel's Theory of Madness* (Albany: State University of New York Press, 1995).

DeVries, Willem A., *Hegel's Theory of Mental Activity: An Introduction to Theoretical Spirit* (Ithaca, NY: Cornell University Press, 1988).

Greene, Murray, *Hegel on the Soul: A Speculative Anthropology* (The Hague: Martinus Nijhoff, 1972).

Laitinen, Arto, and Constantine Sandis, eds, *Hegel on Action* (New York: Palgrave Macmillan, 2010).

Quante, Michael, *Hegel's Concept of Action*, trans. Dean Moyar (New York: Cambridge University Press, 2004).

Stepelevich, Lawrence S., and David Lamb, eds, *Hegel's Philosophy of Action* (Atlantic Highlands, NJ: Humanities Press, 1983).

Stern, David S., ed., *Essays on Hegel's Philosophy of Subjective Spirit* (Albany: State University of New York Press, 2013).

Yeomans, Christopher, *Freedom and Reflection: Hegel and the Logic of Agency* (Oxford: Oxford University Press, 2011).

Philosophy of Right

Avineri, Shlomo, *Hegel's Theory of the Modern State* (Cambridge: Cambridge University Press, 1972).

Brod, Harry, *Hegel's Philosophy of Politics: Idealism, Identity, and Modernity* (Boulder, CO: Westview Press, 1992).

Brooks, Thom, ed., *Hegel's Philosophy of Right* (Malden, MA: Wiley-Blackwell, 2012).

Brooks, Thom, *Hegel's Political Philosophy: A Systematic Reading of the Philosophy of Right* (Edinburgh: Edinburgh University Press, 2013).

Browning, Gary K., *Hegel and the History of Political Philosophy* (Basingstoke: Macmillan, 1999).

Brudner, Alan, *The Unity of the Common Law: Studies in Hegelian Jurisprudence* (Berkeley: University of California Press, 1995).

Buchwalter, Andrew, *Dialectics, Politics, and the Contemporary Value of Hegel's Practical Philosophy* (New York: Routledge, 2012).

Buchwalter, Andrew, ed., *Hegel and Global Justice* (Dordrecht: Springer, 2012).

Colletti, Lucio, *Marxism and Hegel*, trans. Lawrence Garner (London: NLB, 1973).

Conklin, William E., *Hegel's Laws: The Legitimacy of a Modern Legal Order* (Stanford, CA: Stanford Law Books, 2008).

Cornell, Drucilla, Michel Rosenfeld, and David Carlson, eds, *Hegel and Legal Theory* (New York: Routledge, 1991).

Cristi, Renato, *Hegel on Freedom and Authority* (Cardiff: University of Wales Press, 2005).

Cullen, Bernard, *Hegel's Social and Political Thought: An Introduction* (New York: St Martin's Press, 1979).

Dienstag, Joshua Foa, *"Dancing in Chains": Narrative and Memory in Political Theory* (Stanford, CA: Stanford University Press, 1997).

Foster, Michael Beresford, *The Political Philosophies of Plato and Hegel* (New York: Russell & Russell, 1965).

Fraser, Ian, *Hegel and Marx: The Concept of Need* (Edinburgh: Edinburgh University Press, 1998).

Geiger, Ido, *The Founding Act of Modern Ethical Life: Hegel's Critique of Kant's Moral and Political Philosophy* (Stanford, CA: Stanford University Press, 2007).

Hardimon, Michael O., *Hegel's Social Philosophy: The Project of Reconciliation* (New York: Cambridge University Press 1994).

Hobhouse, L. T., *The Metaphysical Theory of the State: A Criticism* (Kitchener, Ontario: Batoche, 1999).

Honneth, Axel, *The Pathologies of Individual Freedom: Hegel's Social Theory* (Princeton, NJ: Princeton University Press, 2010).

Kaufmann, Walter, ed., *Debating the Political Philosophy of Hegel* (New Brunswick, NJ: AldineTransaction, 2010).

Kaufmann, Walter, ed., *Hegel's Political Philosophy* (New York: Atherton Press, 1970).

Kedourie, Elie, *Hegel and Marx: Introductory Lectures* (Oxford: Blackwell, 1995).

Knowles, Dudley, *Routledge Philosophy Guidebook to Hegel and the Philosophy of Right* (New York: Routledge, 2002).

Kotkavirta, Jussi, ed., *Right, Morality, Ethical Life: Studies in G. W. F. Hegel's Philosophy of Right* (Jyväskylä, Finland: SoPhi Academic Press, 1997).

Lakeland, Paul, *The Politics of Salvation: The Hegelian Idea of the State* (Albany: State University of New York Press, 1984).

Levine, Norman, *Marx's Discourse with Hegel* (Basingstoke: Palgrave Macmillan, 2012).

MacGregor, David, *The Communist Ideal in Hegel and Marx* (Toronto: University of Toronto Press, 1984).

MacGregor, David, *Hegel, Marx, and the English State* (Boulder, CO: Westview Press, 1992).

Maker, William, ed., *Hegel on Economics and Freedom* (Macon, GA: Mercer University Press, 1987).

Marcuse, Herbert, *Reason and Revolution: Hegel and the Rise of Social Theory*, 2nd edn (Boston: Beacon Press, 1960).

Marx, Karl, *Critique of Hegel's "Philosophy of Right"*, trans. Annette Jolin and Joseph O'Malley (Cambridge: Cambridge University Press, 1972).

Moland, Lydia L., *Hegel on Political Identity: Patriotism, Nationality, Cosmopolitanism* (Evanston, IL: Northwestern University Press, 2011).

Moyar, Dean, *Hegel's Conscience* (New York: Oxford University Press, 2011).

Neuhouser, Frederick, *Foundations of Hegel's Social Theory: Actualizing Freedom* (Cambridge, MA: Harvard University Press, 2000).

Nicolacopoulos, Toula, and George Vassilacopoulos, *Hegel and the Logical Structure of Love: An Essay on Sexualities, Family and the Law* (Aldershot: Ashgate, 1999).

Pelczynski, Z. A., ed., *Hegel's Political Philosophy – Problems and Perspectives: A Collection of New Essays* (Cambridge: Cambridge University Press, 1971).

Pippin, Robert B., *Hegel's Practical Philosophy: Rational Agency as Ethical Life* (New York: Cambridge University Press, 2008).

Pippin, Robert B., and Otfried Höffe, eds, *Hegel on Ethics and Politics* (New York: Cambridge University Press, 2004).

Prokopczyk, Czeslaw, *Truth and Reality in Marx and Hegel: A Reassessment* (Amherst: University of Massachusetts Press, 1980).

Ritter, Joachim, *Hegel and the French Revolution: Essays on the Philosophy of Right*, trans. Richard Dien Winfield (Cambridge, MA: MIT Press, 1982).

Rose, David, *Hegel's Philosophy of Right: A Reader's Guide* (New York: Continuum, 2007).

Ross, Nathan, *On Mechanism in Hegel's Social and Political Philosophy* (New York: Routledge, 2008).

Rózsa, Erzsébet, *Modern Individuality in Hegel's Practical Philosophy*, trans. Tamas Nyirkos (Leiden: Brill, 2012).

Ruda, Frank, *Hegel's Rabble: An Investigation into Hegel's Philosophy of Right* (New York: Continuum, 2011).

Salter, Michael, *Hegel and Law* (Burlington, VT: Ashgate/Dartmouth, 2003).

Siebert, Rudolf J., *Hegel's Concept of Marriage and Family: The Origin of Subjective Freedom* (Washington, DC: University Press of America, 1979).

Smith, Steven B., *Hegel's Critique of Liberalism: Rights in Context* (Chicago: University of Chicago Press, 1989).

Steinberger, Peter J., *Logic and Politics: Hegel's Philosophy of Right* (New Haven, CT: Yale University Press, 1988).

Taylor, Charles, *Hegel and Modern Society* (New York: Cambridge University Press, 1979).

Verene, Donald Phillip, ed., *Hegel's Social and Political Thought: The Philosophy of Objective Spirit* (Atlantic Highlands, NJ: Humanities Press, 1980).

Walsh, W. H., *Hegelian Ethics* (Bristol: Thoemmes Press, 1998).

Waszek, Norbert, *The Scottish Enlightenment and Hegel's Account of "Civil Society"* (Dordrecht: Kluwer Academic, 1988).

Weil, Eric, *Hegel and the State* (Baltimore: Johns Hopkins University Press, 1998).

Williams, Robert R., ed., *Beyond Liberalism and Communitarianism: Studies in Hegel's Philosophy of Right*, (Albany: State University of New York Press, 2001).

Wood, Allen W., *Hegel's Ethical Thought* (New York: Cambridge University Press, 1990).

Philosophy of History

Buck-Morss, Susan, *Hegel, Haiti, and Universal History* (Pittsburgh: University of Pittsburgh Press, 2009).

Comay, Rebecca, *Mourning Sickness: Hegel and the French Revolution* (Stanford, CA: Stanford University Press, 2011).

Dudley, Will, ed., *Hegel and History* (Albany: State University of New York Press, 2009).

Gallagher, Shaun, ed., *Hegel, History, and Interpretation* (Albany: State University of New York Press, 1997).

Gillespie, Michael Allen, *Hegel, Heidegger, and the Ground of History* (Chicago: University of Chicago Press, 1984).

Gray, J. Glenn, *Hegel and Greek Thought* (New York: Harper & Row, 1968).

Guha, Ranajit, *History at the Limit of World-History* (New York: Columbia University Press, 2002).

McCarney, Joe, *Routledge Philosophy Guidebook to Hegel on History* (New York: Routledge, 2000).

Nuzzo, Angelica, *Memory, History, Justice in Hegel* (Basingstoke: Palgrave Macmillan, 2012).

O'Brien, George Dennis, *Hegel on Reason and History: A Contemporary Interpretation* (Chicago: University of Chicago Press, 1975).

Perkins, Robert L., ed., *History and System: Hegel's Philosophy of History* (Albany: State University of New York Press, 1984).

Aesthetics

Desmond, William, *Art and the Absolute: A Study of Hegel's Aesthetics* (Albany: State University of New York Press, 1986).

Geulen, Eva, *The End of Art: Readings in a Rumor after Hegel*, trans. James McFarland (Stanford, CA: Stanford University Press, 2006).

James, David, *Art, Myth, and Society in Hegel's Aesthetics* (New York: Continuum, 2009).

Kaminsky, Jack, *Hegel on Art: An Interpretation of Hegel's Aesthetics* (Albany: State University of New York Press, 1962).

Maker, William, ed., *Hegel and Aesthetics* (Albany: State University of New York Press, 2000).

Pillow, Kirk, *Sublime Understanding: Aesthetic Reflection in Kant and Hegel* (Cambridge, MA: MIT Press, 2000).

Rutter, Benjamin, *Hegel on the Modern Arts* (Cambridge: Cambridge University Press, 2010).

Wyss, Beat, *Hegel's Art History and the Critique of Modernity*, trans. Caroline Dobson Saltzwedel (New York: Cambridge University Press, 1999).

Religion

Anderson, Deland S., *Hegel's Speculative Good Friday: The Death of God in Philosophical Perspective* (Atlanta: Scholars Press, 1996).

Calton, Patricia Marie, *Hegel's Metaphysics of God: The Ontological Proof as the Development of a Trinitarian Divine Ontology* (Burlington, VT: Ashgate, 2001).

Crites, Stephen, *In the Twilight of Christendom: Hegel versus Kierkegaard on Faith and History* (Chambersberg, PA: American Academy of Religion, 1972).

De Nys, Martin J., *Hegel and Theology* (New York: T & T Clark, 2009).

Fackenheim, Emil L., *The Religious Dimension in Hegel's Thought* (Bloomington: Indiana University Press, 1967).

Hodgson, Peter C., *Shapes of Freedom: Hegel's Philosophy of World History in Theological Perspective* (New York: Oxford University Press, 2012).

Il'in, Ivan A., *The Philosophy of Hegel as a Doctrine of the Concreteness of God and Humanity*, trans. Philip T. Grier (Evanston, IL: Northwestern University Press, 2011).

Labuschagne, Bart, and Timo Slootweg, eds, *Hegel's Philosophy of the Historical Religions* (Leiden: Brill, 2012).

Olson, Alan M., *Hegel and the Spirit: Philosophy as Pneumatology* (Princeton, NJ: Princeton University Press, 1992).

O'Regan, Cyril, *The Heterodox Hegel* (Albany: State University of New York Press, 1994).

Stewart, Jon, *Kierkegaard's Relation to Hegel Reconsidered* (Cambridge: Cambridge University Press, 2003).

Thulstrup, Niels, *Kierkegaard's Relation to Hegel*, trans. George L. Stengren (Princeton, NJ: Princeton University Press, 1980).

Williamson, Raymond Keith, *Introduction to Hegel's Philosophy of Religion* (Albany: State University of New York Press, 1984).

Yerkes, James, *The Christology of Hegel* (Albany: State University of New York Press, 1982).

Index

'Abduh, Muhammad, 125
absolute
  absolute knowing, 41–2, 78, 93,
    141–2, 147–8
  absolute spirit, 11, 76, 102, 103
  Aristotle, 37–8
  British Idealism, 142
  Hegelian concept, 22, 34–6, 38
  historical concept, 22–3
  prime mover, 21–2
  Schelling on, 34–5
  Spinoza, 35
  subject and substance, 24
  see also God
actuality/reality, 91
Adorno, Theodor, 2, 146–7
aesthetics, 11, 14, 102, 107, 119,
  127–31
Africa, 124–5
Agamben, Giorgio, 122
AIDS, 40
Akbar the Great, 124, 125
Althusser, Louis, 149, 153
Analytic Hegelianism, 2, 77, 142–6
ancient Greece, 16–21, 36, 62, 71–2,
  120, 128
ancient Rome, 72, 73, 120
Anglo-American philosophy, 1–2
anthropology, 102, 103, 105

appearance, 89, 90
architecture, 128
Aristotle
  experience, 26
  on friends, 39
  God, 1, 37–8
  influence on Hegel, 16, 19–22
  science, 51
  society, 21, 37, 40
  soul, 103
art, *see* aesthetics; classical art;
    romantic art; symbolic art
atheism, 14, 133–4, 137

Baillie, J. B., 37
Barthes, Roland, 136–7
beautiful soul, 75–6, 110
Beauvoir, Simone de, 2, 148
bees, 21, 37
being
  being-for-itself, 87
  determinate being, 81, 87
  Logic, 10, 81, 82, 83, 85, 85–90, 92
  measure, 87, 89
  Parmenides, 17, 18, 22
  quality, 87–9
  quantity, 87, 89
Berlin, Isaiah, 120, 123
Bernasconi, Robert, 125

bondsmen, 39, 62, 63, 64, 105, 141, 148–9
Bosanquet, Bernard, 142
Bradley, Francis Herbert, 142
Brandom, Robert, 2, 144
Brecht, Bertolt, 11
Brokmeyer, Henry Conrad, 141
Buddhism, 132
bureaucracy, 114
Burkhardt, Christiana, 13, 14
Butler, Judith, 153

Caesar, Julius, 39, 121, 122
Caird, Edward, 142
Camus, Albert, 156n23
Canada, 125
capitalism, 139, 146–7, 149, 150, 152
Carroll, David, 2
castes, 125
causality, 26, 89, 91
censorship, 109, 111, 114–15
Chalmers, David, 40
change, 18, 146
chemism, 92, 93
China, 1, 124
Christianity, 23, 59, 76–7, 131–4, 137–8, 140
Churchland, Pamela Smith, 145
Churchland, Paul, 145
civil society, 111, 112–13
civil war, 115
clairvoyance, 104
Clark, Andy, 40
classical art, 128, 130
climate, 103, 125
climate change, 152
coherentism, 82
Collingwood, Robin George, 142
colonialism, 116–17, 121, 148, 149
communism, 1, 152
concept/notion (*Begriff*), 10, 83, 85–6, 88, 92–3
conscience, 67, 75, 102, 117
conscientious objection, 117

consciousness
  force and understanding, 58–61
  perception, 56–8
  Phenomenology of Spirit, 52–61, 85, 94
  Philosophy of Nature, 97
  self-consciousness, 97
    lordship and bondage, 39, 61–2, 63, 64, 105, 141, 148–9
    Philosophy of Spirit, 105
    Stoicism, 62–3
  sense-certainty, 52–6, 57, 144
  shapes of consciousness, 95
Conway, Moncure Daniel, 141
Cooper, Barry, 122, 123
cosmopolitanism, 115–16
culture
  ethics and, 29
  Herder on, 29, 32
  nature and, 11
  reason and, 32
  self-alienation, 72–3, 85
  spirit, 3, 22, 37, 102
  see also spirit (*Geist*)

Darwin, Charles, 99
Davidson, Thomas, 141
Deleuze, Gilles, 2, 149
democracy, 25, 149, 150
Derrida, Jacques, 2, 149
Descartes, René, 9, 23–4, 26, 46–7, 57, 84
determinate being, 81, 87
determinate negation, 48, 56
Dewey, John, 142
dialectics, 2, 3–4, 33, 39, 51, 76–7, 98, 146–7
Diderot, Denis, 73
dogmatism, 49
Dove, Kenley, 51
Drydyk, Jay, 110
dualisms, 5, 7–8, 23, 28, 142

economics, 112–13
Elements of the Philosophy of Right, see Philosophy of Right

empiricism, 25–6
Enclosure Laws, 149
Encyclopaedia of the Philosophical Sciences, see Logic
Enlightenment, 4–5, 24–5, 73–4, 125
equality, French Revolution and, 25, 74
essence, 10, 83, 85–6, 88, 89–92, 92
ethnicity, 122, 123
Euclid, 27, 82
Eurocentrism, 123–4
evolution, 99
extended mind, 40
external criticism, 33, 48
externalism, 80

family, 111–12
Fanon, Frantz, 148–9
fascism, 146
feeling soul, 104
feudalism, 139
Feuerbach, Ludwig, 14, 138
Feyerabend, Paul, 70
Fichte, Johann Gottlieb, 29–30, 140
Fischer, Georg Ludwig Friedrich, 13, 14
Forster, Michael N., 31, 44, 69, 79
Foucault, Michel, 2, 119, 149
foundationalism, 53, 54, 80, 82
France
    philosophy, 2, 153
    Revolution, 13, 25, 74
Frankfurt School, 146–7
freedom
    absolute freedom, 74
    Christianity and, 23
    free will, 24, 35
    French Revolution and, 25
    historical progress, 20–1, 38, 120–1, 122, 125, 130, 152
    Kant on, 27
    negative liberty, 123
    positive liberty, 120, 123
    reason and, 121
    religious freedom, 135

frenzy of self-conceit, 67
Freud, Sigmund, 146
Fukuyama, Francis, 122, 123, 152–3

Gandhi, Mahatma, 70, 121
Geist, see spirit
gender, 111, 113, 148
geology, 100
Germanic World, 20, 29, 120, 122, 128, 130, 132, 141, 148
global warming, 152
Gnosticism, 133
God
    absolute, 34
    Aristotle, 1, 37–8
    death of God, 133–4
    Descartes, 23
    Feuerbach on, 138
    Hegelian concept, 132–5
    Holy Spirit, 38
    Kant, 15, 27
    Left Hegelianism, 14
    pantheism, 108
    personalism, 1
    Phenomenology of the Spirit, 31, 76–7, 121
    positive qualities, 64
    Protestantism, 23
    rationalism, 26
    skepticism, 5–6
    Spinoza, 24, 34–5
    topsy-turvy world and, 60
    see also absolute; religion
Gorgias, 17, 85
Greco-Roman World, 29, 38, 120, 121, 122, 128, 132, 141
Green, Thomas Hill, 142
guilds, 112–13, 116, 150

Habermas, Jürgen, 2, 147
habit, 104–5
Halliburton, 40
Hardimon, Michael, 96–7, 110
Harris, William Torrey, 141
Hegel, Christiane Luise, 13
Hegel, Georg Ludwig, 13

Hegel, Georg Wilhelm Friedrich
  academic debate, 14–16, 132–3
  biography, 13–14
  importance, 1–11
  influences on, 16–30
  posthumous influence, 1, 136–53
  works, 13–14
  see also specific works and
    subjects
Hegel, Immanuel Thomas
    Christian, 13
Hegel, Karl Friedrich Wilhelm, 13
Heidegger, Martin, 2, 51, 147–8
Heraclitus of Ephesus, 18
Herder, Johann Gottfried von, 16,
    29, 32
Hill, Joe, 14
Hinduism, 77, 108, 131, 132
history
  Africa and India, 124–6
  art, 128, 129
  development of freedom, 20–1,
    38, 120–1, 122, 124, 125, 130,
    152
  end of history, 122, 123, 130,
    152–3
  Eurocentrism, 123–6
  Hegelian optimism, 134
  lordship and bondage, 39, 62, 63,
    64, 105, 141, 148–9
  Marxist theory, 149
  meaning, 119–20, 124
  Nietzsche, 141
  original history, 118
  outsiders, 122–3
  periods, 38, 122, 128
  Phenomenology of Spirit, 8, 10
  philosophic history, 118
  philosophy and, 7, 33
  prehistory, 120
  progress, 96, 151
  reason, 32, 36, 112
  reflective history, 118
  religion, 131
  scope, 122–3
  slaves and masters, 148–9

  socio-economic conditions and,
    112
  state and, 120
  truth and, 3
  West, 95
  world-historic individuals, 39,
    122
  see also Philosophy of History
Hölderlin, Johann Christian
    Friedrich, 13, 30, 34
Holy Spirit, 38, 76, 77, 133
Homer, 128, 140
Hume, David, 25–6, 27, 57
Husserl, Edmund, 86
Hutchins, Edwin, 40–1

Idea, 92, 93
Idealism
  British Idealism, 141, 142–3
  German Idealism, 1, 68, 143
imagination, 106
imperialism, *see* colonialism
India, 16–17, 121, 124–6
individuality, 68–70
insanity, 104
internal criticism, 33, 46, 48
internalism, 80
intuition, 26, 46, 52, 75, 144
Ireland, 120
Islam, 108, 132
Italian Renaissance, 125

Joachim, Harold Henry, 142
Judaism, 140

Kant, Immanuel
  antinomies, 91–2
  British Idealism and, 142
  cosmopolitanism, 115–16
  dualisms, 7, 28
  empiricism and rationalism,
    26–7
  Enlightenment and, 25
  epistemology, 9, 15, 46, 47, 140,
    144
  ethics, 27–9, 74, 133, 134

Fichte and, 29
individuality, 68
influence on Hegel, 15–16, 24–9,
    31, 32, 61
moral law, 69
reason, 32, 91–2
sense-certainty, 52–3
structure of reality, 83
thing-in-itself, 47, 83, 91
Kaufmann, Peter, 141
Keynes, John Maynard, 139, 150
Kierkegaard, Søren, 137–8
King, Martin Luther, 1, 70, 151–2
Knorr Cetina, Karin, 40, 41
Kojève, Alexandre, 62, 64, 122, 123,
    148, 149, 151
Kripke, Saul, 42, 53–4
Kuhn, Thomas, 70

Lacan, Jacques, 153
language
    absolute and, 35
    Herder on, 29, 32
    mysticism and, 53
law, 102
law of heart, 67
Left Hegelians, 14, 137, 138
legislature, 113, 114
Lehrer, Keith, 80
Lenin, Vladimir Ilyich, 1, 146
Levinas, Emmanuel, 149
Lewis, David Kellogg, 145
liberty, *see* freedom
Locke, John, 25, 40, 57
Logic
    being, 81, 82, 83, 85, 85–90, 92
    concept/notion, 83, 85–6, 88,
        92–3
    essence, 10, 83, 85–6, 88, 89–92
    interpretations, 119, 137
    metaphysics, 83–4
    Nature, 94
    nature of work, 79–80, 83–4,
        94–6
    on Parmenides and Zeno, 17
    publication, 10, 13, 14, 79

structure, 83, 85, 88
survey, 79–93
logical positivism, 70
lordship and bondage, 39, 62, 63,
    64, 105, 141, 148–9
Louis XIV, 72–3
Louis XVI, 25
Lukács, György, 146
Luther, Martin, 23, 134–5
Lutheranism, 14, 38, 131–4, 137
Lyotard, Jean-François, 2, 149

MacIntyre, Alasdair, 66
Marcuse, Herbert, 146
Marie Antoinette, Queen, 25
Marx, Karl, 1, 2, 14, 138–9, 149
Marxism, 2, 146–7, 148
mathematics, 100, 101
McDowell, John, 2, 77, 144
McTaggart, John, 142
mechanism, 92, 93
memory, 106–7
mental illness, 104
mereology, 45
metaphysics
    Analytic Hegelianism and, 145
    ancient and medieval thought,
        46
    British Idealism, 142
    Logic, 10, 83–4
    priorities, 37
    reading of Hegel, 14–16
    Spinoza, 24
Mexico, 40
Miller, Arnold, 37
monarchy, 113, 114, 132, 151
monism, 18, 24, 108, 142
Montaigne, Michel de, 23
Moore, G. E., 2, 142
morality
    beautiful soul, 75–6, 110
    conscience, 75
    death of God, 133
    Nietzsche, 140–1
    Phenomenology of the Spirit, 74–6,
        102

Muirhead, John Henry, 142
Mukherjee, Neel, 67
Mure, Geoffrey Reginald Gilchrist,
    142
mysticism, 15, 38, 53, 54
myth, 74, 76, 107, 128, 129, 132–3

Nāgārjuna, 85
Napoleon I, 13, 25, 39, 121, 122
nature, *see Philosophy of Nature*;
    science
necessity, 9, 43–5, 48, 51, 67
Nelson, Lynn Hankinson, 40, 41
Neoplatonism, 1, 22–3
Newton, Isaac, 27
Niethammer, Friedrich Immanuel,
    13
Nietzsche, Friedrich, 2, 5, 139–41
Nigeria, 40
nominalism, 20
notion, *see* concept/notion

object, *Logic*, 92, 93
Oriental World, 20, 29, 38, 120, 121,
    122, 128, 141
Orwell, George, 65, 156n23

Paquette, Gabriel, 117
paraconsistent logic, 60–1
Parmenides, 17–18, 22
perception, *Phenomenology of Spirit*,
    56–8
Phenomenology of Spirit
  absolute knowing, 41–2, 78, 93,
    147–8
  basic concepts, 32–46
  consciousness, 52–61, 85, 94
    force and understanding,
      58–61
    perception, 56–8
    self-consciousness, 61–8
    sense-certainty, 52–6, 57, 144
  context, 32
  difficulties, 8–10
  Enlightenment, 4–5
  Heidegger and, 147–8

hidden essences, 19
Introduction, 46–52
introduction to philosophical
    system, 78, 79, 83
knowledge, 9–10, 49–50
nature of work, 79–80, 94–7
perspectives, 10
phenomenology, 102, 105
Preface, 24, 32–3, 52, 75
publication, 8, 13
reason, 85
  individuality, 68–70
  observing, 64–7
  rational self-consciousness,
    67–8
religion, 76–7, 85
self-consciousness, 85
  lordship and bondage, 39,
    61–2, 63, 64, 105, 141, 148–9
  rational self-consciousness,
    67–8
  skepticism, 63–4
  Stoicism, 62–3, 64
spirit
  absolute freedom and terror, 74
  Enlightenment, 73–4
  ethical order, 70–2
  morality, 74–6
  self-alienation, 72–3, 85, 106
  structure, 31
  subject and substance, 24
  survey, 31–78
philosophy
  discussion in *Philosophy of Spirit*,
    102, 107–8
  Hegelian concept, 34, 129
Philosophy of History
  Hegelian strategy, 118–19
  influence, 1, 152
  objective spirit, 11
  publication, 14
  survey, 118–26
  see also history
Philosophy of Nature
  argument, 11, 93, 100–1
  Hegelian strategy, 118

Heidegger and, 147
nature of work, 94–8
structure, 100
see also science
Philosophy of Right
   censorship, 109, 111, 114–15
   civil society, 111, 112–13
   colonialism, 116–17
   conscientious objection, 117
   conservative text, 109, 111
   context, 109–11
   family, 111–12
   French Revolution, 25
   Hegelian strategy, 118
   justification of war, 116
   nature of project, 96–7
   objective spirit, 11
   Preface, 109–11
   publication, 14
   punishment, 115
   state, 111, 113–17
   structure, 111
   survey, 109–17
Philosophy of Spirit
   arguments, 11, 102–8
   nature of work, 102
   structure, 102
   see also spirit (*Geist*)
phrenology, 65–6, 83–4
physical soul, 103
physics, 100, 101
physiognomy, 65–6
Plant, Raymond, 122, 123
Plato, 18–19, 22, 59–60, 61
Platonism, 143
pleasure, 67
Plotinus, 1
poetry, 128
Popper, Karl, 98
positivism, 70
poststructuralism, 149–51
prehistory, 120
presuppositions, 81–2
prime mover, 21–2
primogeniture, 112
progress, *see* history

Protestantism, 76, 131–4
Prussia, 14, 96, 110–11
psychology, 102, 105–6
punishment, 115
Pythagoras, 18

race, 103, 125, 148–9
Rancière, Jacques, 99
rationalism, 25, 26
reason
   culture and, 32
   freedom and, 121
   Habermas on Hegelian reason,
      147
   Hegelian concept, 36
   Herder, 32
   history, 32, 36, 112
   individuality, 68–70
   Kant, 32, 91–2
   observing, 64–7
   paraconsistent logic, 60–1
   Phenomenology of Spirit, 64–70,
      85
   rational self-consciousness, 67–8
   spirit and, 70–2
   understanding and, 41–2, 58–9
reconciliation, 2, 5, 76, 96, 102, 147
Redding, Paul, 77
Reformation, 125
religion
   Enlightenment and, 4–5, 24–5,
      73–4
   history, 131
   lectures, 11, 119, 131–5
   myth, 76, 107, 128, 129, 132–3
   Phenomenology of Spirit, 76–7, 85,
      102
   religious freedom, 135
   state and, 135
Right Hegelians, 14, 137
rights, 105
Rockmore, Tom, 144–5
Roman Empire, 72, 73
romantic art, 128, 130–1
Royce, Josiah, 141–2
Ruda, Frank, 150

Rushdie, Salman, 125
Russell, Bertrand, 2, 53, 142, 143

Sartre, Jean-Paul, 2, 133, 148–9
Schelling, Friedrich Wilhelm
    Joseph, 1, 13, 16, 30, 34–5,
    135, 137, 142
science
  categories, 100
  Hegelian concept, 33
  Philosophy of Nature, 95–101
  theory and experience, 50–1
Science of Logic, see Logic
sculpture, 128
self-consciousness
  history and, 120
  lordship and bondage, 39, 61–2,
    63, 64, 105, 141, 148–9
  Phenomenology of Spirit, 61–8, 85
  Philosophy of Nature, 97
  Philosophy of Spirit, 105
  rational self-consciousness,
    67–8
  skepticism, 63–4
  Stoicism, 62–3, 64
Sellars, Wilfrid Stalker, 143–4
sense-certainty, 52–6, 57, 144
sensuous medium, 127–8, 131–2,
    137
sexuality, 104, 111
skepticism, 5–7, 23, 47, 48, 63–4, 72,
    84, 140
slaves, 39, 62, 63, 64, 105, 141,
    148–9
Smith, Adam, 67, 112
Snider, Denton, 141
society
  absolute spirit, 11
  acceptance of institutions, 139
  Aristotle, 21, 37, 40
  civic organizations, 113
  civil society, 111, 112–13
  French Revolution and, 25
  Hegelians, 142
  Kant, 29
  Locke, 40

masters and slaves, 39, 62, 63,
    64, 105, 141, 148–9
  objective spirit, 11
  social change, 146
  socio-economics, 112–13, 138, 146
Socrates, 19, 20, 22, 59–60, 61, 72
Sophocles, 71–2, 130
South Africa, 126
Soviet Union, 1, 152
Spinoza, Benedict de, 16, 24, 26, 34,
    35–6
spirit (*Geist*)
  absolute freedom and terror, 74
  absolute spirit, 11, 76, 102, 103
  Enlightenment, 73–4
  ethical order, 70–2
  Hegelian concept, 2–3, 37–9, 41, 66
  Holy Spirit, 38, 76, 77, 133
  human culture, 3, 22, 37, 102
  lectures, 11
  morality, 74–6
  Nature and, 96–101
  nature and, 102
  objective spirit, 11, 102–3, 107
  self-alienation and culture, 72–3,
    85
  subjective spirit, 11, 102–3
  theoretical spirit, 105–6
  translations, 37
  see also absolute; *Phenomenology
    of Spirit*; *Philosophy of Spirit*
spiritual animal kingdom, 68–9
Staal, Frits, 155n7, 157n7
Stallo, John Bernhard, 141
state, 111, 113–17, 120, 135
Stoicism, 39, 62–3, 64, 72, 105
subject, substance and, 24
substance
  dualism, 23–4
  Logic, 89, 91
  monism, 18
  Spinoza, 24, 35
  subject and, 24, 36, 108
Swedenborg, Emmanuel, 15
syllogism, 92
symbolic art, 128

Taylor, Charles, 36
teleology, 92, 93, 139–40, 149, 151
thing-in-itself, 47, 64, 83, 91
topsy-turvy world (*verkehrte Welt*),
    59–61
Transcendentalists, 141
Tucher, Marie Helena Susanna, 13
Twain, Mark, 67

understanding
    force and, 58–61
    reason and, 41–2, 58–9
United Kingdom, 113, 117, 120,
    121, 124, 149
United Nations, 123
United States, 40, 117, 141–2
universals, 19–21, 52, 52–6

Verene, Donald Phillip, 68
virtue, 19, 20, 67–8

Wallace, William, 142
war, 116
warlords, 115
way of the world, 67–8
welfare capitalism, 152
Wilde, Oscar, 16, 146
Williams, Robert, 106
Willich, August, 141
Wittgenstein, Ludwig, 60, 85
women, 111, 113, 122, 148
World War I, 1

Zeno of Elea, 17
Žižek, Slavoj, 66, 75, 153